THE
GOOD
LIFE

THE GOOD LIFE

Helen and Scott Nearing's
Sixty Years of Self-Sufficient Living

Schocken Books   New York

Library of Congress Cataloging-in-Publication Data

Nearing, Helen and Scott.
  [Living the good life]
  The good life : Helen and Scott Nearing's sixty years of self-sufficient living / by
Helen and Scott Nearing
      p.   cm.
  Reprint (1st work). Previously published: Living the good life. New York :
Schocken Books, 1970.
  Reprint (2nd work) Previously published: Continuing the good life. New York :
Schocken Books, 1979.
  Includes bibliographical references.
  ISBN 0-8052-0970-0
  1. Country life—Vermont. 2. Country life—Maine—Harborside. 3. Nearing,
Helen. 4. Nearing, Scott, 1883–   . I. Nearing, Scott, 1883–   . II. Near-
ing, Helen. Continuing the good life. 1989. III. Title.
S521.5.V5N4   1989   974.3'042—dc20   89-43162

Manufactured in the United States of America

CONTENTS

a section of photographs follows page 70

A WORD FROM HELEN

To live the good life has been the aim of countless millions through the ages. We (Helen and Scott) took part in this mutual endeavor during the last half of this twentieth century. Our contribution was but a dot in the whole scene, but it was earnestly meant and steadfastly and joyously and compatibly pursued for more than fifty years.

Now Scott has gone on, at the honorable age of one hundred, and I am left to round out my life and then go on myself. I keep open house at our Forest Farm on the coast of Maine, to help others see that a good life can still be maintained by a woman alone, in her eighties.

The good life is best attempted by a couple or a group of like-minded people, with purposes in common and sufficient capabilities and perseverance to tackle the work involved. For work it is, especially for the aged person I have become. But a lone woman can live productively, fend for herself, gardening and wood-toting and housekeeping and living in nature with a sense of fulfillment and purpose, and round out a life that once included an outstanding partner. Read his biography, *The Making of a Radical*, and agree with me that from Scott's youth to his old manhood he was an exemplar for all of us, with his competence, his industry, idealism, rectitude, and good humor.

When we are long gone, may the search for the good life go on in the lives of our fellow countrymen and countrywomen and may our efforts in buildings and books remain for a while to help others along the way.

Helen K. Nearing

Harborside, Maine
July 2, 1989

Living

THE GOOD LIFE

Irene Strauss

INTRODUCTION

THIS is a book about a twentieth century pioneering venture in a New England community. Most of the subject matter is derived from twenty years of living in the backwoods of Vermont. The book aims to present a technical, economic, sociological and psychological report on what we tried to do, how we did it, and how well or ill we succeeded in achieving our purposes.

During the deepest part of the Great Depression, in 1932, we moved from New York City to a farm in the Green Mountains. At the outset we thought of the venture as a personal search for a simple, satisfying life on the land, to be devoted to mutual aid and harmlessness, with an ample margin of leisure in which to do personally constructive and creative work. With the passage of time and the accumulation of experience we came to regard our valley in Vermont as a laboratory in which we were testing out certain principles and procedures of more general application and concern.

It was, of course, an individual experience, meeting a special need, at a particular time. When we moved to Vermont we left a society gripped by depression and unemployment, falling a prey to fascism, and on the verge of another world-wide military free-for-all; and entered a pre-industrial, rural community. The society from which we moved had rejected in practice and in principle our pacifism, our vegetarianism and our collectivism. So thorough was this rejection that, holding such views, we could not teach in the schools, write in the press or speak over the radio, and were thus denied our part in public education. Under these circumstances, where could outcasts from a dying social order live frugally and decently, and at the same time have sufficient leisure and energy to assist in the speedy liquidation of the disintegrating society and to help replace it with a more workable social system?

We might have followed the example of many of our compatriots, moved to Paris, Mexico or Paraguay, and allowed the United States to go its chosen way to destruction. We could not accept this alternative because our sense of responsibility as teachers, and as members of the human race, compelled us to do what we could (1) to help our fellow citizens understand the complex and rapidly maturing situation; (2) to assist in building up a psychological and political resistance to the plutocratic military oligarchy that was sweeping into power in North America; (3) to share in salvaging what was still usable from the wreckage of the decaying social order in North America and western Europe; (4) to have a part in formulating the principles and practices of an alternative social system, while meanwhile (5) demonstrating one possibility of living sanely in a troubled world. The ideal answer to this problem seemed to be an independent economy which would require only a small capital outlay, could operate with low overhead costs, would yield a modest living in exchange for half-time work, and therefore would leave half of the year for research, reading, writing and speaking. We decided these tasks could better be performed from a Vermont valley than from a large city or from some point outside the United States. As it turned out, we saved enough time and energy from the bread labor and the association required by our Vermont experiment to take an active though minor part in United States adult education and in the shaping of public opinion, at the same time that we were living what we regarded as a self-respecting, decent, simple life.

We had tried living in several cities, at home and abroad. In varying degrees we met the same obstacles to a simple, quiet life, —complexity, tension, strain, artificiality, and heavy overhead costs. These costs were payable only in cash, which had to be earned under conditions imposed upon one by the city,—for its benefit and advantage. Even if cash income had been of no concern to us, we were convinced that it was virtually impossible to counter city pressures and preserve physical health, mental balance and social sanity through long periods of city dwelling. After careful consideration we decided that we could live a saner, quieter, more worthwhile life in the country than in any urban or suburban center.

We left the city with three objectives in mind. *The first was economic.* We sought to make a depression-free living, as independent as possible of the commodity and labor markets, which could not be interfered with by employers, whether businessmen, politicians or educational administrators. *Our second aim was hygienic.* We wanted to maintain and improve our health. We knew that the pressures of city life were exacting, and we sought a simple basis of well-being where contact with the earth, and home-grown organic food, would play a large part. *Our third objective was social and ethical.* We desired to liberate and dissociate ourselves, as much as possible, from the cruder forms of exploitation: the plunder of the planet; the slavery of man and beast; the slaughter of men in war, and of animals for food.

We were against the accumulation of profit and unearned income by non-producers, and we wanted to make our living with our own hands, yet with time and leisure for avocational pursuits. We wanted to replace regimentation and coercion with respect for life. Instead of exploitation, we wanted a use economy. Simplicity should take the place of multiplicity, complexity and confusion. Instead of the hectic mad rush of busyness we intended a quiet pace, with time to wonder, ponder and observe. We hoped to replace worry, fear and hate with serenity, purpose and at-one-ness.

After twenty years of experience, some of it satisfactory and some of it quite the reverse, we are able to report that:

1. A piece of eroded, depleted mountain land was restored to fertility, and produced fine crops of high quality vegetables, fruits and flowers.

2. A farm economy was conducted successfully without the use of animals or animal products or chemicalized fertilizers.

3. A subsistence homestead was established, paying its own way and yielding a modest but adequate surplus. About three-quarters of the goods and services we consumed were the direct result of our own efforts. Thus we made ourselves independent of the labor market and largely independent of the commodity markets. In short, we had an economic unit which depression could affect but little and which could survive the gradual dissolution of United States economy.

4. A successful small-scale business enterprise was organized and operated, from which wagery was virtually eliminated.

5. Health was maintained at a level upon which we neither saw nor needed a doctor for the two decades.

6. The complexities of city existence were replaced by a fairly simple life pattern.

7. We were able to organize our work time so that six months of bread labor each year gave us six months of leisure, for research, travelling, writing, speaking and teaching.

8. In addition, we kept open house, fed, lodged, and visited

with hundreds of people, who stayed with us for days or weeks, or much longer.

We have not solved the problem of living. Far from it. But our experience convinces us that no family group possessing a normal share of vigor, energy, purpose, imagination and determination need continue to wear the yoke of a competitive, acquisitive, predatory culture. Unless vigilante mobs or the police interfere, the family can live with nature, make themselves a living that will preserve and enhance their efficiency, and give them leisure in which they can do their bit to make the world a better place.

Among the multitudes of friends, acquaintances and strangers who visited us in Vermont, many were so impressed with the project that they wondered whether it would be possible for them to launch a similar undertaking. Some of them discussed the matter with us, and others, who had heard of but had not seen the Vermont place, wrote asking us about it. Interest in the enterprise was stimulated by the publication of several magazine articles commenting on phases of the experiment, and by the appearance, in 1950, of *The Maple Sugar Book,* in which we wrote down the history and described the technical processes of the industry which provided us with our cash income.

Maple syrup and sugar production was only one phase of an experiment which had other and more important aspects. We suggested some of these in Part III of *The Maple Sugar Book,* especially in Chapter Ten, "Pioneers, O Pioneers" and Chapter Twelve, "A Life as Well as a Living". In the present volume we are presenting a report on the entire Vermont enterprise, omitting the sugaring details and dealing with the project as a whole. It is our hope that a novice, with the background of experience

recorded in this book, can establish and maintain a health-yield-
ing, harmless, self-contained economy. Such a handbook is
needed for the many individuals and families, tied to city jobs
and dwellings, who yearn to make their dreams of the good life
a reality. May they be encouraged and inspired to attempt such
ventures, and may they enjoy them and benefit from them as
much as we have done.

"It is my purpose to lay out unto you the waies so to dwell upon, order, and maintaine a Farme, as that it may keepe and maintaine with the profit and encrease thereof, a painefull and skilfull Husbandman, and all his Familie."

Gervase Markham, The Countrey Farme, 1616

"Useful Arts are sometimes lost for want of being put into Writing. Tradition is a very slippery Tenure, and a slender Pin to bear any great Weight for a long Time . . . Whoever has made any observation or Discoveries, altho' it be but a Hint, and looks like a small Matter, yet if pursued and improved, may be of publick Service . . . I am sure I should have been glad of such an History of Facts (as imperfect as it is). It would have afforded me Light, Courage and Instruction."

Jared Eliot, Essays upon Field-Husbandry in New-England, 1760

"There can be no doubt but that many of the articles which follow in this work will appear to men who have devoted their lives to the arts and those sciences which are most immediately connected with them, as trite and little worthy of notice. But what might seem to such persons as merely commonplace information may, perhaps, prove valuable to others, whose time may have been devoted to pursuits of a different nature."

Thomas Green Fessenden, The Register of Arts, 1808

"For want of records, much useful knowledge is continually lost. Though many individuals have derived advantages to themselves from experiments, but few have recorded them. Even those who make experiments are liable to forget them, so as to give incorrect representations of them when they attempt to relate them."

Leonard E. Lathrop, The Farmer's Library, 1826

"The principal object of this work is to save young housekeepers the pain and trouble of buying their own experience; and though it is particularly addressed to those residing in the country, I have had the satisfaction of finding that it has been in many cases almost equally useful to those living in towns."

Jane Loudon, The Lady's Country Companion, 1852

"This is not to be the history of the working of a great farm run by some rich man regardless of expense, with model buildings, model machinery, and the rest. On the contrary, here is but a modest place, modestly, if sufficiently, furnished with the necessary buildings, capital, instruments, and labour. Possibly for this very reason the details connected with it may prove of the more value to readers interested in the subject."

Rider Haggard, A Farmer's Year, 1899

"Arise, come, hasten, let us abandon the city to merchants, attorneys, brokers, usurers, tax-gatherers, scriveners, doctors, perfumers, butchers, cooks, bakers and tailors, alchemists, painters, mimes, dancers, lute-players, quacks, panderers, thieves, criminals, adulterers, parasites, foreigners, swindlers and jesters, gluttons who with scent alert catch the odor of the market place, for whom that is the only bliss, whose mouths are agape for that alone."

Francesco Petrarch, De Vita Solitaria, 1356

"My friend, if cause doth wrest thee, ere follie hath much opprest thee:
Farre from acquaintance kest thee, Where countrie may digest thee.
Let wood and water request thee, In good corne soile to nest thee,
Where pasture and meade may brest three, And heathsom aire invest thee.
Though envie shall detest thee, Let that no whit molest thee.
Thanke God, that so hath blest thee, And sit downe, Robin, and rest thee."

Thomas Tusser, Five Hundredth Pointes of Good Husbandrie, 1573

"Would not amoungst roses and jasmin dwel,
    Rather than all his spirits choak
With exhalations of dirt and smoak?
And all th' uncleannes which does drown
In pestilentiall clowds a populous town?"

Abraham Cowley, Chertsea, 1666

"Such is the superiority of rural occupations and pleasures, that commerce, large societies, or crowded cities, may be justly reckoned unnatural. Indeed, the very purpose for which we engage in commerce is, that we may one day be enabled to retire to the country, where alone we picture to ourselves days of solid satisfaction and undisturbed happiness. It is evident that such sentiments are natural to the human mind."

John Loudon, A Treatise on Forming, Improving and Managing Country Residences, 1806

"I have been seeking through all the valleys to acquire some isolated pasturage which will yet be easily accessible, moderately clement in temperature, pleasantly situated, watered by a stream, and within sound of a torrent or the waves of a lake. I have no wish for a pretentious domain. I prefer to select a convenient site and then build after my own fashion, with the view of locating myself for a time, or perhaps for always. An obscure valley would be for me the sole habitable earth."

E. P. de Senancour, Obermann, 1903

CHAPTER I

WE SEARCH FOR THE GOOD LIFE

A change of life—World conditions—Alternative affirma-
tions—Values essential to the good life—Where to live the
good life—A setting found in Vermont—From summer folk
to all-year-rounders—We buy timberland, and give it away
—We hear of mapling—The means of livelihood

MANY a modern worker, dependent on wage or salary, lodged in
city flat or closely built-up suburb and held to the daily grind
by family demands or other complicating circumstances, has
watched for a chance to escape the cramping limitations of his
surroundings, to take his life into his own hands and live it in
the country, in a decent, simple, kindly way. Caution, consideration for relatives or fear of the unknown have proved formidable
obstacles, however. After years of indecision he still hesitates.
Can he cope with country life? Can he make a living from the
land? Has he the physical strength? Must one be young to start?
Where can he learn what he needs to know? Can he build his
own house? Can he feed his family from the garden? Must he
keep animals? How much will a farm tie him down? Will it be
but a new kind of drudgery all over again? These and a thousand

11

other questions flood the mind of the person who considers a break with city living.

This book is written for just such people. We maintain that a couple, of any age from twenty to fifty, with a minimum of health, intelligence and capital, can adapt themselves to country living, learn its crafts, overcome its difficulties, and build up a life pattern rich in simple values and productive of personal and social good.

Changing social conditions during the twenty years that began in 1910 cost us our professional status and deprived us of our means of livelihood. Whether we liked it or not we were compelled to adjust to the new situation which war, revolution and depression had forced upon the western world. Our advancing age (we were approaching fifty) certainly played some part in shifting our viewpoint, but of far greater consequence were the world developments.

Beyond these social pressures our choices were in our own hands, and their consequences would descend upon our own heads. We might have stayed on in the city, enduring and regretting what we regarded as essentially unsatisfactory living conditions, or we might strike out in some other direction, perhaps along a little-used path.

After a careful first-hand survey of developments in Europe and Asia, as well as in North America, we decided that western civilization would be unable henceforth to provide an adequate, stable and secure life even for those who attempted to follow its directives. If profit accumulation in the hands of the rich and powerful continued to push the economy toward ever more catastrophic depressions; if the alternative to depression, under the existing social system, was the elimination of the unmarketable surplus through the construction and uses of ever more deadly war equipment, it was only a question of time before those who depended upon the system for livelihood and security would find themselves out in the cold or among the missing. In theory we disapproved of a social order activated by greed and functioning through exploitation, acquisition and accumulation. In practice, the outlook for such a social pattern seemed particularly unpromising because of the growing nationalistic sentiments among colonial peoples and the expanding collectivist areas. Added to this, the troubles which increasingly bedeviled western man were most acute at the centers of civilization and were multiplying as the years passed. Under these conditions we decided that we could not remain in the West and live a good life unless we were able to find an alternative to western civilization and its outmoded culture pattern.

Was there an alternative? We looked in three directions for an answer. First we considered and rejected the possibility of living abroad as refugees from what was for us a revolting and increasingly intolerable social situation. Even two decades ago, in the early 1930s, movement was far easier than it is today. In a very real sense, the world lay open before us. Where should we go in search of the good life? We were not seeking to escape. Quite the contrary, we wanted to find a way in which we could put more into life and get more out of it. We were not shirking obligations but looking for an opportunity to take on more worthwhile responsibilities. The chance to help, improve and rebuild was more than an opportunity. As citizens, we regarded it as an assignment. Therefore, we decided not to migrate.

As a second alternative to staying in the urban culture pattern of the West, we checked over the possibilities of life in a cooperative or an intentional community. In the late 1920s the chances of such a solution were few, far between and unpromising. We would have preferred the cooperative or communal alternative, but our experience, inquiries and investigations convinced us that there were none available or functioning into which we could happily and effectively fit.

Finally, we decided on the third alternative, a self-sufficient household economy, in the country, and in the United States, which we would try to make solvent, efficient and satisfying. Having made this decision, our next task was to define our purposes and adjust them to the possibilities of our situation.

We were seeking an affirmation,—a way of conducting ourselves, of looking at the world and taking part in its activities that would provide at least a minimum of those values which we considered essential to the good life. As we saw it, such values must include: simplicity, freedom from anxiety or tension, an opportunity to be useful and to live harmoniously. Simplicity, serenity, utility and harmony are not the only values in life, but they are among the important ideals, objectives and concepts which a seeker after the good life might reasonably expect to develop in a satisfactory natural and social environment. As things stand today, it is not this combination of values, but rather their opposite (that is, complexity, anxiety, waste, ugliness and uproar) which men associate with the urban centers of western civilization.

Our second purpose was to make a living under conditions that would preserve and enlarge joy in workmanship, would give a sense of achievement, thereby promoting integrity and self-respect; would assure a large measure of self-sufficiency and thus make it more difficult for civilization to impose restrictive and coercive economic pressures, and make it easier to guarantee the solvency of the enterprise.

Our third aim was leisure during a considerable portion of each day, month or year, which might be devoted to avocational pursuits free from the exacting demands of bread labor, to satisfying and fruitful association with one's fellows, and to individual and group efforts directed toward social improvement.

Our search for the good life brought us face to face with several immediate questions: Where to live the good life? How to finance the enterprise? And finally there was the central problem of how to live the good life once we had found the place and the economic means.

Where in the United States should we turn? There were countless possibilities. Multitudes were flocking to the sunny southlands, to the Carolinas, Florida, Arizona, New Mexico, California. Others were going north-west. We decided in favor of the north-east, for various reasons. *Aesthetically,* we enjoy the procession of the seasons. In any other part of the country we would have missed the perpetual surprises and delights to which New England weather treats its devotees: the snow piled high in winter and the black and white coloring from December to March; the long lingering spring with its hesitant burgeoning into green; the gorgeous burst of hot summer beauty combined with cool nights; and the crisp snap of autumn with its sudden flare of color in the most beautiful of all the seasons. The land that has four well-defined seasons cannot lack beauty, or pall with monotony. *Physically,* we believe the changing weather cycle is good for health and adds a zest to life. We even enjoy the buffeting that comes with extreme winter cold. *Geographically,* we found New England in closer contact with the Old World, from which we did not wish to sever connections.

We took our time, and during many months looked through the north-eastern states. Finally we settled on Vermont. We liked the thickly forested hills which formed the Green Mountains.

The valleys were cosy, the people unpretentious. Most of the state was open and wild, with little of the suburban or summer vacation atmosphere.

We also picked Vermont for economy's sake. In New York, New Jersey and Eastern Pennsylvania, where we first inquired, land values were high, even in the depression years. By comparison, the prices and costs in Vermont were reasonable.

Where should we go in Vermont? On the map it is a small state compared with some of its big neighbors. From a distance it seemed an easy matter to take a run through the area and check its possibilities, but when we reached the Green Mountains with their steep, curving highways and began to thread our way through the endless mazes of back roads or went on foot from valley to valley, along logging roads and trails which lost themselves in the thickets of underbrush which choke the hillsides, Vermont looked big and baffling. We decided that we needed help. We read the farm ads, gratefully accepted suggestions from friends, and finally fell into the amiable clutches of ex-farmer and present real-estate salesman, L. P. Martin of Newfane, Vermont.

Luke Martin may or may not have been a good farmer, but he was a born realtor. The fulsome descriptions he penned, the small talk and tall tales he traded and the tricks he played must have made him number one man on Beelzebub's roster of real-estaters. Luke boasted that he and his boys sold more Vermont farms than all of the other operators in that area put together. Luke talked steadily, while Gray and Winchester took turns driving the car. After escorting us around the southern part of the state for three consecutive days, they sold us a farm in the town of Winhall. Actually, we bought the first farm they showed us, but between that first view and the purchase we looked at dozens of others. None appealed to us as much as the old Ellonen place, in the Pikes Falls valley which covers part of three townships—Stratton, Winhall and Jamaica. So we went back there on a chill day in the autumn of 1932, and signed an agreement to buy the place.

Its setting and view are lovely. Nestled against a northern slope, the Ellonen place looks up at Stratton Mountain and "The Wilderness", a name applied to the 25,000 acre pulp reserves owned by paper companies. Stratton is a wild, lonely, heavily wooded 4,000 foot mountain, inhabited by 50 or 60 people, where in Daniel Webster's time there had been 1500. "A few score abandoned farms, started in a lean land, held fiercely so long as there was any one to work them, and then left on the hill-sides. Beyond this desolation are woods where the bear and the deer still find peace, and sometimes even the beaver forgets that he is persecuted and dares to build his lodge."[1]

Our new place was a typical run-down farm, with a wooden house in poor repair, a good-sized barn with bad sills and a leaky roof, a Finnish bath house, and 65 acres of land from which the timber had been cut. "Conveniences" consisted of a pump and a black iron sink in the kitchen and a shovel-out backhouse at one end of the woodshed. The place had a plenteous spring of excellent water, a meadow, a swamp or two, and some rough land facing south and stretching perhaps a third of a mile up Pinnacle Mountain, which lay to the east of Stratton. The farm was located on a dirt road seven miles from the Jamaica Post Office and two miles from the hamlet of Bondville. Both villages together had under 600 people in them, and along our ten mile stretch of back-road there were not more than a dozen families.

Peter Ellonen, a Finn, and previous owner of the farm, had

[1] Rudyard Kipling, *Letters of Travel*, N. Y.: Doubleday Page, 1920 p. 11

been killed while working in a feed mill. Most of the children had married and gone away. That left Mrs Peter and her son, Uno, with the farm, which was running down hill and growing up to brush. They were anxious to get out, and sold to us for $300 cash and a Federal Land Bank mortgage of $800.

With the transaction completed, and the deed registered in the name of the new owners, we began to realize what a plunge we had made. The road from New York City to the wilderness was short in miles but far-reaching in social consequences. We were leaping from the economic and social sophistication of a metropolis to a neighborhood in which few of the adults and none of the youngsters had ever visited a large city, in which every house was heated with wood and lighted with kerosene, and in which there was not a single flush toilet. In the first year of our stay we piled the children of several neighbor families in the back of our truck and took them to get their first glimpse of the ocean, to see their first train, to attend their first movie and treated them to their first icecream soda. Coal was an object the children had never known. They handled a piece with interest but could not see how it would burn. They were as removed from modern civilization as if they had been born in some remote Alpine village. We had crossed a wide chasm when we moved from downtown New York to this isolated spot.

We started as "summer folk", who are usually looked on by the native population as socially untouchable and a menace to agriculture. These "foreigners" come with a little or a lot of money, and do not intend to stay long or work much.

In so far as summer residents occupy abandoned land or marginal land unfit for agriculture, they do no great harm. Usually they cultivate little or no land beyond small vegetable and flower gardens. Their pastures go back to wood lots and the wood lots grow timber without benefit of selective cutting. They need no income from the land, or they count on its future income.[2] In so far as summer residents occupy productive land, take it out of use and let it revert to brush, they are a detriment to the agriculture of the state. Certainly this is true in the more productive valleys.

Another thing the summer residents do to Vermont agriculture is to put a premium on factory goods and specialties shipped in from out of state, have them carried in the stores and thus help to persuade Vermont residents that it is easier and cheaper to get dollars, exchange them for canned goods sold in the stores, and abandon long-established gardens in the course of the turnover. Thus the state is made less dependent upon its own agriculture and more dependent on dollars, many of which will be used to buy out-of-state produce.

If this process goes far enough, Vermont will develop a suburban or vacationland economy, built on the dollars of those who make their income elsewhere and spend part of it during a few weeks or months of the Vermont summer. Such an economy is predominately parasitic in terms of production, although income and expense accounts may be in balance. Carried to its logical conclusion, it would make Vermonters sell their labor-power to summer residents, mowing their lawns and doing their laundry, thus greatly reducing their own economic self-dependence. Such an economy may attract more cheap dollars to the state, but it will hardly produce self-reliant men.

Summer people do more than upset Vermont's economy. By living on their places during the summer and closing them for

[2] "Some rich theorists let the property they purchase lie unoccupied and unproductive, and speculate upon a full indemnity from the future rise in value, the more so as they feel no want of the immediate profits." William Cooper, A Guide in the Wilderness, Dublin: Gilbert & Hodges 1810 p. 20

the balance of the year, they turn sections of the State into ghost
towns. Neighborhoods, to be meaningful, must have continuity.
Part-time towns are parasitic dead towns. "No dwellers, what
profiteth house for to stand? What goodnes, unoccupied, bringeth
the land?"[3]

The social consequences of turning the countryside into a
vacationland are far more sinister than the economic results.
What is needed in any community is individuals, householders,
villagers and townsmen living together and cooperating day in,
day out, year after year, with a sufficient output of useful and
beautiful products to pay for what they consume and a bit over.
This is solvency in the best social sense. Solvency of this nature
is difficult or impossible except in an all-year-round community.

We decided to develop a means of livelihood as soon as possible, so that we could live and work in Vermont through all the
year. For a while we shuttled back and forth every two or three
months from New York and its New Jersey suburbs to the Vermont farm. Commuting eight or ten times a year across the 216
miles that separated Winhall, Vermont from New York and New
Jersey was unsatisfactory, to say the least, and we finally came to
the conclusion that our probationary period was over and we
would take the plunge. We moved up our belongings in our small
truck and passed from part-time summer people to all-year-
rounders.

We were not quite sure how newcomers should behave in
Vermont, except that we agreed with Captain Basil Hall who
wrote in 1829, "I think it should be a rule for persons coming
to a new country, always first to follow the customs of that
country as closely as possible, reserving their improvements till

[3] Thomas Tusser, *Five Hundredth Pointes of Good Husbandrie*, Lon.:
Tottell 1573 p. 11

they get firmly established, and see good reason to apply them."⁴ Rather timidly, not wanting to disturb things too much, we cut some poplars near the house and split them up for firewood. It turned out to be the poorest wood on the place. Then we picked the wrong spot and laid out a garden. There was little choice for garden ground on this sixty-five acres, most of which was covered with brush. On the cleared land, flat places were wet or swampy, and dry places were so steep that showers would speedily carry off the topsoil.

The land we picked for gardening did not look too bad in the autumn. It sloped gently to the south and south-west, as a good Vermont garden should, seemed reasonably dry and had a heavy sod deep rooted in black soil. The next spring we learned the reason for the heavy sod and the black soil. A spring opened in the high side of the garden. It dried up in the summer but flowed copiously while the snow was melting and the spring rains were falling. Do what we would, that garden spot was a quagmire until late in the season. We ditched the water around the garden and finally dug a drain across the entire patch, following the slope of the land. Through eternal vigilance and considerable sweat, we coped with the difficulties of drainage, cleared the patch of witch-grass, and in the eight years during which we used that plot, produced some fairly good crops.

Only the well-to-do can go to the country, buy a farm, install a water supply, a bathroom, a refrigerator and electricity, tear down the chicken coop and pig pen, convert the barn into a studio and garage, paint the entire place white, leave on Labor Day and return the second week of the following June. We were not well-to-do, and we had burned our bridges and moved to the wilds on a year-round basis. How were we to keep going?

⁴ *Travels in North America*, Phil.: Carey, Lea & Carey, 1829, Vol. I, p. 176

We had thought the matter over and hoped to make our living by the development of a forest and the selective cutting of timber and pulp wood. Forest reproduction is rapid in the Green Mountains and the market for forest products is close at hand. With this in mind, soon after our move we bought a large tract of cut-over land on Pinnacle Mountain, adjoining our place and lying back from the town road. The cost was three dollars an acre. John Tibbets, a Newfane lumberman who owned the tract, had lumbered it off in 1916–19 and had no desire to pay the taxes on the land for twenty or thirty years until another crop of timber was ready for cutting. Cut-over land which does not border on a public road and has no buildings on it can still be bought in this section of Vermont in blocks of a hundred or more acres for under ten dollars an acre.

When lumbermen cut over a tract, they take out only the trees that contain at least one twelve foot log, or the spruce and fir which can be cut into four foot lengths and sold for paper pulp. The land and trees that are left are useless to a lumberman who slashes off timber in a big way, but they offer possibilities as a source of steady cash income for one or two people who are not out to strike it rich, and who are satisfied with a modest cash return.

On the piece of cut-over land, when we bought it, there were many beech, birch and maples with short or crooked or partly rotted trunks, which would not make logs but which would yield a cord or more of firewood per tree. It is possible to convert these cull trees into cordwood, to take out inferior trees such as poplar, soft maple and beech, to cut up the trees which fall in every winter storm, to cull out spruce and fir seedlings into Christmas trees or decorations, to thin young spruce and fir groves for pulp wood and to cut the better trees into logs and cordwood as they mature.[5] Cut-over land, weeded and thinned, and cut selectively as trees become marketable, will yield a man a small, steady income for an indefinite period. Probably he will make less cash on such a project than he could get in wages from a professional lumberman, but he is his own boss and can do the work when it fits best into his own economy.[6]

Such cut-over or "sprout" land had one supreme advantage for people in our position. It required only a small capital outlay and frequently could be bought for an insignificant down payment. To be sure, a lumber company which has slashed the timber from a piece of land and is willing to sell it for a few dollars an acre, will not bother to lay out less than a hundred acres. When Norman Williams tried to buy a piece of cut-over land to the east of Pikes Falls from the Smith Lumber Company, they offered him a hundred acres for $300. He and one of the Smith boys drove four corner stakes around the piece, "by guess and by God". Later we surveyed the piece for them and found that it contained 125 acres. The Smith boys did not worry, however. An extra 25 acres of $3 land was a negligible detail as far as their accounts were concerned. And when Charlie Wellman asked Norm to sell him an acre, Norm obliged, driving stakes at the four corners of a square, 206 by 206 feet. For this acre Charlie paid Norm $3, at a time when a good axe was worth $4.50.

[5] In *The Maple Sugar Book*, Chapters Four and Eleven, we discussed in detail work on the woodlot, and the place of wood cutting in a self-contained rural economy.

[6] "There are few farms in the United States where it is not convenient and profitable to have one or more wood lots attached. They supply the owner with his fuel, which he can prepare at his leisure; they furnish him with timber for buildings, rails, posts and for his occasional demands for implements; they require little attention, and if well managed, yield more or less forage for cattle and sheep. The trees should be kept in a vigorous, growing condition, as the profits are as much enhanced from this cause as any of the cultivated crops." R. L. Allen, *The American Farm Book*, N. Y.: Saxton 1849 p. 295

These rather fantastic figures give an idea of the relatively low price at which cut-over land could be bought and sold in Vermont between 1932 and 1945.

As things turned out, we never got into the timber business, nor did we make use of the Tibbets tract. After paying taxes on it for about eighteen years, we found that it carried an estimated two and a half million board feet of merchantable timber and the lumber barons were after it. The great increase in lumber prices due to the war of 1941–45 had made the Tibbets tract worth more than ten times the amount we paid for it in 1933. Since this increment was due, not to any efforts of ours, but to the growth of the United States in population and wealth, and particularly to participation in war, we made up our minds that we would not profit in any way from the butchering of the trees.

We knew that European towns, in wooded regions, frequently own timber tracts which are forested collectively. These forests are an excellent source of cash income for the towns, and provide enduring and useful monuments which one generation may pass on to its successors. A Vermont State law authorizes towns to own municipal forests, provided that cutting is done under the direction of the State Department of Forestry. So we deeded the entire Tibbets tract to the Town of Winhall in 1951. The next year the Town began cutting one quarter of the area selectively, and under State supervision. If the tract is well handled it should provide the Town with a sizeable income for an indefinite period.[7]

[7] "Though we cannot expect to find many in this Age publick-spirited enough to have such regard to the general Good, as to prefer it before their private Interest; yet the particular Profit that Timber brings to the Owners of it, as well as its Advantage to the Publick, might if it had not caused more Care in propagating of it, have at least prevented those that have had opportunities of experiencing its Advantages, from making that destruction and general spoil that hath everywhere of late been made of Woods." J. Mortimer, *The Whole Art of Husbandry*, Lon.: Mortlock 1712 p. 294

A new possibility had presented itself which turned our minds from lumbering. The first spring after we moved into the Ellonen place, the Hoard boys who lived with their mother, Mercy Hoard, on the next place north of us, burned over their pastures. When they got down in our direction, we noted with alarm that while the two houses were almost half a mile apart, the Hoard land ran to within about a dozen feet of our house and not much farther from our barn. The boys kept the fires under control that day, but the flames came too close for comfort.

We decided to ask Mercy Hoard to sell us a strip of land that would protect our house and barn from future pasture burnings. We found she wanted to move away and she then and there offered us her entire place with its down-at-the-heels buildings, its better than average sugar bush and its decrepit sugarhouse. She wanted a year to cut the 60,000 feet of logs which she estimated were on the place, and after that sold us the farm quite reasonably.

Frank Hoard had been dead for some time when we bought this new place. All of the children except Rodney were grown up and leaving home, and Mercy and the boys had pretty well given up farming. The sugar bush, overgrown with softwood and thick with brush, was being sugared on shares by Floyd Hurd, his wife Zoe, and such of their eleven children as were big enough to lend a hand when sap began to run in the spring. We talked things over with Floyd and Zoe, and continued the original share arrangement. That first year, without raising a finger, we got one-quarter of the syrup crop for the use of the tools and the bush and some fuel. Not knowing what else to do with that amount of syrup, we stored it in gallon cans in an old horse stall in the Ellonen barn. That summer, however, we discovered that maple syrup in Vermont is better than cash. It sells readily and does not depreciate. Here was something on which we had not counted. In a syrup season lasting from four to eight weeks, owning only the maple trees, the sugar house and some poor tools, and doing none of the work, we got enough syrup to pay our taxes and insurance, to provide us with all the syrup we could use through the year, plenty to give away to our friends and to sell. We realized that if we worked at sugaring ourselves, syrup would meet our basic cash requirements.

We were surprised and delighted to learn that here might be the answer to our problem of making a living amid the boulders scattered over the green hills of Vermont. We had been counting on cutting over the woodland as a source of cash income, but there in the barn, before our eyes, stood row upon row of shining cans of maple syrup, all saleable for immediate cash. Up to that moment we had not given a thought to syrup production. We had scarcely noted the sugar houses which dotted the hills all about us, and we had certainly never considered the possibility of our making syrup and sugar. The excellent maple crop in the spring of 1934 opened our eyes to new prospects and put hopes of a solid economic foundation under our Vermont project.

The finding of a spot in Vermont which appealed to our reason, enthusiasms and pocketbooks answered our first question: *where to live the good life.* The possibility of sugaring for a living answered the second question: *how to finance the good life.* Our next job was to determine *the way in which the good life was to be lived.*

"When the sun rises, I go to work,
When the sun goes down, I take my rest,
I dig the well from which I drink,
I farm the soil that yields my food,
I share creation, Kings can do no more."

Ancient Chinese, 2500 B.C.

"O God! methinks it were a happy life,
To be no better than a homely swain,
To set upon a hill, as I do now . . .
So many hours must I tend my flock;
So many hours must I take my rest;
So many hours must I contemplate;
So many hours must I sport myself;
Ah, what a life were this, how sweet! how lovely!"

William Shakespeare, King Henry VI, 1623

"I am retired to Monticello where . . . I enjoy a repose to which I have been long a stranger. My mornings are devoted to correspondence. From breakfast to dinner, I am in my shops, my garden, or on horseback among my farms; from dinner to dark, I give to society and recreation with my neighbors and my friends; and from candle-light to early bedtime, I read. My health is perfect, and my strength considerably reinforced by the activity of the course I pursue; perhaps it is as great as usually falls to the lot of near 67 years of age. I talk of plows and harrows, of seeding and harvesting with my neighbors, and of politics too, if they choose, with as little reserve as the rest of my fellow citizens, and feel, at length, the blessing of being free to say and do what I please, without being responsible to any mortal."

Thomas Jefferson, Letter to Kosciusko, Feb. 26, 1810

"No man is born in possession of the art of living, any more than of the art of agriculture; the one requires to be studied as well as the other, and a man can no more expect permanent satisfaction from actions performed at random, than he can expect a good crop from seeds sown without due regard to soil and season . . . Nothing is more conducive to happiness, than fixing on an end to be gained, and then steadily pursuing its attainment."

J. C. Loudon, An Encyclopedia of Agriculture, 1825

"There are two ways of living: a man may be casual and simply exist, or constructively and deliberately try to do something with his life. The constructive ideas implies constructiveness not only about one's own life, but about that of society, and the future possibilities of mankind."

Julian Huxley, Essays of a Biologist, 1923

CHAPTER 2

OUR DESIGN FOR LIVING

Our assets—We make a ten year plan—Free of price-profit
—Not out to make money—No I.O.U.'s—Cooperation
wherever possible—Build up a sugar business—Share other
farm products—Keep no animals—We will tear down old
buildings and pick sites for new—We will build of rock,
gathering materials beforehand—The essential gravel pit
and its ramifications—Order heaven's first law—Good tools
will last—Self discipline necessary—Work schedules

THINGS were moving fast—perhaps too fast. We were getting in
deep. Was it too deep? We had acquired three neglected farms
and were starting off at sugaring, of which we knew nothing.
Where were these events leading us? Did the sweeping changes
in our way of life mean commitments and entanglements which
we would regret later on? We had to be wary as well as watch-
ful. Our situation could be summed up in three paragraphs.

We were in the country. We had land. We had all the wood
we could use, for the cutting. We had an adequate supply of
food from the gardens. We had time, a purpose, energy, enough
ingenuity and imagination, a tiny cash income from maple and
a little cash money on hand.

29

We were on a run-down, run-out farm. We were living in a poorly built wooden house through which the winter winds swept like water through a sieve. We owned a timber tract that would come into its own only in twenty to thirty years. We owned the place next door, another run-down farm, equipped with wretched buildings. Our soil was swampy, rough and rocky, mostly covered with second growth, but there was a small amount of good timber left on it. Our gardens were promising, but the main garden was too low and wet to be really productive.

We were in good health. We were solvent in that we had no debts. We were fairly hopeful of the future, but inexperienced in the ways of subsistence living and somewhat uncertain as to how we should proceed. After due consideration and in the spirit of the times, we drew up a ten year plan.

This plan was not made out of whole cloth, all at once. It was modified by experience, as we went along. It was flexible, but in principle and usually in practice we stuck to it. Suppose we set down the main points which the plan covered when we outlined it in the middle 1930's.

1. *We wish to set up a semi-self-contained household unit, based largely on a use economy, and, as far as possible, independent of the price-profit economy which surrounds us.*

The Great Depression had brought millions of bread-winners face to face with the perils which lurked for those who, in a commodity economy based on wage-paid labor, purchase their livelihood in the open market. The wage and salary workers did not own their own jobs, nor did they have any part in deciding economic policy nor in selecting those who carried policy into effect. The many unemployed in 1932 did not lose their jobs through any fault of their own, yet they found themselves workless, in an economy based on cash payment for the necessaries and decencies. Though their incomes had ceased, their outgo for food, shelter and clothing ate up their accumulated savings and threw them into debt. Since we were proposing to go on living in this profit-price economy, we had to accept its dread implications or find a workable alternative. We saw that alternative in a semi-subsistence livelihood.

We would attempt to carry on this self-subsistent economy by the following steps: (1) Raising as much of our own food as local soil and climatic conditions would permit. (2) Bartering our products for those which we could not or did not produce. (3) Using wood for fuel and cutting it ourselves. (4) Putting up our own buildings with stone and wood from the place, doing the work ourselves. (5) Making such implements as sleds, drays, stone-boats, gravel screens, ladders. (6) Holding down to the barest minimum the number of implements, tools, gadgets and machines which we might buy from the assembly lines of big business.[1] (7) If we had to have such machines for a few hours or days in a year (plough, tractor, rototiller, bull-dozer, chain-saw), we would rent or trade them from local people instead of buying and owning them.

2. *We have no intention of making money, nor do we seek*

[1] All through the years in Vermont we had one expensive, indispensable machine, a half-ton pick-up truck. The first one was a Dodge; later came Fords and Chevrolets, until we got a Jeep, which proved incomparably superior to the others because of its four-wheel drive. If we had done our driving on concrete highways, the four-wheel mechanism would have been superfluous, but on back roads, across fields and through the woods, up and down hills, in mud, snow, slush and on ice, the four-wheel drive paid for its extra cost in one season. Occasionally there might be something, logs, for example, which we could not handle in a pick-up with a body 48 inches wide by 78 inches long, though we did rig up a device that enabled us to carry easily and in quantity, standard iron pipe lengths 21 feet long and even longer poles. The pick-up handled lumber, gravel, stone, lime, cement, topsoil, cord wood and sugar wood, freight and express. It also delivered our sugar products, and carried us many thousand miles each year

wages or profits. Rather we aim to earn a livelihood, as far as possible on a use economy basis. When enough bread labor has been performed to secure the year's living, we will stop earning until the next crop season.

Ideas of "making money" or "getting rich" have given people a perverted view of economic principles. The object of economic effort is not money, but livelihood. Money cannot feed, clothe or shelter. Money is a medium of exchange,—a means of securing the items that make up livelihood. It is the necessaries and decencies which are important, not the money which may be exchanged for them. And money must be paid for, like anything else. Robert Louis Stevenson wrote in *Men and Books*, "Money is a commodity to be bought or not to be bought, a luxury in which we may either indulge or stint ourselves, like any other. And there are many luxuries that we may legitimately prefer to it, such as a grateful conscience, a country life, or the woman of our inclination."[2]

People brought up in a money economy are taught to believe in the importance of getting and keeping money. Time and again folk told us, "You can't afford to make syrup. You won't make any money that way." One year a neighbor, Harold Field, kept a careful record of the labor he put in during the syrup season and of the sale price of his product, and figured that he got only 67 cents an hour for his time. In view of these figures, the next year he did not tap out because sugaring paid less than wage labor. But, during that syrup season he found no chance to work for wages, so he didn't even make the 67 cents an hour.

Our attitude was quite different. We kept careful cost figures, but we never used them to determine whether we should or should not make syrup. We tapped our trees as each sap season

[2] Lon.: Chatto & Windus 1888 p. 143

came along. Our figures showed us what the syrup had cost. When the season was over and the syrup on hand, we wrote to various correspondents in California or Florida, told them what our syrup had cost, and exchanged our product for equal value of their citrus, walnuts, olive oil or raisins. As a result of these transactions, we laid in a supply of items at no cash outlay, which we could not ourselves produce. Our livelihood base was broadened as the result of our efforts in the sugar bush and the sap house.

We also sold our syrup and sugar on the open market. In selling anything, we tried to determine exact costs and set our prices not in terms of what the traffic would bear but in terms of the costs,—figuring in our own time at going day wages.

Just as each year we estimated the amount of garden produce needed for our food, so we tried to foresee the money required to meet our cash obligations. When we had the estimated needs, we raised no more crops and made no more money for that period. In a word, we were trying to make a livelihood, and once our needs in this direction were covered, we turned our efforts in other directions,—toward social activities, toward avocations such as reading, writing, music making, toward repairs or replacements of our equipment.

3. *All of our operations will be kept on a cash and carry basis. No bank loans. No slavery to interest on mortgages, notes and I.O.U's.*

Under any economy, people who rent out money live on easy street. Whether as individuals or banking establishments, they lend money, take security and live on a rich harvest of interest and the proceeds of forced sales. The money lenders are able to enjoy comfort and luxury, without doing any productive labor. It is the borrowing producers who pay the interest or lose their

property. Farmers and home owners by the thousands lost everything they had during the Great Depression because they could
not meet interest payments. We decided to buy for cash or not
at all.

4. *We will make our cash crop from maple syrup and will work
out a cooperative arrangement wherever possible.* We made a
cooperative agreement with Floyd Hurd and his family under
which we would work together and divide the syrup crop in
proportion to land and tools owned and the work done by each
party. We began this arrangement in 1935 and continued it for
six years with the Hurds, later carrying it on with other people.

5. *We will put syrup production on an efficient basis, replace
the old Hoard sugarhouse with a modern building and equip it
with new tools.* We did this in 1935, we building the new sugarhouse and the Hurds buying a large new evaporator. We also
decided to convert part of our syrup crop into maple sugar, for
which there was a ready sale. The complete story of this effort
has been told in detail in *The Maple Sugar Book.*

6. *So long as the income from the sale of maple syrup and sugar
covers our needs we will not sell anything else from the place.
Any garden or other surpluses will be shared with neighbors and
friends in terms of their needs.*

This latter practice was carried out generally in the valley. Rix
Knight had extra pear trees. In a good season he distributed
bushels to any of us who had no pears. Jack Lightfoot let us
pick his spare apples and let others cut Christmas greens, free of
charge. We brought firewood to those who needed it, and many
garden products. Our chief delight was growing, picking and
giving away sweet peas. We grew these in profusion,—double
rows 60 to 100 feet long, each year. Whenever taking a trip to
town in blooming season (July to frost of late September) we

filled baskets and basins with dozens of bunches and gave them out during the day to friends and strangers alike. Grocers, dentist friends, gas station attendants, utter strangers on the street,—all were the delighted recipients of the fragrant blossoms. One woman, after endeavoring to pay for a large bunch, was heard to go off muttering, "I've lived too near New York too long to understand such practices."

7. *We will keep no animals.* Almost without exception, Vermont farmers have animals, often in considerable variety. We do not eat animals, or their products, and do not exploit them. We thus escape the servitude and dependence which tie both farmer and animal together. The old proverb "No man is free who has a servant" could well read "No man is free who has an animal."

Animal husbandry on a New England farm involves building and maintaining not only sheds but barns and the necessary fences, and also the cutting or buying of hay. Into this enterprise goes a large slice of the farmer's time. Farm draft animals work occasionally but eat regularly. Many of them eat more than they produce and thus are involuntary parasites. All animals stray at times, even with the best of fences, and like all runaway slaves, must be followed and brought back to servitude. The owners of horses, cattle, pigs and chickens wait on them regularly, as agrarian chamber maids, feeding, tending them and cleaning up after them. Bernard Shaw has said: "Millions of men, from the shepherd to the butcher, become mere valets of animals while the animals live, and their executioners afterwards."

We believe that all life is to be respected—non-human as well as human. Therefore, for sport we neither hunt nor fish, nor do we feed on animals. Furthermore, we prefer, in our respect for life, not to enslave or exploit our fellow creatures. Widespread and unwarranted exploitation of domestic animals includes rob-

bing them of their milk or their eggs as well as harnessing them
to labor for man. Domestic animals, whether cows, horses, goats,
chickens, dogs or cats are slaves. Humans have the power of life
or death over them. Men buy them, own them, sell them, work
them, abuse and torture them and have no compunctions against
killing and eating them. They compel animals to serve them in
multitudinous ways. If the animals resist, rebel or grow old, they
are sent to the butcher or else are shot out of hand.

Cats and dogs live dependent subservient lives under the table
tops of humans. Domestic pets kill and drive away wild creatures, whose independent, self-respecting lives seem far more
admirable than those of docile, dish-fed retainers. We enjoy the
wild creatures, and on the whole think they are more lithe, beautiful and healthy than the run of cats and dogs, although some
of our best friends in Vermont have been canine and feline
neighbors.

While remaining friends with all kinds of animals, we preferred to be free from dependents and dependence. Many a
farmer, grown accustomed to his animal-tending chores and to
raising food for animals instead of for himself, could thus find his
worktime cut in half.

8. *We will not waste time making over old buildings. We will
use them as long as necessary, repair them if we must, but in
general we realise they are on the skids. If they have no function,
we will tear them down at the first opportunity. Only if they are
useful and necessary, will we replace them.*

We wanted a fireplace in the Ellonen house. The only practicable way to get it was to add a room; there was no other possible space. So we built a 12 x 12 foot stone-walled addition, with
a stone fireplace, a stone floor and pine-panelled walls. With that
exception, we made only urgently necessary repairs to the old

Ellonen buildings, although we lived in the house for nine years before we moved into new quarters.

Some of our friends and neighbors cry out in protest: "But the lines on these old houses!" Our answer is simple, and in three parts. (1) If we are worth a snap of the fingers, we can build with lines as good or better than our great-grandfathers. If we cannot, we do not deserve to live in a well-designed house. (2) The refurbishing of an old building will often cost as much, and sometimes more, in time and money than the construction of a new one.[3] (3) When you get all through with the old building you still have an old framework, which means old and often rotten sills, studs, plates, floor joists and rafters. Corners or lines may never be square or true, and the style and planning are not really custom-fitted to the modern occupant. "He that alters an old house is as tied as a translator to the original, and is confined to the fancy of the first builder."[4]

A dozen times, since we moved to Vermont, we have watched relatives and friends remodel old buildings. We think that the three points in the preceding paragraph applied in every instance.

9. *We will pick out the sites for a permanent house and other necessary buildings, and for gardens which can be terraced for drainage during wet seasons and can be irrigated in dry spells.* Chapter Three "Building a Stone House" and Chapter Four "Our Good Earth" give details of the way we put this ninth proposition into practice.

10. *We will build of natural stone and rock. This can be done*

---

[3] "I may remark here, in way of warning to those who undertake the renovation of slatternly country places with exuberant spirits, that it is a task which often seems easier than it proves." D. G. Mitchell, *My Farm of Edgewood*, N.Y.: Scribner 1863 p. 57

[4] Thomas Fuller, *The Holy State and the Profane State*, Cambridge: Daniel 1632 p. 166

most efficiently by gathering the materials long beforehand. We
will sort all stone that we have to move, establish piles for wall
stones, corner stones, chimney stones, floor stones, terrace stones
and fireplace stones to prepare for the years when we can build.

From the birth of our idea of building a stone house we started
collecting these rocks.[5] From roadsides, from our garden, gravel
pit, old stone walls, on walks in the woods, all over the countryside we kept our eyes open for well-shaped rocks, of any cartable
size. We followed old Thomas Tusser's advice: "Come home
from land, with stone in hand", said he.[6] "Where stones be too
manie, annoieng thy land, Make servant come home with a
stone in his hand. By daily so dooing, have plentie yee shall, Both
handsome for paving and good for a wall."[7] Some desirable stone
we even trucked in from out-of-state. Neighbors became interested, and turning up good rock with the plow or the pick,
contributed them to our growing piles.

We set aside a convenient locality, out of the way of building
or hauling, but handy to our site. We put up rough sign-boards
labelled "Corner", for stones having one 90° angle; "Blue Ribbon",
for those having a good flat face; "Floor", for thin, large rocks
having a smooth flat surface; "Chimney", for regular blocks, with
well-set corners if possible; and "Uglies", for just plain stone,
of odd sizes and shapes, which could be used for foundations or
for fillers. Stone gathering became a real preoccupation on our

[5] "A great part of the cost of a stone building is the expense of collecting
the materials . . . If the materials should be collected in winter, or at any
leisure time, and be handy to the spot, it is presumed that the cost of a neat
and handsome house would not exceed much, if any, the expense of a wooden
building, when the timber and the boards are to be purchased and carted
from some distance." J. M. Gourgas, in *The New England Farmer*, April 4,
1832, p. 298

[6] *Five Hundred Pointes of Good Husbandrie*, Lon.: Tottell 1573 p. 96
[7] *Ibid.*, p. 99

walks or drives, and it was a rare day when we did not come back "with stone in hand."

11. *First among the new buildings to be erected in our construction program will be a lumber shed where our green lumber can be stored and dried under the best conditions. This will give us air-dried lumber when we come to build.* As it turned out, our supply of lumber put in the shed in 1933–36, provided us during the years from 1938–43 (when we did most of our building), with $25 lumber at a time when the same lumber, green at the mill, was hard to get at $125 per thousand feet.

12. *Since building with concrete requires sand and gravel, we will need a dependable source of good gravel and sand.* This was a must! So we set out in 1934 in search of a satisfactory gravel pit.

We were not alone in our search for gravel. We lived on a dirt road, which the town had to patch continually, repair and rebuild with gravel. The town roadmen told us that there was only one good gravel pit within easy hauling distance. They had made repeated tests elsewhere in the valley, they said, but without success. The available pit belonged to an estate administered by Dr. Heflon of Jamaica. It was in this pit that the roadmen got their supply. For a time we hauled sand and gravel from that pit. Then the estate was sold to some New Yorkers who said they did not want any gravel trucks running through their front yard, and they forbid entrance. The closing of this pit meant hauling gravel from the other side of the mountain. We took this in our stride and began getting it from miles away, but the material was very fine and mixed with quicksand and clay, both of which spoil concrete.

While we were puzzling over this problem, Charlie White happened to stop us one day on a trip to Jamaica. "You don't want

to buy a piece of land up your way?" he asked. We said we had
plenty, but as an afterthought inquired where it was. It turned
out to be a 13 acre tract adjoining the place on which the New
York owners had closed the gravel pit. We looked it over, tested
it in several places, decided that it contained good gravel and
asked the owner, Sadie Clayton, how much she wanted for it.
She said her price was $100. "But", she said, "Merrill Stark has
put down $25 on the place and he was going to buy it. His option
has run out and he hasn't any money. I don't want to pay taxes
on it, so I'm going to sell it."

Here was a bear-trap. Merrill Stark, of the famous Vermont
Stark family, lived at Pikes Falls, two miles south of us. There
were the makings of a neighborhood feud here if we bought the
land he wanted. How could we get it amicably?

After discussion, we made Sadie Clayton this offer: We will
give you a check for $100 drawn to you, a check for $25 drawn
to Merrill Stark, and we will pay the back taxes on the tract,
which amounted to about $10. Sadie Clayton accepted, Merrill
Stark got back his $25 and was friendly and neighborly to us
until his death several years later, and we got a badly needed
gravel pit.

Of course we had no use for 12 acres of gravel. One acre was
enough. So we opened up a pit at a place that seemed handiest to
the road, staked off something less than two acres at this end of
the tract and divided the remainder of the land into two pieces.
On one of these we built a small log cabin, an experiment for
us in this kind of building, and sold it for $600. We learned a
lot in the building of it, and the principal lesson was not to build
again of logs.[8] On the other piece of land we built a four room,

---

[8] "If I were commencing life again in the woods, I would not build anything
of logs except a shanty or a pig-sty; for experience has plainly told me that

one-story stone building with a stone springhouse at the back, which we sold for $2,000. Into the latter building, which was located about 100 yards from the gravel pit, went the rocks which were coming in large quantities from the stone piles remaining after we had taken out sand and gravel. We built stone fireplaces and chimneys into both houses.

We look upon profits and the profit system as iniquitous. Therefore we kept careful expense accounts on these two houses, allowed ourselves day wages for the time we put in on them, added land costs, material and building costs, and thus arrived at a profit-free selling price. The building and sale of the two houses brought us much experience and a small amount of capital which we promptly invested in our other building projects.

Gravel pit yields included sods and topsoil with which we built up our terraced gardens and compost piles; subsoil and boulders which we used for fill on construction jobs; stone and sand and gravel which went into walls, floors and chimneys. We kept the top of the pit skinned back to reduce the likelihood of organic matter getting into the underlying clean gravel and sand. We constructed a rough gravel screen which separated pit material into three grades—sand, gravel up to 1½ inches in diameter, and small stones. These stones were ideal for road work. They solidified mudholes and made hard wheel tracks. In eighteen years, beside a small amount of material used by the town, and some

---

log buildings are the dirtiest, most inconvenient, and the dearest, when everything is taken into consideration. As soon as the settler is ready to build, let him put up a good frame, roughcast, or stone house, if he can possibly raise the means, as stone, timber, and lime cost nothing but the labour of collecting and carrying the materials. When I say that they 'cost nothing', I mean that no cash is required for these articles, as they can be prepared by the exertion of the family." Samuel Strickland, 27 *Years in Canada West*, Lon.: Bentley 1853 Vol. I. pp. 170-1

given to friends and neighbors, we removed 5,050 pick-up truck loads of material from the gravel pit.

During the course of years we took out enough good earth to enlarge the truck-garden, enough non-building rocks and even roots and other coarse material to fill a swamp so that we could drive around the sugarhouse woodshed, and enough subsoil and rough stones to build and add to many roads round the place. All material was used, from loam down through the various strata to fine gravel. The fill behind the sugarhouse woodshed, for instance, was a deep drop that could absorb anything up to four feet in diameter.

Projects of this type, rushed to completion in a few months, would have involved a heavy outlay of time and would have led to delay in the fulfillment of other more essential features of our over-all plan. Actually, the third and final unit of the truck garden was completed and put into full production eleven years after the first unit of the truck garden was begun. When finished, it was about 75 feet long by 28 feet wide. It was divided into three units or terraces by concrete and stone retaining walls. Into this garden we put about 300 truck loads of soil. We built the first unit immediately as an urgent project, because we needed the food supply. After that, we built the truck garden only as we had available materials. The lower side of the garden consisted of a fill which in some places was six feet deep. Into such a deep fill we could put almost any type of subsoil. As we approached the garden level, however, we used only first grade topsoil.

We aimed never to move stones, earth or any material more than once—directly to its final resting place. We had many projects going on at the same time, in various stages of completion. Thus, the finishing of these successive units was a by-product of the wastes from other projects. In a sense they cost us nothing, because it was necessary in any case to move these materials. In another sense they were a dividend, because had we moved these superfluous materials and dumped them just anywhere, we would have ended up with a littered, unsightly landscape, whereas with our procedure, each load of material from foundation or gravel pit was ticketed in advance to a specific destination and for a specific purpose. In a very real sense the truck garden was not built, it grew, over a decade, as a part of a general plan aimed toward a place for everything (including wastes), and everything to its place.

These twelve points were the essentials of our ten year plan,—the items in our card catalog. They made up the Constitution of our household organization. We also drew up by-laws of household procedure, the first of which called for order.

We were planning a functioning homestead, not a business; nevertheless we tried to be as systematic as though we were handling a large-scale economic project. Our card index of activities had a place for "jobs to be done", divided into "clear weather jobs" and "rainy day jobs", for "construction planned", and for "finished projects". Each project had its cost cards with records of materials used and money outlay for specific purposes. Separate loose-leaf books for gardening and sugaring contained the plans, current activity reports and records from previous years.

Under "Winter Evenings" in *The Farmer's Calendar*,[9] Arthur Young advises the farmer thus: "Every work for the next day is to be arranged, whether for fine or rainy weather, and the farm-books to be made up for the transactions of the past day. Besides these, he should have another book, for miscellaneous observa-

[9] Lon.: Phillips 1805 pp. 51-2

tions, queries, speculations, and calculations, for turning and comparing different ways of effecting the same object . . . Loose pieces of paper are generally lost after a time, so that when a man wants to turn to them to examine a subject formerly estimated or discussed, he loses more time in searching for a memorandum, than would be sufficient for making half a dozen new ones; but if such matters are entered in a book, he easily finds what he wants, and his knowledge will be in a much clearer progression, by recurring to former ideas and experience."

We tackled our practical problems one by one, as we reached them. In each case we followed a pattern which began with a survey of the situation, continued with a discussion or series of discussions which led to a decision, often written down in memorandum, black on white. The decision was elaborated into a plan, also written out and often revised. Finally the plan was checked and coordinated with our ten year plan, adopted as a project and fitted into the work schedule.[10]

Some of our readers will feel that such a life pattern is over-organized. They would not wish to plan their activities so completely. After having tried it out, day after day, and year after year, we know it is the way to get things done. Two people can accomplish much in a day or a month or a year if they have defined objectives, agreed plans, if they work on the program systematically and conscientiously, giving as much attention to details as to the over-all plan.

Take an illustration from the handling and conditioning of

[10] Native Vermonters are wary of lawyers and they shy off at the sight of legal documents. Only under pressure will they put their names on a "paper". On several occasions, when considerable detail was involved, as in the division of maple syrup among those cooperating in its production, we talked the matter over, made notes of the points on which we agreed, typed the notes with carbons and handed around copies of the memorandum. In such cases no one signed, but the memorandum was a useful record.

tools. We had a place for each tool. Shovels, hoes, rakes and bars were in racks on the right as we entered the tool shed. There were as many holes in the racks as there were tools. No one ever had to hunt for a shovel or a hoe. If one was missing, a glance showed its absence and we searched until we located it. If we could not find it, we replaced it. Actually, with this system, we almost never lost a tool.

After each job which was completed in less than a working day, the tools went back into their places. At the end of each day's work we followed the same procedure. Consequently, tools which were not in place were in actual use and tools not in use were in place. We tried to follow this practice even though a tool was used on several jobs in the course of one working day. To further classify and locate tools, we painted a bright stripe of color on their handles. If left in the grass or on top of a job they were easy to see and identify.

Our neighbors, knowing we were well supplied, borrowed many tools. Of these, we tried to keep duplicates as otherwise we were often left short-tooled. Gervase Markham advocated this practice in 1616 in his *Countrey Farme*.[11] "He must have Tooles and Instruments twice so manie in store as he useth to have Workmen, to the end they need not to borrow anything of their neighbours, for otherwise hee shall lose more in dayes workes not fulfilled than would pay for the buying of his yron Tooles."

Ordinarily, capital goods should last a lifetime. Our cement mixer, for instance, bought new in 1933 for $20 was still doing good work when we passed it on to Herbert Leader twenty years later. We cleaned it up after each job and oiled it and housed it over the winter. It was a hand mixer, and many a visitor told us

[11] Lon.: Adam Flip p. 22

how we could hook it up with a gas engine or an electric motor. We continued to operate it by hand, however, and the capital outlay of twenty dollars for the mixer (minus its considerable value in 1953) spread over twenty years, came to less than one dollar per year.

Incidentally, our refusal to convert our hand mixer into a power tool had several noteworthy results. (1) We saved the time, labor, capital outlay, upkeep and replacement costs incident to the operation of all power tools. (2) We saved the outlay for gasoline or electricity. (3) We avoided the anxiety, tension, frustration and loss of time caused by mechanical breakdowns. Advocates of mechanization do not like to face the fact that a machine gets tired, gets sick and dies during its life cycle, and that a machine tender must be prepared to meet these emergencies in the life of a machine in much the same way that he must meet them in the life cycle of a domestic animal such as a horse or of any other slave. (4) Turning the mixer with first one hand and then the other, we got balanced muscle-building, invigorating, rejuvenating physical exercise in the fresh air, under the open sky,—one important ingredient in the maintenance of good health. (5) We had the satisfaction of participating directly in the project, instead of wet-nursing a machine and inhaling its oil fumes and carbon monoxide.

At this point some reader may ask us two quite reasonable questions. First, if we seek to avoid machinery, why not use a shovel instead of a hand mixer? Our reply is that much of the time we did. All of our pointing mixtures were made by hand. Also on all small jobs we mixed concrete in a steel wheelbarrow. It is easier to lug a wheelbarrow to a job than it is to lug a mixer. Furthermore, a barrow can be washed up in a quarter or a fifth of the time that it takes to wash up a mixer.

The second question might be "If you were building Hoover Dam, would you mix concrete in a wheelbarrow?" Our answer: Probably not. The machine has its function, especially on gigantic undertakings. Our project was not gigantic, but minute. We were busy setting up and maintaining a self-sufficient household. In such an enterprise machine tools are, on the whole, a liability rather than an asset.

Mankind has worked for ages with hand implements. Machine tools are a novelty, recently introduced into the realm of human experience. There can be no question but that machines have more power than humans. Also there can be no question but that they have watered down or annihilated many of the most ancient, most fascinating and creative human skills, broken up established institutions, pushed masses of "hands" into factories and herded droves of anonymous footloose wanderers from urban slum to urban slum. Only the historian of the future will be able to assess the net effect of the machine age on human character and on man's joy in being and his will to live.

We were saying that the cost of capital goods can be spread over a great period of time when we allowed ourselves to digress into a discussion growing out of a reference to our faithful and long-suffering cement mixer. We continue with our argument.

The surveyor's level and compass transit which we used in our grading and building we inherited from a grandfather. Both were made by Stackpole and Brother (long-since deceased) in the middle of the nineteenth century. Both sufficed for our simple engineering needs. Many of our hammers, saws, planes, shaves and metal tools had been well cared for and had served the needs of two and three generations. Had this equipment been left, even for brief periods, out in the weather, its life would have been shortened. Had it remained outside through the late fall and winter, it would have been soon unfit for use.[12]

We argued this point, to little purpose, with several of our neighbors. Invariably they replied that it was easier to leave the tools "handy to the field" than it was to bring them in. Many of these men had shed room and simply failed to use it.

In some ways exposure to the weather is more disastrous for the metal on tools than for the wood. Wood also suffers, however. One summer we had a job that involved handling clay in a $35 rubber-tired contractor's wheelbarrow. At the end of each day's work we washed the barrow with a hose and put it under cover for the night. Although the wooden handles of the barrow had been painted, within a month they showed serious deterioration as a result of repeated wetting and drying. We countered with generous doses of old engine-oil and saved the day.[13]

In our tool shed, at the right side of the shovel rack, hung two pieces of burlap sacking on nails. As each shovel came from a job it was wiped clean and dry with the burlap. In the winter each shovel got a coat of oil, applied in half a minute with a rejected paint brush. The shovels were never rusty, therefore clay and loam did not stick to them, nor did they require banging and scraping on the job. Clean tools do more work with less labor.

[12] "A farmer, by the nature of things, ought to be a man of strict economy. His aim ought to be habitually to prevent waste, in anything, and in all things. After he has paid $70 for his ox wagon, and $45 for the cart, they should not be left exposed to the ardent sun, nor to the rain, but carefully housed under sheds, when not in use. Plough and tools should be secured in the same way." J. M. Gourgas, in *New England Farmer*, 1/25/1828 p. 209

[13] Tool handles and other wooden parts may be painted to advantage, but the paint wears off speedily. A more effective treatment is to brush on a coat of engine oil whenever openings begin to show between the grains of the wood. A bit of fine dust, rubbed on when the oil is applied, gives the handle a pleasantly smooth surface and seals the wood pores against moisture penetration.

Axes were in a compartment next to the shovels. Each night after work, the axes went into their places. If they were dull, they were sharpened. There is more difference on a job between a dull axe and a sharp axe than there is between night and day.

With care, capital costs can be held down and capital goods can be made to last so long that the annual outlay for upkeep and replacement is reduced close to zero. Bought new, they require considerable cash expenditure, especially if purchased on installments and left out in the weather or turned over to children for playthings.

During the autumn months, as we gave the gravel pit a final once-over, inspected the sap pipelines, swept out the tool shed, sowed rye in the big garden, stored the root vegetables and the apples, and put the snow-stakes along the road and beside the culverts, we asked ourselves: "Well, what is our project for next year?" In the course of weeks or months, we talked over various possibilities, decided between them, put our decisions on paper, drew our plans, filed them in the appropriate place and were ready well ahead of time to start on them when spring came. If we found we were short of lumber for some building operation, we cut logs during the winter, put them on skids and sent them to the mill as soon as roads hardened up in the spring. We aimed to keep our lumber shed full of miscellaneous pieces for odd jobs or big projects. Our woodsheds too were filled ahead of time. We considered dry wood under cover better than money in the bank. Our inventories for the sugar business were kept well filled so that needs were anticipated and crises due to lack of essential materials were avoided. When we had money, we put it into building. If we could not finish a building one year, we stopped at a planned point and finished it the next year.

In order to carry out our various plans we had to use a certain amount of self-discipline, and expected it of those who lived with us. There were three kinds of work to be done on the farm: (1) household routine: the getting of meals, washing up, and keeping the house clean; (2) organized homestead activities: bread labor such as gardening, wood-cutting, repairs, replacements, capital construction on plant, buildings and equipment; and (3) work on the cash crop or crops.

Amongst the various people who shared our life at Forest Farm were, first, those who dropped in for a day or two. These we regarded as guests and did not try to fit them into the pattern of the place, except to let them help prepare meals and wash up.

Second, were those who stayed over a week. These we dubbed transients, and let them help with organized homestead activities for half of their time.

Last, came the permanent residents. They helped in labor categories *one* and *two,* shared all food produced on the place and could build living quarters for themselves,—we providing the building site, materials and help with plans and labor. Initiative and responsibility rested with the permanent resident. When they wished to participate in the production of the cash crop, they shared on an agreed cooperative basis.

All guests and transients were put up in our guesthouse and ate their meals with us. We aimed to make the mealtime a social event. Friends staying with us or visitors who happened to drop in knew that meals were social occasions. Whoever was present when a meal was announced—be it customer, stranger or friend— was invited to breakfast, lunch or supper. Frequently it was necessary to set a second table in our combination kitchen-dining-room.

Each day was divided into two main blocks of time—four morning hours and four afternoon hours. At breakfast time on week-days we first looked at the weather, then asked "How shall we arrange the day?" Then by agreement we decided which of these blocks of time should be devoted to bread labor and which to personally determined activities. Of necessity the weather was the primary factor in making the decision.

Suppose that the morning was assigned for bread labor. We then agreed upon the tasks that each member of the group should take on—in the garden, in the woods, on construction, in the shop, at sugarmaking or packing. If one's bread labor was performed in the morning, the afternoon automatically became personally directed. One might read, write, sit in the sun, walk in the woods, play music, go to town. We earned our four hours of leisure by our four hours of labor.

There is another very important point to remember about our projects. We were not in a hurry, except occasionally when it threatened to shower or when sap buckets were running over, or on special Christmas rush orders. All such emergencies we tried to anticipate as much as possible, in order to avoid haste, which according to the old saying, results in waste. We took our time, every day, every month, every year. We had our work, did it and enjoyed it. We had our leisure, used it and enjoyed that. During the hours of bread labor we worked and worked hard. We have never worked harder and have never enjoyed work more, because, with rare exceptions, the work was significant, self-directed, constructive and therefore interesting.[14]

There was no boss. No one pushed anyone else around. When Hank Mayer worked with us, he came from a big construction job. After the first day, he said skeptically, "I don't see how you get anything done around here. Nobody is yelling at anyone else."

[14] "What is the good of life if its chief element, and that which must always be its chief element, is odious? No, the only true economy is to arrange so that your daily labour shall be itself a joy." Edward Carpenter, *Non-Governmental Society*, Lon.: Fifield 1911 p. 15

Each was expected to contribute according to his energy and ability and for the most part, each did. There was little idling or shirking. Occasionally our difficulty was not to get people to work, but to keep them from it. The garden was a special temptation. There is always something to do in a garden. After a morning of planting or thinning, there would be some ragged edges that were not cleaned up by noon. It was so easy to slip down to the garden after lunch, intending to plant just one more row or put in those few tomato stakes. Before you knew it, half the afternoon was gone and still the garden beckoned.

When Jacob Apsel came to stay with us, he was a bit restless and uncertain as to his future and what he wanted to do. His nervousness found release in working. So day after day he would take on a morning of bread labor, and then after lunch go on with an afternoon of the same. It was a month or six weeks before we could persuade him to put his free half-day into reading or some other activity not associated with the production of our livelihood. After a time he caught on and enjoyed his four hours leisure as much as his four hours of bread labor. Jacob learned the lesson that to get things done, leisure is often as important, or, in case a person is over-tense, more important than work.

Each person on our project took vacations—blocks of time ranging from weeks to months, which were set off against equal periods of bread-labor time. We talked these matters over well in advance, arranging the vacation schedules in a way that made sense in terms of work urgency on one side and personal preference on the other. Our aim was to get a year's livelihood in return for half a year of bread labor. We were quite flexible in arranging the details. Occasionally we would work steadily for months and then take off months away from work.

On Sundays we varied our schedule by having no schedule and by doing no regular bread-labor. Usually there was a period of music Sunday morning and often a group discussion Sunday evenings. Other evenings there was a period of reading aloud by someone while the others cracked nuts, shelled beans or did some personal chore like darning or knitting. We adhered generally to this daily and weekly routine, but not fanatically. However, unless there was a good and sufficient reason, we did not depart from it.

Need we say that our Vermont neighbors were appalled by such a planned and organized life? They were accustomed to a go-as-you-please existence. They usually ate at noon, but that was the one fixed point in the day unless someone was working out on a regular job and had to report at a specified hour. They got up and went to work, or did not go to work, as a result of accident or whim. If someone came along and wanted to visit, they would turn from almost any job and chat, sometimes for hours. When they did decide to work, they let inclination determine the object of their efforts. When they got through with a tool, they dropped it. When they wanted it again, sometimes half the day was wasted in search. If the morning looked like rain or snow, they "sat on their heels" in the local vernacular. They naturally regarded our regulated life as self-imposed torture. "Those people work on a treadmill", said the neighbors pointing in our direction. "Why, they go on a schedule, like a train or a bus."

So we did, but we kept a schedule because we had definite goals toward which we were working and which we planned to reach. No job is overwhelming if you have a general idea of what you are about, break the project into manageable units, put through these units one at a time and have the thrill of fitting them into the over-all pattern.

"Would I a house for happiness erect, Nature alone should be the architect. She'd build it more convenient than great, And doubtless in the country choose her seat."

Horace, First Book, 20 B.C.

"There is some of the same fitness in a man's building his own house that there is in a bird's building its own nest. Who knows but if men constructed their dwelling, with their own hands, and provided food for themselves and families simply and honestly enough, the poetic faculty would be universally developed, as birds universally sing when they are so engaged? But alas! we do like cowbirds and cuckoos, which lay their eggs in nests which other birds have built."

Henry Thoreau, Walden, 1854

"I count it a duty to make such use of the homely materials at hand, as shall insure durability and comfort, while the simplicity of detail will allow the owner to avail himself of his own labor and ingenuity in the construction."

D. G. Mitchell, My Farm of Edgewood, 1863

"One of the greatest pleasures of life is to build a house for one's self . . . I notice how eager all men are in building their houses, how they linger about them, or even about their proposed sites. When the cellar is being dug, they went to take a hand in it; the earth evidently looks a little different, a little more friendly and congenial than other earth. When the foundations walls are up and the first floor is rudely sketched by rough timbers, I see them walking pensively from one imaginary room to another, or sitting long and long, wrapped in sweet reverie, upon the naked joist."

John Burroughs, Signs and Seasons, 1914

"In the home-built house, life goes on enriched by a sense of beauty and an innate dignity that are left over from an older time, when hard work and infinite care, not money, were spent to beautify a house and its furnishings."

K. and D. N. S., Adobe Notes, 1930

"Nature, to my mind, gave men three materials, to serve him in the course of his life: earth, in which to grow food; wood, from which to fashion furniture; and stone, of which to build his home."

Frazier Peters, Houses of Stone, 1933

CHAPTER 3

WE BUILD A STONE HOUSE

Why stone?—Our rules for architecture—Selecting a house
site—Pick and shovel work—Planning the forest farmhouse
—The Flagg system—Building, setting and filling the forms
Window and door frames—Changing the forms—Pointing
and concrete finish—Fireplaces—Passion for stones—Roofs
and roofing—Interior decoration—The whole building plan

WE BEGAN this book by describing our trek to Vermont and our
buying first the Ellonen place and later the Hoard place. It was
on the latter farm that we planned to build a home—a forest
farmhouse.

The Hoard place had on it a half-dozen run-down but still
usable buildings—a house and woodshed, a cow and hay barn
with out-buildings, a horse stable, a pig pen and chicken-house.
These buildings were designed to provide for the needs of a
general Vermont farm, based upon animal husbandry. Since we
had decided to keep no animals, most of the buildings were un-
suited to our purposes, quite aside from their ramshackle appearance and condition. At the earliest possible moment, therefore, we gave the cow and hay barn, pig pen and chicken-house
to John Korpi, who lacked these buildings and wanted them as

much as we wanted to get rid of them. He and his son took them down and hauled away all of the usable material. The horse barn we kept as a temporary tool shed. The old house was used as a carpenter shop and storage space for lumber and cement during part of our building operations, before it too was torn down and given away.

We decided to replace these old Hoard structures with a group of functional buildings, all to be constructed of stone. We chose stone for several reasons. Stone buildings seem a natural out-cropping of the earth. They blend into the landscape and are a part of it. We like the varied color and character of the stones, which are lying around unused on most New England farms. Stone houses are poised, dignified and solid—sturdy in appear-ance and in fact, standing as they do for generations. They are cheaper to maintain, needing no paint, little or no upkeep or repair. They will not burn. They are cooler in summer and warmer in winter. If, combined with all these advantages, we could build them economically, we were convinced that stone was the right material for our needs.

We are not trained architects and know next to nothing of the details of that profession. We have read on the subject, and have put up over a dozen buildings. In view of this experience, we take our courage in our hands, and state four general rules which we think should govern the architecture of domestic establish-ments.

Rule I: *Form and function should unite in the structure.* The symmetry and harmony of a building are not skin deep. They arise out of its innermost being. Neither utility nor beauty can be added to a building, as icing is added to a cake. The building should be so designed that it fulfills its economic purpose and does so without unnecessary expenditures of materials and labor.

Utility and beauty must be part and parcel of its line and form. As a rule, exterior decoration detracts from architectural beauty, although there are exceptions. Frank Lloyd Wright comments, "I have great faith that if the thing is rightly put together in true organic sense, with proportions actually right, the picturesque will take care of itself."[1]

Rule II: *Buildings should be adapted to their environment,* merging with it and becoming so indistinguishable a part of it that the observer must look twice before he decides where the environment ends and the building begins.[2] Both utility and beauty are qualities possessed by wholes rather than parts. If the environment permits of utility and is a thing of beauty, the building must continue the lines of that utility and fill out the exquisite balance and harmony which give rise to that beauty. "A building should appear to grow easily from its site and be shaped to harmonize with its surroundings if nature is manifest there, and if not, try to make it as quiet, substantial and organic as she would have been were the opportunity hers."[3]

Rule III: *Local materials are better adapted than any other to* create the illusion that the building was a part of the environment from its beginnings and has been growing up with the environment ever since. "The owner who sends far overland for unusual marbles or granites with which to build his house does not

[1] *On Architecture*, N.Y.: Duell, Sloan & Pearce 1941, p. 39

[2] "There is nothing obtrusive about old cottages. They do not dominate the landscape, but are content to be part of it, and to pass unnoticed unless one looks specially for their homely beauties. The modern house, on the other hand, makes a bid for your notice. It is built on high ground, commands a wide range of country, and is seen from far and wide. But the old cottage prefers to nestle snugly in shady valleys. The trees grow closely about it in an intimate, familiar way, and at a little distance only the wreath of curling smoke tells of its presence." Stewart Dick, *The Cottage Homes of England*, Lon.: Arnold 1909 p. 11

[3] Frank Lloyd Wright, *Ibid.*, p. 34

thereby achieve individuality, but the one who, for reasons of economy, digs up the forgotten local stone of the country—he does!"[4] "I was particularly anxious to demonstrate not only the possibility of employing the humblest materials at hand, but also of securing durability and picturesqueness in conjunction with a rigid economy."[5]

Rule IV: *The style of a domestic establishment should express the inmates and be an extension of themselves.* "A man's character emerges in the building and ordering of his house,"[6] says Richard Weaver. In a short story, "They", Rudyard Kipling writes, "I waited in a still nut-brown hall, pleasant with late flowers and peace. Men and women may sometimes, after great effort, achieve a creditable lie; but the house, which is their temple, cannot say anything save the truth of those who have lived in it."

With our four general rules in mind, we planned a long low building of native stone and local hand-hewn timbers. We would leave the natural ground levels and run the house along an uneven rocky ledge on the side of a hill. Three outside doors would have stone patios. A brown-stained balcony would front the house and look over Stratton Mountain. The roofs would be low-lying, broad eaved and stained moss green.

Snow conditions led New England farmers to locate their houses close to the public roads. The Hoard place buildings were farther back from the road than average, but they were on a low, wet flat, ill-adapted for housing purposes. Since good drainage is an essential feature of any structural operation, we were on the lookout for another building site.

[4] Edwin Bonta, *The Small-House Primer*, Little Brown 1925 p. 79
[5] D. G. Mitchell, *My Farm of Edgewood*, N.Y.: Scribners 1863 p. 84
[6] *Ideas Have Consequences*, Chicago: Univ. of Chicago Press 1948 p. 146

Skiing down the hillside above the Hoard place buildings, we ran through some brush and came onto what seemed like a low rock precipice. "It is as plumb as the wall of a house", we said. After the snow went off that spring we pushed our way back through the underbrush to view the rock. It was a split boulder, with an even face 26 feet from north-west to south-east, as vertical as though it had been set with a level, and, as it turned out later after we had cut down the trees in front of it and taken off some of the top soil, it was more than nine feet high. The back of the boulder was sunk in the hillside on the north-east. Its front faced Stratton Mountain to the south-west as accurately as though it had been set with a compass. (On a number of occasions, visitors who were not engineers asked us how we moved that great wall of rock into place.)

We had found our site. The split boulder would make the back wall of the new house. It became part of our living room and a faithful friend, whose twenty-foot-wide body kept out the north wind; who was cool to lean against in summer, and who brought a living part of nature into the home. From our second floor in back, the same rock formed a massive base for a stone patio which linked house and hill. The rock had answered the question of where to put our house.

We surveyed the surroundings. The thicket included some hemlock and white birch trees. We would leave them. Along the steep hillside above the site other boulders were scattered in wild profusion among the forest trees. The house would become a part of that setting.

The neighbors were horrified. "You don't mean to try and build up in that rock pile and brush heap!" they exclaimed. They called it "a bear garden", "a zoo", and, as the stone house went up, "a blacksmith shop". However, a comment from an 1863 volume fits our forest farmhouse. "I am gratified to perceive that the harshest observers of my poor cottage in the beginning, have now come to regard it with a kindly interest. It mates so fairly with the landscape,—it mates so fairly with its purpose; it is so resolutely unpretending, and carries such an air of permanence and durability, that it wins and has won upon the most arrant doubters."[7]

Our first building project was a lumber shed to house the boards and timbers for the building operations. Like all our buildings, it too was to be of stone. A decision to build a mere lumber shed of stone may seem too ambitious and formidable. Would not any old shelter do for lumber? Actually, the lumber-shed was an integral part of our whole plan. In Holland we had stayed in Eerde Castle, where two long low sheds fronted both sides of the roadway that swept up to the moat. We were building no castle, but the idea stayed with us. Eventually we had two long low buildings opposite each other (one, a garage and lumbershed, the other a guesthouse and toolshop) on the road that swept up to the main house. Building the lumber shed, the first of the stone buildings on the Hoard place, taught us many lessons.

Alex Crosby and his family were living for part of that summer as our guests in an unused schoolhouse which we rented from our neighbors, the Youngs. Alex was a newspaper man with a yen for creative manual work. "Isn't there some project you could assign me?" he asked, when they came up from Nyack. "Something I could do myself, at my own pace and in my own time?"

"Sure", we told him. "You might dig the foundations for the lumber shed."

[7] D. G. Mitchell, *My Farm of Edgewood*, N.Y.: Scribners 1863 p. 88

Alex went to work and made a fine job of it, under rather difficult conditions. For no sooner had he begun the digging than he ran on a shelving loose ledge which extended for many feet under one end of the building site. As we were planning to build with stone, we were forced to go down below the level where water would settle between the loose layers of this ledge, freeze to ice in the winter, heave and crack the walls.

As a matter of record, we did not get the foundation trench deep enough under one corner. Frost did heave the wall at that spot and gave us the one really bad wall crack in any of our stone-concrete buildings. This was not Alex' fault, however. During his digging, which lasted through several days, we all consulted over the knotty problems which broken ledges of loose rock always present to builders.

The lumber shed was 17 by 30 feet. That meant digging a trench 20 inches wide and about 90 feet along the four sides, getting out the dirt, removing loose rocks, of which there were many, and clearing off the exposed ledge so that foundation concrete would stick to it. We have helped dig many foundation trenches and seen many others dug in the rough terrain around that district. We have never seen a nicer looking job than Alex' trench when he had it ready for the concrete. He was justly proud of it.

While we are on this subject, we might note that many people use the phrase "pick and shovel work" with a curl of the lip. Make no mistake; digging to specifications is an art which few have mastered. Alex Crosby is one of the few we have met. Jack Lightfoot, one of our neighbors who helped us frequently and effectively with our building, is another.

The walls of the lumber shed were stone-faced outside, backed by concrete inside, built 10 inches thick. Door and window frames were made of hand-hewed spruce timbers, 6 × 6 inches, with plates of the same. Rafters were round spruce poles. Nailing strips, 1 × 6 inches, which went horizontally across the rafters, 16 inches apart, center to center, were the only milled materials in the building except for the lumber of which we built the doors. The windows, of course, we bought. To this building we later attached a 20 foot-long two-car garage, making the whole a synchronous 50 foot line.

We decided to construct the main house in three units,—a dwelling of livingroom, two bedrooms, bathroom, kitchen and cellar; a glassed-in passageway and pantry connecting to a large woodshed, half of which would consist of two rooms for sugar-packing and storage.

We wanted no complicated roof lines, so we designed two simple rectangular units with the long lines running from front to back. The passageway and pantry was a long, low narrow building joining the two main units. A second-story balcony and low overhanging eaves would give the structure an Alpine appearance. We planned to heat by fireplaces or stoves, with no radiators or central heating. We felt that steam heat, plumbing and electricity were not necessary for our comfort. Later, as electricity came into the valley we added electric light. Plumbing was to be taken care of by a running water toilet flushed with a pail, and a pump in the kitchen, which meant no pipes to freeze in winter. Our bathroom was to combine the Hindu and Finnish way of bathing. A slab of marble formed a bench against the parent rock, which became one wall of the bathroom. The floor we made with a central drain, and covered the concrete with a wooden grill. A chunk-stove heated the small room to 95° in a short time, and vessels of hot and cold water were used for washing and pouring and splashing. This built-in "Sauna" proved effective and enjoyable.

We wanted a farmhouse, not an imitation suburban or city home. We would build for utility and comfort and let convention shift for itself. We had, for instance, no front door. One entered directly into a roomy kitchen, low of ceiling, with exposed hand-hewn rafters, brown-stained panelling, wood stove and a pine plank table under broad windows facing the mountain. In the whole house there was to be no wall paper, plastering or paint. The walls were all to be wood panelled, the floors to be of stone. A colorful tapestry of books in rows of shelves, and the view through the windows, were to provide the decoration. Furniture of the simplest was to be home-made and built in wherever possible.

The first summer we contented ourselves with clearing away the brush, cutting the trees, and digging some foundation trenches. This sounds easy and simple. When we tackled it, we faced some formidable tasks. The trees, including apple and white ash, stood close together and were deep-rooted in the silt and rock-wash that had poured over the big boulder in successive freshets and floods.

There was an obvious location for the fireplace—in the east corner of the living room, right against the great rock. At that exact spot stood a sturdy white ash tree about 18 inches in diameter. White ash is proverbially well rooted. This one was no exception. We had to dig out the entire stump root by root. As the silt and loose rock offered us no satisfactory foundation for a fireplace and chimney, we went down seven feet before we reached hard-pan. Through the entire seven feet we chopped out ash roots. Along every foot of foundation trench we encountered stumps and roots, big and little. To make the work more exacting, the roots were woven and tangled through a never-ending maze of large and small ledge-chips and boulders.

The following spring we had to build a road to the new house site. In places the hill sloped steeply—as much as 15 to 20 percent. In going up this hill the truck wheels slid sidewise on the new grass, ground into the soft spring earth and then skidded on the resulting mud. We brought in stone and coarse gravel from the gravel pit and built up the road on the low side, load by load, until we got to the house site level. There we faced a new transportation problem. There was no spot large enough and level enough on which to turn the truck around. To meet this need we hauled up more stone and gravel and built a fill extending out away from the woodshed end of the house site. On its low side this fill was over six feet deep. Rock and earth from the foundation trenches and from the cellar helped us with this rather extensive project.

Like the foundation digging, the cellar looked easy. We proposed to put the cellar under the 11 by 22 foot kitchen, with its north-east end toward the big boulder. The ground was soft on top and we hoped that the silt and rock wash which lay along the boulder would extend far enough to make the cellar excavation a minor task. Alas, we had no sooner removed the top soil from the south-west end of the proposed cellar hole than we ran into a ledge of soft granite that went down to the cellar bottom. Fortunately the ledge was soft enough to be split off and removed with picks and bars. And by double good fortune these ledge slabs, exposed to the air, hardened up sufficiently to make acceptable wall-stone.

When we had cut the ledge down to cellar floor level we turned our attention to the other end of the cellar. We found no ledge there, and the washed-in dirt came out easily, but halfway back there was a good-sized boulder, five to six feet in diameter. We dug around it, decided that we could not lift it out of the cellar, voted against blasting it, inched it to the back of the cellar with bars, and walled it up, leaving a small but workable cellar about 12 feet square.

We found a spring in the back of the cellar-hole which might have made trouble for us. We concreted the sides and ran a pipe up to the kitchen sink. So we had an addition to the water supply which we piped down from a spring farther up the hill.

Having found running water, we faced the problem of getting rid of the overflow through a cellar drain. The land between the cellar and the hill slope was littered with boulders. With considerable difficulty we managed a ditch which missed the larger boulders and involved moving only the smaller ones. All went well until, about a foot above the cellar bottom we struck a hard granite ledge. One way out of the difficulty was to drill and blast—a matter of perhaps twenty feet. Instead, we filled up that ditch and dug another somewhat longer ditch which avoided the ledge and gave us sufficient grade for cellar drainage. Building operations, like true love, never run smoothly.

Our method of stone building was based largely upon the "Flagg system." Ernest Flagg was a New York architect who believed that people of limited means and experience could build permanent, beautiful dwellings out of native stone. They had done it in many parts of the world where stone was plentiful and Mr. Flagg felt that they should be able to do it in the United States. He therefore set about devising a method that would do away with the prohibitively expensive cut-stone, hand-laid masonry. His stone walls are concrete with field-stone facing,—the two being constructed simultaneously, as one unit. Instead of laying up masoned walls with trowel and level, he proposed to build a wall of sticky concrete, between two wooden forms, with stone facing to the front. The stone was to be not a veneer, but bonded into the concrete wall, with the rock often extending through three-quarters or more of the wall. Through years of practise Flagg successfully demonstrated that stone houses could be effectively and artistically constructed and at a reasonable cost.[8] "The Flagg methods enable the ordinary person, contractor, or clerk, to build a house of stone at a saving of one third the cost."[9]

Flagg laid down four basic propositions[10]:—(1) Stone buildings should be kept low, because after they reach a height of five feet, the cost of lifting the stone and concrete increase progressively with the height. If a second story is needed, it should be based on dormer construction. (2) Cellar space should be reduced to a minimum and all possible floor areas should be of concrete, laid on the earth. If it is desired, other types of flooring may be used over the concrete. Heating pipes and wires can be laid in conduits or channels. (3) The house should be a unit, with door and window frames of solid material, built into the stone and concrete walls, and without trim. (4) The walls are to be built in movable forms.

We would like to add three other points based on our experience in using aspects of this system. (5) Keep the roof lines as simple as possible,—few if any dormers or extra angles. (6)

[8] "Little accustomed as we are to stone buildings, it may be thought by many to erect such an one would be a great undertaking, yet it may be done without either great expense, nor much difficulty. Hammered or chiseled stone is adapted to public buildings, or the houses of the wealthy, and is expensive; but comfortable, decent houses may be built with common stone, such as we would use for good field walls. Such stones laid in strong mortar, will make an excellent building, either by facing the wall with stones, if fit for the purpose, or by rough casting the wall after it is built." J. M. Gourgas, in *New England Farmer*, 1/25/1828 p. 209

[9] Harold Cary, *Build a Home—Save a Third*, N.Y.: Reynolds 1924 p. 105

[10] *Small Houses*, N.Y.: Scribners 1921

Make all shapes as regular as possible, eliminating excrescences and cutting corners down to a minimum. (7) Build large enough, because stone walls once built are hard to break down if additions are desired.

Flagg's most important innovation was his fourth point—movable forms. Forms are scaffoldings built to hold concrete while it is setting. When the concrete has hardened, the forms are removed. Forms must be sturdy enough and braced enough to contain the fresh concrete without bulging or buckling. If they move from their assigned place, irregularities appear in the hardened concrete. Usually the forms are built by setting up a framework of dimension timbers, fastening boards on the side of the timbers next to the proposed concrete mass, pouring the concrete, and then removing the scaffolding. Form building is expensive because much of the lumber that goes into the ordinary form is used once, for a few days, and then discarded. Flagg decided to use movable forms. He erected studs around his projected building, bored holes in them at frequent intervals, put wooden pins in the holes, rested his forms on the wooden pins and fastened them to the studs. The studs were on the inside of the wall, consequently the concrete was poured around them so that they became part of the wall and were anchors for the furring strips needed for paneling or lathing. Flagg's forms were made of 2×6 or 2×8 inch timbers, cleated together side by side. It took two or three men to handle a 2×18 or 2×24 sixteen foot form, especially on a scaffolding.

We experimented with various types of forms and finally adopted one easy to make and light to handle. Its greatest advantage was the elimination of Flagg's expensive bored studs. Our improved form was exactly 18 inches wide, and made of three six inch boards. We tried making forms wider than 18 inches, but found that they were very heavy and unwieldy, and were so deep that it was difficult to place the bottom layer of stone with precision.

The boards for a six foot form were cut to length and assembled. (The problem of weight has been met in much construction work by using metal forms or forms built of plywood. We used ⅞ inch white pine or spruce wood. Pine is lighter, but expands more when it is wet. Spruce is tougher and expands less than pine.) At each end we nailed a 2×3×16¼ inch stud with the 2 inch side next the boards, and flush with the board ends. On the ends of the studs we nailed a piece ⅞×3×6 feet, thus making a shallow box, exactly 6 feet long, 18 inches wide, and 3 inches deep on the inside. We then put in two more studs, 2×3×16¼ inches, 24 inches from center to center and centered in the form, thus dividing our shallow box into three compartments. We finally brushed onto the form a generous coating of used engine oil, and it was ready to set up. In constructing these forms we used six penny common nails because it is sometimes necessary to take a form apart, and six penny nails can be pulled and re-driven with little or no damage to the form boards.

Our forms ranged in length from 15 inches to 14 feet. All were exactly 18 inches wide. In the longer forms the studs were placed every 24 inches, from center to center. The end studs of each form were bored, to pattern, with two ½ inch holes, 16 inches apart, centered both ways. Since all forms were bored with the same pattern, all holes were opposite one another when forms were assembled. We used ⅜ inch bolts, some 4 and some 5 inches long, washers and wing nuts to fasten the forms together. For corners, we left one end of a form "open." Instead of a 2×3 stud, we cut a ⅞ inch board, 4 inches wide and 18 inches long, nailed it in place, bored it with the usual pattern, fitted it over the form at the other side of the corner and bolted it in place. For this purpose, on the inside forms, we used flat head or carriage bolts. Otherwise we used square head or machine bolts. The latter are easier to tighten and loosen.

These forms were so light that one person could handle a 14 foot form, though they went up more quickly if two people worked on them. In planning buildings we aimed to place our window and door frames so that our inside forms fitted exactly between the frames. Sometimes, but rarely, we made special forms for particular places.

Having built a set of forms, we were ready to put them in place. The foundations of the building had been poured, and evened up without making them smooth. (We always left the top of the day's work rough or rocky to form a surer bond with the next day's work.) Within a day or two, while the foundations were still damp, we attached a set of strings to the nails in the batter-boards and began setting the forms.

If the building was a small one, say 12×16 feet or less, we set forms around all four sides. If it was larger, we selected a corner, set forms opposite to each other, with the smooth side facing toward the prospective wall. If possible, we set up at least two corners and connected them with forms, because two corners are self-bracing. To separate the two wall forms, we placed inside spacer sticks of hardwood, 1×1 inch, cut to the width of the wall, say 12 inches. Next we fastened the forms together top and bottom with light telephone wire which went through ¼ inch holes bored in the forms, around a 2×3 stud if one was close by, otherwise around a 1×2×16 inch piece set vertically across the outside of the form. We usually inserted tie-wires at the top and the bottom around each stud, which placed wires every two feet along the forms. These wires were then tightened by twisting them, inside the forms, with a 20 penny nail, until they were taut. If the twist comprises 3 or 4 wraps of wire on each side of the nail, the wire will not untwist when concrete is poured. If it is less than 3 or 4 wraps, it is better to leave the twisting-nail in place and let it remain in the concrete.

We now had an open double form, 18 inches high, 12 inches wide inside, bolted loosely together and extending around two corners of the foundation. The next job was to tighten the connecting bolts and level the forms. On an irregular foundation, this required staking and building up under the bottom of the leveled form. At the same time the form was plumbed.

If door or window frames were to go in at this level, allowance had to be made for the sills. If panelling, lath, plaster or wall board was to be used for inside finish, furring strips had to be placed in the forms at proper intervals. If there were door or window frames, we fastened furring strips to the sides of the frames.

When this operation was completed, we had a level, plumb, braced form, sufficiently tight underneath to hold sticky concrete. We were ready to fill the forms.

Let us assume that the building is to have a stone face outside and panelled walls inside. Furring strips are placed at necessary intervals in the forms, and held in position by 6 or 8 penny nails, driven in lightly from outside. Scrap nails, driven into the side of the furring strips, will hold them solidly in the set concrete. If the furring strips are set carefully, they can be cut to several feet in length. Once their bottoms are set in hard concrete, they provide an excellent anchor for the forms.

Over the surface of the foundation about two inches of "sticky" concrete should be spread,—slightly drier than brick mortar and yet moist enough to work into the spaces between stones without running over their outside faces and leaving cement stains.

The original Ellonen farmhouse.

"Our new place was a typical run-down farm."

Setting supports for pea vines.

The most formidable problem was not the soil but the climate.

Scott Nearing tending a vegetable garden.

Preparing natural compost.

Shoveling a path to the woodshed.

Maple sap must be gathered before it ferments.

Boiling sap in the sugarhouse.

Driving through the sugarbush.

Building with stone.

The first completed cabin.

The authors.

"Usually there was a period of music Sunday mornings."

"The food we produced kept us in good health."

There was a constant stream of visitors.

The upper garden.

"We built a house of stone."

Forest Farm, Vermont.

Flagg favored a concrete composed of 10 shovels of gravel, 5 sand and 1 cement. For most of our foundation and wall work we have used 6 gravel, 3 sand and 1 cement. Either formula will give a slow-setting, solid wall, if the gravel and sand are free from clay or loam. Under either formula a wall can be put up that is surprisingly cheap and sufficiently hard to be permanent.

Into the two inches of sticky concrete on the foundation surface we put a line of wall stones, placing the flattest faces against the outside form and fitting them as closely together as possible, yet not quite touching. There should be room for some mortar between. The larger and thicker these stones are, the better. Limit of size is determined by the cross wires which hold the forms and the 10 inch form space left by the presence of a 2 inch furring strip. Occasionally we moved furring strips or cut wires to get in a particularly desirable and large rock. Behind these stones, sticky concrete is shoveled, then tamped solidly against the inside form, under and between the stones and around the furring strips. The tamped concrete should slope at 20 or 30 degrees upward from the placed stones, toward the back form. This sloping bank of concrete enables the builder to lay a stone with a good face against the outside form, snug it into place with a few light blows from trowel or stone hammer, and then push the surplus concrete all around the stone, with fingers or trowel. Once laid in sticky concrete, such a stone will not move unless the form gives.

If the wall stones faced against the outside form are 6 to 8 inches in thickness, very little concrete will be required to complete this filling operation. If they are thinner, leaving areas or pockets of concrete, push ugly stones into this concrete—being sure they do not touch the form or the wall stones. The larger the ugly stones the better, because they take the place of concrete and strengthen the wall.

In all mason work it is better to begin with the corners and work toward the open walls, because the corners are more limited as to size and shape of stones. It is easier to find a wall-stone which will fill the final gap than it is to find just the right corner stone for the end of a wall operation.

We now had a line of wall stones stretching between two corners and for a short distance around each corner, backed by an up-sloping bank of sticky concrete. We next pressed some reinforcing metal into the concrete bank around each corner. The reinforcing should extend at least three feet each way from the corner. It may be standard ¼ inch reinforcing rods; iron pipe or any other iron or steel scrap with a minimum length of 6 feet will do. We have used doubled barbed wire with good results. We like to put in corner reinforcings every four or five inches as the form is filled. As with the stones, the concrete around the reinforcing should be tamped carefully to prevent air pockets.

Our next move was to put in a second line of corner and wall stones, facing the forms and fitted as closely as possible into the first layer. One stone should not be laid directly on top of another, but should cross the intersection, thus binding together the under-lying stones. A little experimenting will show how to get the desired pattern. The corners should be especially well tied-in, with alternate stone overlapping on each tier. As these stones are placed, our trowels brought the sloping concrete around them and tamped them solidly. Additional concrete was shoveled along the inside form and the operation was repeated until the form was full.

Our practice was to place a layer of stone along the entire length of form, or at least 12 to 20 feet, fill up holes, due to irregularities in the stones with small chinkers faced against the outside form and tucked into the concrete. If the job was well done, there would be several fairly level places on top of this line of stone. If there was such a spot 22 inches long (the distance between studs and wires) we picked a stone 22 inches in one direction and perhaps 10 or 11 inches in the other, set it in place and braced it temporarily. We did this at every possible point, so that the big open spaces were filled by big stones. Then we filled the intervals with smaller stones. In this way big stones got into the wall and gave a less choppy appearance, the forms were filled quickly, concrete was saved and pointing minimized.

With a good selection of well-shaped stones, it was sometimes possible, between tie wires, to fill the entire 18 inches of the form with one or two stones. A little care resulted in attractive arrangements of the stone making up the outside wall, and it was always exciting when the forms first came off to see the varied patterns and colors. It was like the unveiling of an art work. We still recognize certain rocks as old friends and delight in many sections of our own buildings. We knew our houses from inside out and placed each rock with loving care.

Experience has convinced us that it is unwise to let stones stick up above the top of the filled form. As surely as we did, when the concrete set, we might find wall stones which extended beyond the outer wall-line. Before the next form could be placed, these protruding stones had to be broken off or removed, with a loss of labor-time and a weakening of the wall.

Filled forms were covered with empty cement bags, or some other protection against sun or rain, and left for 48 hours. In the meantime, if enough forms were available, we set them around the other two corners of the building, and proceeded as before. "Observe in working up the Walls," says a builder of 1712, "that no side of the house, nor any part of the Walls be wrought up three Feet above the other, before the next adjoining Wall be wrought up to it, that so they may be all join'd together and make a good Bond, or else what is done first will be dry, so that when they come to settle, one part being moist and the other dry, it will occasion it's settling more in one place than another, which causes cracks and settlings in the Wall, and much weakens the Buildings."[11] It is good practice to have all four walls of a structure go up at about the same rate, making it possible to check dimensions.

Regular door and window frames (unless they are metal) are made of 2 × 3 or 2 × 4 inch material, which in its turn, is covered by trim. In practice, the trim is beveled, beaded and otherwise varied and decorated, giving a fussy, over-dressed effect. Cutting and placing the trim is time-consuming. Flagg proposed that the frames be made of solid timber, be built into the structure and not trimmed at all.

We decided to use 7 × 7 inch local white pine for door and window frames. We had the timbers sawed ¼ inch over-size, stuck up in a lumberyard over winter and planed to size the following spring. When the planing was done we put them under cover in our new lumbershed.

All frames were made in our workshop, with halved-corner joints. They were bored at each corner with a pattern which put two holes, slanted at 45 degrees to the right angle, at each corner. Inch dowel pins were then driven into these holes. The frame was squared, braced and taken to its place in the building. One or two of the larger window frames were too heavy to handle in one piece. They were built in the shop, assembled, tested for square, taken apart and reassembled on the job.

We prepared for either a door or window frame by making a concrete sill of the desired dimension, beveled away from the

[11] J. Mortimer, The Whole Art of Husbandry, Lon.: Matlock 1712 p. 280

building at the outside to carry off water. We usually gave a sill 48 hours to harden. We then put a layer of mortar on the part of the sill designed for the frame, set the frame in place, leveled it, plumbed it and braced it solidly in position.

The position of the frame on the sill depended on thickness of wall and the type of inside finish. Our dwelling unit had 12 inch walls and was panelled inside in a way that placed the surface of the panelling 1⅝ inches from the inside face of the wall. The 7 inch frame was set on the sill so that it was recessed 7 inches from the outside face of the wall, and therefore extended 2 inches beyond the inside face of the wall. When the panelling was put in place, the inside face of the frame extended ⅜ of an inch beyond the face of the panelling, thus breaking the line of panelling at the frame and setting off the frame from the panelling. There was no other trim.

Following this method of construction, we soon discovered that after the building was finished, the different rate of expansion for concrete and wood pulled the two apart at times, leaving a small crack between the frame and the concrete wall. We remedied this in later construction by cutting a square groove all around the outside of the frame and inserting a small strip of wood which projected ¼ inch or a little more beyond the center of the frame into the concrete. Later we improved this method still more and cut a groove half an inch deep with a bench-saw and set a piece of galvanized metal ¾ of an inch wide into the groove. This took less time than inserting the wood strip and served the same purpose of bridging the crack between frame and concrete.

When the frame was in position, we drove a row of scrap spikes into the frame where it was to come into contact with the concrete, and poured the concrete against the frame. As the concrete hardened, the spikes were embedded in it, making the frame an inseparable part of the concrete and stone walls.

After some trial and error, we learned that the house plates should be bolted down into the walls. The technique was simple. As we reached the top of the last form, we placed half-inch machine bolts heads down in the concrete, with a good sized washer held in a vice and hammered until it tightened around the head of the bolt. The bolt was set in the concrete so that its top end would be even with the top of the plate. If the plate was a 6×6, the bolt would stand up 6 inches above the wall top. A ⅝ inch hole through the plate and a small notch, made with a chisel, would bring the nut snugly even with the plate-top. One such bolt for each 8 or 10 feet would insure against the plate shifting sideways when the rafters went on.

Frequently door or window frames came up to the plate. In that case we put an inch wooden dowel through the plate and 4 or 5 inches into a 6 inch frame timber, effectually anchoring the plate, since the frames were built securely into the stone-concrete walls.

After 48 hours, we went back to the filled forms, removed the cement bags and set another set of forms on top of the first, evening the faces and driving 8 penny nails through the 1×3 inch flanges. If the filled forms were properly levelled, the second layer of forms also would be level. It remained only to bolt, space and wire them, plumb them, brace them, and fill them in turn with stone and concrete. After another 48 hours, the wires were cut and the bolts removed from the lower level of forms. The forms were taken off, and put on top of the upper forms and filled in their turn. Thus, 18 inches at a time, the wall went up. It is rather like the children's game of hand over hand.

With three dozen forms, ranging in length from 15 inches to

14 feet, we built some eight or nine stone buildings at Forest Farms over a period of thirteen years. At the moment of writing they are being used by a neighbor for building a stone house. In addition we have used the same forms for garden retaining walls, concrete culverts, swimming pool and the like. Each time we finished a job we scraped the forms, made minor repairs, oiled them with used engine oil, and stored them in a dry level place. With minor breaks and a few patches they are almost as good as brand-new forms. The form-cost per foot of wall space constructed with their aid has been almost negligible.

Finishing the wall was a simple matter. When the forms were removed from the outside of the wall, we were confronted with a straight, plumb wall cut up by openings between the stones. Sometimes stones fitted badly or were irregular, leaving holes as big or bigger than a goose-egg. Our first job was to snip off all the extending wires. Then we went over the wall with a hammer, clearing off flakes of concrete which adhered to the wall-face. Next we went over the wall with a pail of small pebbles and stone-flakes, filling the larger holes to within a half-inch of the wall-face. Then, with a whitewash brush and pail of water, or with a hose if one was available, we wet the wall thoroughly. We were now ready for pointing.

Using a metal wheelbarrow, we mixed three shovels of well-sifted, sharp, clean sand, with somewhat less than a shovel of cement (3½ to 1 is a good pointing mixture) and very little water. The mortar for this purpose should be slightly stiffer than brick mortar. It may be mixed with lime to whiten it or with some pigment to color it. We merely used a light colored cement. On a large building, with much pointing to do, care should be taken to get cement from the same carload for the entire pointing job. At the very least the cement should be of the same brand; otherwise there may be splotchy or linear variations in the color of the pointing.

The pointing mortar is placed on a hawk (a piece of flat board or metal 8 or 10 inches square, with a short, round handle at right angles underneath). The hawk is held against the wall, slightly below the opening to be filled, and the mortar is pushed and packed with the back of the pointing trowel, a bit at a time, into the opening until the mortar is flush with the wall face. There are several ways to finish pointing. One can make stylized and formal lines. We pointed the simplest way,—even with or slightly above the wall-face, letting each stone tell its own story in its own form and color.

Pointing mixtures made with our formula set rapidly. On a clear, dry day, within three or four hours, the pointing would be hard enough to resist a light shower dashing against it. If there was any danger of rain immediately after the pointing was done, the area was covered, as wet mortar washes out easily, smearing and streaking the wall with cement stains. If this does happen, muriatic acid will wash off the stain.

Where much pointing is to be done, it will be well to have a standard pointing trowel, supplemented with one or two cheap small trowels from the five and ten cent store. With a pair of sturdy tin shears the blades of these cheap pointing trowels can be snipped down to ⅜ and ½ inch width. These narrow trowels come in handy for all pointing operations. Friends and visitors are invariably fascinated with the filling-in job, and love to stand with hawk in hand, pecking away at the wall with one of these trowels and dropping mortar all over the place.

We enjoy open fires, so we planned fireplaces for every room. Even in mild weather there is something indescribably attractive and satisfying about the flickering glow of a wood fire. The heat thrown off may be negligible, but the live coals vitalize the atmosphere and the leaping flames enliven the surroundings. In cold weather, open fires contribute the tangy perfume of burning wood as well as welcome warmth. Thoreau considered his fire a friend: "My house was not empty though I was gone. It was as if I had left a cheerful housekeeper behind."[12] A room without an open fire in winter is almost as desolate as a room without windows.

Building one's own fireplace is a satisfying and rewarding experience. We rarely let a year go by without putting one up in a house, of our own or some one else's. Our friends called it a recurring disease. Kipling would have understood our passion. He wrote in *Something of Myself*, "How can I turn from any fire on any man's hearth-stone? I know the wonder and desire that went to build my own."[13]

We lived in an area of rapid forest reproduction, where beech, yellow birch and hard maple were abundant. Wood was our only fuel, and fireplaces were our chief means of heating, just as they were of the original settler. We agree with the squire of Edgewood who said, "The days of wood fires are not utterly gone; and as long as I live, they never will be gone."[14]

Since an old-fashioned fireplace allows something like nine-tenths of the heat to go up the chimney, we used manufactured metal forms in most of our fireplaces. These reflect and distribute the heat quite economically, drawing the air from floor level through the scientifically designed boiler-plate chambers, heating it and circulating it. With any one of the several types of fireplace forms on the market, the problem of design and engineering is

[12] *Walden*, Boston: Ticknor & Fields 1854 p. 272
[13] N.Y.: Doubleday 1937 p. 191
[14] D. G. Mitchell, *My Farm of Edgewood*, N.Y.: Scribner 1863 p. 8

eliminated. The builder simply encloses the metal form with stone or brick to the mantle level, and then constructs the chimney. Anyone following the directions cannot possibly go wrong. Also, for ten cents one can get a United States *Farmers Bulletin* giving careful directions for stone or brick fireplace building.

With two exceptions we used tile in our chimneys. They reduce fire hazard and decrease the amount of creosote which sticks to the inside of a flue. They also make it more difficult for mice and squirrels to get up and down. When a chimney becomes well-coated with creosote, mice and squirrels can travel it as easily as you travel a woodland path.

Our fireplaces and chimneys were built with stone, but rarely was the stone cut. Occasionally we knocked a projecting piece from a rock. In chimney construction, where good corners are essential, we did a bit of stone trimming. But in the course of our whole building program, during which we used many thousand stone, almost all of the rock were "wild stone, untamed by hammer or chisel."[15] In his account of building Edgewood Farm, Mr. Mitchell says "I insisted that no stone should be touched with a hammer; and that, so far as feasible, the mossy or weather sides of the stone should be exposed."[16]

The best-shaped stone we could find were put in the fireplace supply pile. Since they were the prize ones, there was always the temptation to pick them over when a particular size and shape of corner or wall-stone was wanted. Occasionally we yielded to the temptation, but usually one or another of us was a self-constituted guardian of the fireplace stone pile and uttered a cry of anguish whenever any builder approached the forbidden area.

Chimneys may be finished, on the inside like the inner walls,

[15] John Burrough, *Signs and Seasons*, N.Y.: Houghton Mifflin 1914 p. 256
[16] *My Farm of Edgewood*, N.Y.: Scribners 1863 p. 84

with panelling, wallboard or plaster. All of our fireplaces were
built with stone chimneys, exposed from mantel to ceiling. We
like the ruggedness of a stone chimney. Also, if a fire is kept day
and night, as in winter, the stones warm up and help in heating
the room.

Some of our fireplaces were built with mantels and some without. The mantel-less fireplace is a bit simpler and more austere.
A mantel, especially a low one, adds cosiness but collects trinkets.
Most of our mantels were stone. Two were of wood. One of
these we hewed with axes out of a curly birch log, 12 inches in
diameter. It was a chore, but an object of beauty when set up.
Some of the spans between the fireplace pylons were held up by
built-in arches. Most of them consisted of lintel stones, thin
enough to allow room for the smoke flue and smoke chamber,
but wide enough and heavy enough to support the weight of the
chimney. In all cases we put a piece of metal reinforcing inside
and under the arch or lintel to help carry the load. The lintel
stone of the 42 inch wide living room fireplace in the main house
was formerly the doorstep of a neighbor's barn. He insisted it was
the best rock for the purpose for miles around, and it was, but it
was part of his barn. At his own insistence and with his help, the
rock was detached with bars, and still aromatic of the barnyard,
was placed in our living room fireplace. Our neighbor, Jack
Lightfoot, now has a proprietary interest in our fireplace and
often comes over to toast his shins in front of a glowing fire and
his rock. His eye still searches for other choice rocks and he often
tells us of new finds.

Others have had this same passion for stones, and a farmer-
author of the middle 1800's writes: "There were, scattered along
the roadside, as along most country roadsides of New England,
a great quantity of small, ill-shapen stones, drawn thither in past

years from the fields, and serving only as the breeding ground for pestilent briars. These stones I determined to convert into a cottage."[17] John Burroughs rhapsodized: "It seems to me that I built into my house every one of those superb autumn days which I spent in the woods getting out stone. . . Every load that was sent home carried my heart and happiness with it. The jewels I had uncovered in the debris, or torn from the ledge in the morning, I saw in the jambs, or mounted high on the corners at night. Every day was filled with great events. The woods held unknown treasures. Those elder giants, frost and rain, had wrought industriously; now we would unearth from the leaf-mould an ugly customer, a stone with a ragged quartz face, or cavernous, and set with rock crystals like great teeth, or else suggesting a battered and worm-eaten skull of some old stone dog. . . Then we would unexpectedly strike upon several loads of beautiful blocks all in a nest; or we would assault the ledge in a new place with wedge and bar, and rattle down headers and stretchers that surpassed any before. I had to be constantly on the lookout for corner stone, for mine is a house of seven corners, and on the strength and dignity of the corners the beauty of the wall largely depends. . . I looked upon the ground with such desire that I saw what was beneath the moss and the leaves. . . With me it was a passionate pursuit; the enthusiasm of the chase venting itself with the bar and hammer, and the day was too short for me to tire of the sport."[18]

We have gone into so much detail on stone construction because we enjoy the solidity and massiveness of stone and we would like others to have a similar opportunity, both of work and enjoyment. We are convinced that anyone who will follow

[17] D. G. Mitchell, *My Farm of Edgewood*, N.Y. Scribners 1863 p. 84
[18] *Signs and Seasons*, N.Y.: Houghton Mifflin 1914 pp. 257-8

these instructions can put up a satisfactory stone building if he is willing and able to take the time. If he does build with stone, he will get a thrill from the day he discovers a blue-ribbon rock and places it in its proper pile, until he finds the right place in wall, floor, fireplace or chimney, and sees his rock set and solid years after, built into his house.

Before building we discussed the roof problem in detail. Stone buildings with non-combustible roofs are proverbially fireproof and are insurable at about half the rate of a frame house. For a time we favored slate roofing, which was produced within a short distance of us. There were difficulties, however. Slate was expensive to buy and to lay; it was heavy; and in winter, water and ice tended to back up under the slate ends, freeze and crack or break the slate, especially on a low-pitched roof such as we intended to build. Wooden shingles were out of the question with us because of the fire hazard. Asbestos shingles blew up and cracked in high winds and were generally not too permanent. Finally we settled on double-v crimp galvanized steel, to be painted moss-green. We have never regretted the decision. The metal was easy to lay, the fire hazard from sparks or chimney fires was nil, and the roofs, painted every three or four years, last indefinitely. Some of our metal roofs have been in place for twenty years; they show practically no signs of wear and the upkeep costs on them are negligible. Metal roofs protect buildings even when no lightning rods are used, especially if tin or iron pipes are connected with the roofs and run into the ground.

We wanted a low roof-pitch. "What constitutes the charm to the eye of the old-fashioned country barn but its immense roof,— a slope of gray shingle exposed to the weather like the side of a hill, and by its amplitude suggesting a bounty that warms the heart. Many of the old farmhouses, too, were modelled on the same generous scale, and at a distance little was visible but their great sloping roofs. They covered their inmates as a hen covereth her brood, and are touching pictures of the domestic spirit in its simpler forms."[19] The Swiss type of house snuggling lowly into the hill pleased us more than the steep-roofed Finnish and American houses. In our district in Vermont all the roofs were steep, because it was said the snow slid off quicker. However, we found that even in a heavy-snow area like ours, metal roofs cleared before any others (and, while we are on the subject, we might note that aluminum clears sooner than iron, but does not hold paint as well and dents more easily). By using a metal roof we were able to lower the roof-pitch and still get rid of the snow without shoveling. We also wanted generous eaves and gable-ends, in the Swiss manner. The low roof pitch helped in this design and yet let light reach the windows, which were placed just below the plates.

Simplicity and convenience were our standards in finishing and furnishing the house. We felt that without frills, trim, painted woodwork, wall paper, curtains, plaster, carved and over-stuffed furniture and bric-a-brac, we would have the basis for a Japanese simplicity that would be beautiful in itself. "The construction," said Claude Bragdon of a lovely room, "was the decoration: when the room was built it was decorated."[20]

First, as to the wall finishing, this was to be an integral part of the house, not a plaster or paper applied later. Into the concrete wall itself, as we were building it, we inserted vertical furring strips. When the roof was on and the house enclosed, we put horizontal strips on the vertical ones. On the horizontal strips went a layer of building paper and over this our pine,

[19] John Burroughs, *Signs and Seasons*, N.Y.: Houghton Mifflin 1914 p. 252
[20] *More Lives Than One*, N.Y.: Knopf 1938 p. 165

spruce or basswood panelling. Thus inside of the stone and
concrete wall was an air space and a layer of building paper for
insulation.

We stained our paneling a different shade in every room. The
walls mellowed with time and formed a fine background for the
tapestried color of our hundreds of books. "The natural color and
grain of the wood give a richness and simplicity to an interior
that no art can make up for. How the eye loves a genuine thing;
how it delights in the nude beauty of the wood. A painted surface
is a blank meaningless surface; but the texture and figure of the
wood is full of expression."[21] "Bring out the nature of the materials," says Frank Lloyd Wright. "Let their nature intimately
into your scheme. Strip the wood of varnish and let it alone;
stain it. Reveal the nature of the wood, plaster, brick or stone in
your designs; they are all by nature friendly and beautiful."[22]

All our floors but the kitchen floor (which was over the cellar)
were laid on the ground and surfaced with smooth flat stone.
The giant boulder backing the fireplace in the living room, and
extending into the kitchen and bathroom, gave further substance
and stability to the monastic simplicity.

When building, even though it was to be a small house, we
aimed at spaciousness so that no room was tight and cluttered.
The living room was 22 feet long, one wall lined with books, 14
feet of rock wall and the fireplace at one end, and 12 feet of
windows at the other. The ceiling was 9 feet high and crossed
with heavy handhewn timbers. No old furniture was dragged in,
or carpets or curtains. As far as possible all furniture was built
into the original design and was an integral part of the architecture. Frank Lloyd Wright says, "The ideal of 'organic sim-

[21] John Burroughs, *Signs and Seasons*, N.Y.: Houghton Mifflin 1914 p. 259
[22] *On Architecture*, N.Y.: Duel, Sloan & Pearce 1941 p. 34

plicity' naturally abolished all fixtures, rejected the old furniture, all carpets and most hangings, declaring them to be irrelevant or superficial decoration.[23] . . . Swift sure lines and clean planes in every way make a better background for living than lace curtains, figured wall paper, machine carved furniture, and elaborate picture frames."[24]

Four summers of interesting, instructive and rewarding work were necessary before we were able to move into the new house unit. Each spring we made syrup and planted a garden. It was June before we could devote time to building. Four or five months later, heavy frosts ended concrete and stone work for the season. When we made our original construction plans we estimated that the building project would cover about ten years. It was eleven years before we completed our entire building program. We had not rushed. We worked at it when we could and were satisfied if we kept moving toward our goal.

During the time we were in Vermont we put up twelve major buildings and many minor constructions. None was of wood, one was entirely concrete, and two were metal sugarhouses. Five of the stone buildings were grouped functionally around the central dwelling house. We might outline here some of those which have not been mentioned previously.

Our first building was the lumber shed which we have already described. Later a 20 foot addition on the west end of the shed gave us a two car stone garage, with storage space for nails, chains, ropes, paints and some miscellaneous tools. The completed building provided a 50 foot stone windbreak on the north side of the truck garden, which extended 28 feet south from the wall.

[23] *Ibid.*, p. 187
[24] *Ibid.*, p. 211

When we got into our new house on the slope overlooking the Hoard place buildings, we gave the Hoard house and woodshed to Vernet Slason who was on the job with us. He hauled them home piecemeal and turned them into a garage-woodshed. We rebuilt the cellar under the Hoard house and readied it for vegetable and syrup storage. Above it we built a 12×12 foot room, which we used temporarily for a workshop. When we were able to do so, we built a 12×20 foot addition with a concrete floor north of the 12×12 workshop, connected the two buildings with a room and stone fireplace, furnished the old shop and connecting room with two double beds and a single one, built in a toilet and used these rooms as a guest house. The far room we equipped as a permanent workshop.

We put up an open-air 12×14 foot woodshed, with a stone and concrete wall on the north side and the other three sides open. Three concrete piers supported handhewn posts on the south side of the building. The woodshed was not expensive. The cash cost was $114.88. It sheltered an abundance of air-dried wood, which was essential to our economy, both for heating the house and cooking our maple sugar. In fact, so important is dry wood in a back-woods farm economy that a Vermont wife can sue, with valid cause for divorce, when her husband supplies her with green wood for cooking and heating.

We cleared off a partly exposed boulder 25 yards west of the dwelling unit, and on it built a 12×16 foot study, stone finished inside and out, with a stone fireplace and a 6×9 foot window overlooking Stratton Mountain. The cash outlay was $553.75.

Finally we pulled down the last of the Hoard place buildings, —the old horse barn, erected an 18×24 foot stone and concrete tool shed in its place, built a 6×18 foot sun-heated greenhouse against the south wall and put a small cabbage and celery storage cellar under the lower end of the building.

As the years went by we constructed a 9×12 foot cabin of concrete on an upper lot, adjacent to the sugar bush. It was just the size of a one-man tent. We put in a tiny fireplace, let guests occupy it in summer, and in winter used it as storage space for sap buckets. We also built a concrete culvert and concrete bridge between the garage and the road, and in front of the house poured a 12×20 foot concrete swimming pool, with permanent granite forming the bottom and the side toward the hill.

Our latest and last building venture in Vermont was a stone cabin in the woods, built for a friend, Richard Gregg, who had lived and worked with us long enough to know he wanted to settle in the valley. We supplied the land and the materials and half of the labor. He did the rest, and lovingly fashioned a house to his own taste and needs.

It goes without saying that we did not do all of this work by ourselves. A very few of our guests proved helpful. Jack Lightfoot, our nearest neighbor, born in London, England, his head brimful of witticisms, criticisms, suggestions and plans, worked with us off and on when he could take his time from his farm and other commitments. In his own words, he was "Jack of all trades, master of none," but an ever-present help in time of need and trouble. Charlie Sage and Adelbert Capen, both from nearby Bondville, two miles over the hill, helped us for several seasons. Both were our friends, handy with the axe and adze, but neither were extra skilled in the art of stone house building.

Vernet Slason, also of Bondville, did more work on the projects than any other person. When we began our building program he had just completed a long session in the hospital and was feeling poorly. He made part of his living at that time by filing saws. We took some saws to him and he did a superior job on them. A few months later we needed someone to help during sugaring. Vernet agreed to try it. He turned out to be extremely ingenious. He had carpentered, painted, fixed clocks and gasoline engines; he was good in the woods; he had sugared. With his help we relaid the pipe system in the sugar bush and built the new sugar house. He did stone work with us, carpenter work, cabinet work, plumbing. For every problem he had a suggested solution, and he worked as fast as he worked well.

We should not close this chapter without a bow to our faithful pick-up trucks, of many years and makes; to our indispensable gravel pit, and the long lines of stone walls, picked from plowland and pasture by our predecessors. All of these were assets of the greatest value in our building program.

Our experience leads us to believe with Flagg, that people of moderate intelligence, little experience and slender means can build with stone if they have the time, patience and the inclination. Once the stone building is in place, it becomes a thing of beauty and lasts indefinitely. Stone construction takes time, but tested by results, it is time well-spent. In any case, here is one way in which a self-sufficient homestead can be established and strengthened.

"I come now to discourse of the pleasures which accompany the labours of the husbandman, and with which I myself am delighted beyond expression. They are pleasures which meet with no obstruction even from old age, and seem to approach nearest to those of true wisdom."

Cicero, De Senectute, 45 B.C.

"The prudent husbandman is found
In mutual duties, striving with his ground,
And half the year the care of that does take
That half the year grateful return does make.
Each fertile month does some new gifts present,
And with new work his industry content."

Virgil, Georgics, Book II, 29 B.C.

"Doe you yet maruaile how I can delight my selfe with this so honest and profitable a quietnes, then which in the judgement of the holiest and wisest men, there is nothing more honest nor better, neither is there beside any trade of life more meet for a Gentleman, nor travaile more acceptable to God, then is the tilling of the ground."

Barnabe Googe, The Whole Art and Trade of Husbandry, 1614

"I consider the kitchen garden as of very considerable importance, as pot-herbs, sallads, and roots of various kinds, are useful in housekeeping. Having a plenty of them at hand, a family will not be so likely to run into the errour, which is too common in this country, of eating flesh in too great a proportion for health. Farmers, as well as others, should have kitchen-gardens: And they need not grudge the labour of tending them, which may be done at odd intervals of time, which may otherwise chance to be consumed in needless loitering."

Samuel Deane, The New England Farmer, 1790

"I have often thought that if heaven had given me choice of my position and calling, it should have been on a rich spot of earth, well watered, and near a good market for the productions of the garden. No occupation is so delightful to me as the culture of the earth, and no culture comparable to that of the garden. Such a variety of subjects, some one always coming to perfection, the failure of one thing repaired by the success of another, and instead of one harvest a continued one through the year. Under a total want of demand except for our family table, I am still devoted to the garden."

Thomas Jefferson, Letter to Charles E. Peale, 1811

"All men eat fruit that can get it; so that the choice is only, whether one will eat good or ill; and for all things produced in a garden, whether of salads or fruits, a poor man will eat better that has one of his own, than a rich man that has none."

J. C. Loudon, An Encyclopedia of Gardening, 1826

CHAPTER 4

OUR GOOD EARTH

Vermont climate—The pitch of the land and terraces—The living soil—Making compost—Laying out a garden—Principles behind our gardening—Extending the garden year— A pit greenhouse—Raspberries—Mulching—Sweetpeas

THE keystone of our economy was our food supply. As food costs are the largest single item in the budget of low income families, if we could raise most of our food instead of buying it on the market, we could make a substantial reduction in our cash outlay and in our required cash income. Was such a project feasible on the thin leached soil of a high Vermont valley? Our concern for home-grown food led to much thought, generous advice from the neighbors and some experimentation, in the course of which we decided to undertake a rather extensive garden project. This decision brought us face to face with three stubborn facts, the Vermont climate, the pitch of the land, and the depleted soil.

The most formidable problem with which we had to deal was not the soil, but the climate. Someone has described the weather in our part of Vermont as eleven months of winter and thirty days of mighty cold weather. Experience showed that the author of this saw was not too far from the truth. "The Spring visiteth

not these quarters so timely . . . Summer imparteth a verie temperate heat."[1]

We were located at an elevation of 1800 feet above sea level,
in a valley surrounded by mountains, where the frost-free growing season was around 85 days per year. In 1947, bean, tomato
and squash plants were damaged by frost in June, July and
August, which meant frost every month in that year. We have
seen our apple trees loaded with blossoms; then, on the 22nd of
May, more than a foot of damp snow has fallen, crushing flowers
and breaking down branches. This May snowfall was followed
by a hard frost. Late in May we have seen the weather-vane shift
into the north after a heavy rain, and in the course of a few
hours have seen the thermometer drop 12 or 15 degrees and
stay around 20° all night, taking fruit, blossoms, seedlings and
even the young leaves of ash, birch, beech and chokecherry. We
have had our last killing frost on June 5th, and on August 25th
we have seen an entire field of potatoes, sturdy and green the
previous day, frozen dead. A nearby fruit grower lost 196 out
of 200 Baldwin apple trees during the cold winter of 1938. They
were fine healthy trees about 35 years old. All these experiences
spelled possible frost twelve months of the year. Could a vegetarian household survive in such a region? After twenty years
of experimentation we can answer that question in the affirmative.

We knew our climatic limitations. If we were careful, there
would be a chance for tender vegetables such as squash and
tomatoes to grow and mature. Hardier crops like potatoes, beets
and carrots surely would get by. Apple trees would survive most
winters. Plum and pear trees might frequently freeze. Cherries
and peaches were out of the picture. The trees that did survive
would bear fruit perhaps two or three years out of five, because

[1] Richard Carew, *The Survey of Cornwall*, Lon.: Iaggard 1602 p. 5

late frost might catch the blossoms. Among the nut trees, only beechnuts and hazels could be counted on, and they bore crops about one year in three. Our food raising, if food raising we did, must be concentrated in a brief period of each year and even then we would be compelled to pick our varieties with care.

We were in Indian country, but in our neighborhood there were few arrowheads or stone axes. Why? The Indians had hunted and fished there, but they had lived in the lower valleys. Their camping sites were in Connecticut, not Vermont. It was too cold, even for Indians, up in those frost-ridden hills. However, we knew the old settlers had conquered the Vermont wilderness, endured the climate, raised large families and prospered. We decided that if farmers had survived in that valley for more than a hundred years, we might also have a try at it. But we had notice. We must watch our step or we might lose our shirts.

The neighbors saved us a deal of time and trouble with welcome advice. Arthur Young, in 1792, counseled the newcomer in farming to "look over his hedges, and see what his neighbors do with their land; let him walk about the country for the same purpose, and compare the practise which he *sees* with the opinions which he *hears*. It would be for his interest to be acquainted with one or two decent sensible farmers, that will not take a pleasure in misleading him; such are everywhere to be found."[2] We had such neighbor-friends. Jack Lightfoot had lived in the valley for thirty-five years. Floyd Hurd was born there, was part Indian and could smell a coming frost. They talked to us of their experiences. Then each spring as planting time approached they apprised and warned. In the autumn they watched for frost as a mountain climber watches for avalanches.

We put our kitchen garden on a level with the house, but,

[2] *Rural Economy*, Burlington, Vt.: Neale 1792 p. 102

thanks to our neighbors' suggestions, we also laid out a garden three hundred feet higher, on a shoulder of Pinnacle Mountain. (Cold air drains from the heights into the valleys. An early frost which wipes out valley vegetation may leave untouched locations only a few hundred feet higher, especially if there are no pockets to hold cold air and retard its normal flow into the valley.) We called this upper garden patch our "insurance garden." There we established an asparagus bed and a raspberry patch. It was there that we grew all of our corn, beans, squashes and turnips, our tomatoes, all of our cabbage family plants, and most of our eating peas and sweet peas. Taking one season with another, we estimate that the insurance garden was frost-free at least three weeks longer than the garden near the house.

Later, as our food needs grew with more people coming to Forest Farm, we started an intermediate garden on a piece of land that had been used by the Hoard family for potato growing. In this garden we grew strawberries, hybrid blueberries and potatoes—all of which thrive in acid soil. The berry and potato garden was open to the south, but protected by forest growths on the north, east and west. The soil of the area was an exceptionally fine sandy loam. The spot had a frost-free growing season slightly longer than that of the house garden.

Land in the narrow Vermont valleys slopes steeply. There are level spots in the valley bottoms, but these are generally swampy or else they are so water-logged in the spring that it takes weeks of good weather before they are dry enough to work.

Most Vermonters meet this problem by planting their gardens on the slopes. Every third year they break up a piece of sod land, cultivate it while the sod holds together enough to protect the soil against wash, and then sow the garden spot to grass or grain and break another piece of sod land. When we talked about terracing our gardens, the neighbors told us "You can't do that. Gardens here are good for about three years. You will no sooner get your terraces made than you will have to move the garden and start all over again."

We listened. But we had seen terraces in the Philippines, in Europe and Asia upon which men had gardened for hundreds and in some cases for thousands of years. If they could do it in China, Japan and Germany, why could we not do it in Vermont? While our neighbors continued to shift their gardens each time the sod rotted, we kept ours in the same place year after year. If land sloped more than two or three feet in a hundred, we put up terraces. We began by building them of loose stone. When we found that weeds and grass were hard to uproot from these loose stone walls, we turned to stone and concrete. Mulches and fall-sown rye helped to reduce top soil wash. We built up our gardens by hauling in any available top-soil and we increased its fertility by consistently making and using compost, which enriched the soil instead of exhausting it.

Soils in eastern United States have been cultivated for any time up to four hundred years. In Vermont the time range is about two hundred years. The farmers who had preceded us in the valley had broken the sod, cultivated crops during the growing season and left the unprotected soil to the mercy of sudden showers, driving rains, melting snows and high winds. Consequently, most of the top soil had been swept off the hills and a good deal of it flushed down the West River and the Connecticut into the sea. What remained of the top soil had been sadly depleted. Year after year the trace minerals had been exhausted, until the land was barely able to produce grasses and the sturdier forms of wild vegetation.

Anyone who hopes to make a good garden must remember

that vegetation draws most of its sustenance from top soil, which is alive. Healthy soil teems with organic life. Top soil is alive in several senses. It is alive because it contains large quantities of organic matter, made up of plant and animal residues,—leaves, twigs, grasses, manures, carcasses. It is alive with microscopic organisms which convert organic matter such as dead leaves and grasses into available plant food. It is alive with earthworms which work the land by passing particles through their bodies, extracting certain nutritive factors upon which they live, and casting forth the remainder to greatly enrich the land. Sir Albert Howard writes, "The casts of the earthworm are five times richer in available nitrogen, seven times richer in available phosphate, and eleven times richer in available potash, than the upper six inches of the soil. Some twenty-five tons of fresh wormcasts are produced every year on each acre of properly farmed land."[3] These castings are "neutral colloidal humus, the only form immediately available to plants."[4] Earthworms ventilate and drain the land as well as transform trash to balanced plant food. Top soil swarms with insect and rodent life. The richer the top soil in organic matter, the larger will be its living population (unless it is drugged or killed with chemical fertilizers, poisonous sprays or dusts) and the more friable for production and use.

Whole food can be grown only upon whole soil. If essential ingredients such as iodine and boron, for instance, are not present, the vegetation grown on the soil and the animals which feed on the vegetation will suffer from the same mineral and dietetic deficiencies.

Eastern people, the Chinese and the Koreans, for example, have been growing food on certain areas for thousands of years.

[3] Letter to the London Sunday Times, 2/27/1944
[4] F. H. Billington, Compost, Lon.: Faber 1942 p. 75

But they have been careful to put back into the soil everything that came from it,—vegetable, animal and human wastes. Western man has been following the opposite practice. He is dumping great quantities of city waste, including human waste, into the rivers or the sea, or else he is burning it. He is abandoning animal husbandry, farming with machinery, thus decreasing the supply of animal manure, harvesting crops and putting back on the land chemical fertilizers which contain little organic matter and only a portion of the elements removed from the soil by cropping. Open cultivation permits water and wind to move the top soil bodily and thus decrease fertility. Such practices erode and demineralize the land. On such depleted lands, whole foods cannot be produced.

Nature has been building soil for ages. It may be found on the floor of forests and in swamps, composed of decaying vegetation, plus the castings of earth worms, the droppings and, occasionally, the bodies of insects, birds and animals. In North American forests an inch of top soil may be built in from three hundred to a thousand years. Its essential ingredient is decomposing organic matter. The chief factor in decomposition is the teeming population of organisms which live in and partly compose the top soil.

Perhaps it would be well, at this point, to note an important fact about the soil of a forest floor. The forest is composed of many species of trees, shrubs and lesser vegetation whose nature is determined by climate, elevation, exposure and soil content. The composition of the forest floor is constantly altered by the demands of the vegetation occupying it. The hard maple requires a considerable amount of calcium. As the calcium is exhausted by the hard maples, the soil becomes less hospitable to maple and more attractive to some other species,—for example, spruce. Consequently, over the years, the hard maple will be replaced by spruce, and a hardwood forest will give way to evergreen. We have seen this transformation taking place again and again in areas devoted to the cultivation of the sugar maple.

Soil, such as one finds on a forest floor, varies in its mineral content and therefore in its capacity to supply the requirements of different types of vegetation. The forest floor mixture being a chance one, local conditions may provide it with an over-supply or an under-supply of essential minerals. Strictly speaking, therefore, to reproduce the conditions of a natural forest is not enough. Each type of vegetation requires soil of a particular mineral make-up.

Must we turn our depleted soils back into forest and wait thousands of years until they are restored to wholeness? Certainly not. We can build whole, living, balanced soil by composting. Compost is a mixture of topsoil and organic matter which has decomposed sufficiently to provide nourishment for vegetation. Man-made compost may be kept, from start to finish, under the control of the composter. Soil testing reveals deficiencies. Deficiencies may be supplied and the proper mineral balance of the soil may be re-established by putting into the compost the proper amounts of the necessary ingredients. Soils may be built and rebuilt with somewhat the same accuracy that metals may be alloyed. Largely, it is a matter of learning the facts and adopting appropriate procedures.

Agricultural experiment stations, located in the state agricultural colleges, will help by providing soil analyses which indicate the mineral ingredients present in soil specimens supplied by the prospective food grower. The analyses will show what minerals are present in sufficient quantity, and what are deficient or absent. With this factual background the compost maker can introduce into his compost the minerals that will restore the balance of a depleted soil.

In our early experiments with compost making, we used animal residues—chiefly manure. Later we changed our practices and made compost as it is made in the forest, with the products of vegetation. We supplemented this vegetation, much of which came from depleted soils, with ground limestone, ground phosphate rock, ground potash rock, marl, or colloidal earth. All of these natural earths contain a considerable variety of the score of trace minerals necessary to maintain the balance that will provide for growth, vitality and health in vegetable and animal life. As our soil was deficient in nitrogen, we also used cotton seed, linseed, soybean or alfalfa meal. The results far exceeded our fondest hopes and expectations. On gardens covering less than a third of an acre we grew enough food to provide everything except grain for half a dozen people.

Our compost making followed the general lines laid down by Albert Howard in his *Agricultural Testament*[5] and *The Soil and Health;*[6] by Ehrenfried Pfeiffer in *Bio-Dynamic Farming and Gardening*[7] and *Soil Fertility, Renewal and Preservation;*[8] by Eve Balfour in *The Living Soil;*[9] and by J. I. Rodale in *Pay Dirt*[10] and *The Organic Front.*[11] We modified their patterns somewhat to meet our particular needs.

We built our compost piles 8 by 8 feet square. For a small family we would suggest 5 by 5, or even 3 by 3 feet. The important point is that the piles should be small enough so that,

[5] N.Y.: Oxford University Press 1940
[6] N.Y.: Devin-Adair 1952
[7] N.Y.: Anthroposophic Press 1938
[8] Lon.: Faber 1949
[9] Lon.: Faber 1943
[10] N.Y.: Devin-Adair 1945
[11] Emmaus, Pa.: Rodale Press 1949

with the available organic matter, each pile can be completed in two or three weeks. Some English composters recommend 2 by 2 foot piles for very small families or single persons. As the volume of the pile grows smaller, its capacity to produce internal heat decreases. Internal heat is one of the essential factors in the destruction of weed seed and the elimination of fungus enemies and in the rapid break-down of organic matter.

For our compost making we picked a well-drained shady spot, dug away the sod, laid it to one side, then took out 6 to 8 inches of top soil and laid that in a separate pile. Into this excavation we put a foot of coarse organic matter—pea vines, corn stalks, hay, straw, weeds, cabbage stalks. If materials destined for compost are wilted by lying at least a day in the sun, so much the better. Fresh cut vegetation, put immediately into a compost pile, is likely to go sour and retard the process of disintegration.

Materials used for compost are likely to be sleazy and messy, and so broken up that they do not pile neatly. Therefore a bin or crib is advantageous if not necessary. After some experimenting we built a type of open log cabin container, of poles 2 to 3 inches in diameter, cut from such inferior wood as poplar, white birch, hemlock or cherry. During our woodcutting season we made a point of converting all suitable straight material into compost poles, and storing them near our compost areas. We began to build our compost bin by laying four 8 foot poles around the sides of the square hole, with the ends of the poles lapping at the corners. As we added material to the pile, more poles were laid up, criss cross, around the pile. We continued this building process until the pile was approximately 5 feet high.

On the first layer of compost material (that is, at about ground level) we set up a ventilating system, consisting of three or four small poles, 8 feet long, bunched together horizontally across the center of the pile, with ends resting on the side poles. With a bar we made holes at two points along these ventilator poles (dividing the distance into three equal sections) and put in two vertical bundles each, containing three or four light poles 5 or 6 feet long. These we fastened together with wire. As the pile grew, air circulated along the horizontal bundle of poles and up through the vertical bundles. Compost piles smaller than 6 × 6 feet require only one vertical ventilator, placed at the center of the horizontal vent poles.

Compost piles are built with the materials at hand. These vary with the locality and the season. In Vermont, near each composting area, we kept a stack of straw or hay, a crib of autumn leaves, a bin of sawdust, a pile of sods and one of topsoil. These materials could usually be had for the hauling. Whenever they became available we picked them up and put them in their respective bins. Hay and autumn leaves were abundant only once each year, when we aimed to store enough to last until the following season.

Each day brought garbage from the house, weeds and tops from the garden, grass cuttings and trash from the flowerbeds. We used every available bit of organic matter,—never paper. These materials went on the current compost pile until they filled about 4 to 6 inches in depth. Since the organisms which break down the organic matter live in top soil, we sprinkled a thin layer of topsoil (half an inch to an inch) on this organic matter. Next we added a sprinkling of ground phosphate rock, followed by a thin layer of forest leaves from the storage pile kept for the purpose, with another sprinkling of top soil, and a light dressing of ground potash sand. Then came a layer of hay or straw, followed by a light dressing of sawdust, a sprinkling of topsoil and of cottonseed or other meal. Next, we applied a thin layer of sod, broken up and turned upside down with a scattering of limestone. That was our sequence. When it was completed we did the same things over again until the pile was breast or chin high. As the pile went up we edged it with the 8 foot compost poles. We topped off the pile with inverted sods and a thick covering of hay or straw to discourage weed growth, retain moisture and shut out direct sunlight.

It is better to build a compost pile a bit at a time, over a period of at least ten days to two weeks. If built in a day or two, it sinks too much. The pile should be damp, but not wet. In a dry spell this means some watering. If it is properly built, within a few days of completion it will heat to around 150°, thus speeding the breakdown of organic matter and disposing of weed seeds by germinating them. Unless the pile heats, the weed seeds may survive and be returned to the garden.

When the pile has cooled a bit, earth worms and worm capsules can be inserted. If the pile is sufficiently moist, the worms will work their way through it, breaking down the organic matter as they go. If no earth worms are available, the pile can be turned by forking or shoveling the material into a new hole dug beside the old pile. Usually we also put into the finished pile a small quantity of herbal activator, which speeds decomposition.

Activators are designed to speed up bacterial action, to attract earth worms and to expedite the disintegration of organic matter. Usually a small quantity is dissolved in water which may be sprinkled on successive layers or poured into holes made by a crowbar from top to bottom of the finished compost pile. After making compost with and without activators, we believe that they speed up the process, but that, if one is in no hurry, equally good compost may be made without them.

If the pile is kept damp and the weather is warm, the compost will be available for use on the garden in from sixty to ninety days. In the course of that period the varied materials composing the pile will be reduced to a rich, sweet-smelling earthy mass closely resembling the black wood dirt picked up on a forest floor. The pile will be more completely broken down if a longer time is allowed. Some organic gardeners recommend leaving compost for as long as three years.

Good compost can be made, as it is on the forest floor, without introducing anything foreign in the way of phosphate rock, potash, cottonseed meal or lime, activator or worms, and without turning the pile, but these elements help speed the breakdown of organic matter. On a piece of depleted demineralized soil, such as ours was, the addition of specific absent or deficient minerals stepped up the restoration of soil balance.

For years we put nothing on our garden except compost. We fed the soil live food, not dead, inert, synthetic or artificial fertilizers. The resulting garden produce was superb in quality, abundant, and of splendid color and flavor. And year by year we added to the volume of top soil as well as to its friability and productivity.

We laid out our garden so that the rows ran north and south, thus allowing the greatest amount of sun to reach the soil between plants. Each row was marked by a numbered stake. In our earlier gardening experiments the stakes were made of sawed lumber and the tops were painted before numbering. Later we used straight 16 inch sections of hard maple or ash saplings, an inch or a little more in diameter, pointed on one end with an axe and having on the opposite end of the stake, a small blaze, made with an axe, on which the number could be written with a lumber pencil. If possible the stakes were given a year to dry before they went into the garden. When gardening was over in the autumn, stakes were pulled, the dirt was shaken off and they were stored, dry, for the winter. Thus treated, they would last for several years. Tomato stakes and bean poles were made from straight saplings and were similarly cared for.

Above each garden we had a storage tank, from which we ran water in pipes to the garden and distributed it in the garden by means of hoses, laid to irrigation ditches between the rows. We did not irrigate regularly—only when the gardens got too dry, between rains. Some seasons we scarcely irrigated at all, but we had the water there if we needed it. In transplanting, the water was invaluable.

For the planning of the garden we employed several simple techniques that kept plans and garden and work in order. We had a loose-leaf notebook labeled "Garden Book" in which we put all information and material dealing with gardening. One section of the book was devoted to garden plans, including a free-hand map of the garden for two years, with proper crop successions and rotations, and a detailed plan, section by section, bed by bed and row by row. Entries in the garden book, under corresponding numbers, showed dates of planting, variety and origin of seeds, methods of treatment and results. We numbered our compost piles too and kept a record of each pile in a section of the garden book. These general records enabled us to test the efficacy of various gardening techniques and the reliability of different seed houses and nurseries. They also distinguished compost made with lime, which was not good for potatoes and berries. Year by year these records were made and filed away in the back of the book. By turning to them we could refresh our memories when we came to plan for succeeding gardens.

In late winter or early spring we planned our garden and ordered our seeds. Frequent changes in plan were necessitated by weather vagaries, and other unexpected events. But at all times we had at our elbows a pattern on paper which we tried to develop in the garden. Such a procedure of "think first, then act" helps to make gardening less haphazard, more interesting, satisfying and effective.

We come now to the principles which governed our gardening. (1) We wanted to live twelve months in the year from a garden which enjoyed barely three months of frost-free weather. (2) We wanted to eat fresh, unprocessed food. (3) We wanted a variety of garden products which would furnish a rounded diet. (4) We wanted to reduce canning and preserving to a minimum. Through the years we have been able to reach all four objectives.

Most difficult among these four assignments was the twelve months of fresh food from the garden. We approached the problem in two ways. The first of these two was eating with the seasons. There is something extravagant and irresponsible about eating strawberries and green peas in a cold climate, every month in the year. Such practices ignore the meaningful cycle of the seasons. Those who dodge it or slight it are like children who skip a grade in school, pass over its drill and discipline, and ever after have the feeling that they have missed something.

We seldom bought anything out of season, such as asparagus, strawberries or corn. Instead, we enjoyed thoroughly each food as it came from the garden. We began early in the spring with parsnips, the first thing available in our garden. As soon as the snow went, we dug them and had them for one meal a day for about three or four weeks. During that period they provided much of our starch and sugar. With parsnips went salsify, celery and parsley root, leeks and chicory. Then came six to eight weeks of asparagus, accompanied by dandelion, chives and multiplier onions. Before the asparagus was finished, we had begun on spinach, radishes, mustard greens, garden cress and early lettuce. Following that we had green peas, beets, standard lettuce, string beans and squash. In the height of the season came corn, tomatoes, shellbeans, broccoli, cauliflower and celery. As autumn approached, we turned to the cabbages, winter squash, turnips, rutabagas, carrots, escarolle, chinese cabbage, collards, with cos lettuce, fall radishes, spinach and beets, and, for the first time, potatoes and dried beans. We cultivated strawberries, raspberries and blueberries and ate them in season. These berries also grew wild in abundance, along with chokecherries, shad and blackberries. For other fruit we had pears, plums and apples.

After the snows, when the gardens were white and frozen, we turned to our vegetable cellars with their winter roots, cabbages, winter squash, potatoes, beets, carrots, turnips, onions, rutabagas, celery root, parsley root and pears and apples. The hardiest of these vegetables would still be fresh and edible up to the time the snow melted and we were digging parsnips once again.

Through this entire twelve month cycle, we ate a great variety of fresh food. It was garden fresh from the first thaw in February-March to the heavy snows of December. The balance of the time it came from an outside vegetable cellar. By following the seasons, we got a succession of foods—each at its peak. We enjoyed each in turn. We tired of none, but always looked forward to its coming in the new growing season.[12]

Gardens in our neighborhood frequently were made in May. By late August or early September they were neglected, weed-filled, insect-ridden and finished for the year. When frost hit us, usually in early September, our kitchen garden was filled to the

[12] Henry Thoreau wrote in his Journal "I love best to have each thing in its season only, and enjoy doing without it at all other times." Dec. 5, 1856

corners with frost-free plants. We are convinced that our early spring and late autumn gardens were more valuable than the summer garden.

Early spring gardens are made by wintering over leeks, chives, multiplier onions, dandelions, parsley, collards, chicory, removing the protecting brush and mulch when heavy frosts are ended and letting the sun bring them along. This gives one mature vegetables even before seed-planting time. Another help for the spring garden is a small, portable coldframe, made with a few boards and some window sash or cold frame sash, in which early radishes, lettuce, cress and mustard greens may be sown. Under favorable conditions radishes mature in three to four weeks. They are hardy and will stand some freezing.

Fall gardens grow out of summer gardens. About July 1st, as we removed radishes, lettuce, early beets and spinach from the garden, we scattered an inch of compost, worked it in and planted onion seed, beets, escarolle, endive, broccoli, chinese cabbage, kale, collards. A little later we planted oak leaf lettuce, cos lettuce, winter celery plants, spinach and finally mustard greens, garden cress and radishes. We did our last planting late in September or early in October.

When our cucumbers, squash, peppers and tomatoes froze, we replaced them with transplants of lettuce, escarolle, broccoli and kale, and with sowings of mustard, cress and radishes. On October first our garden was prolific, and greener than it was in August, because it was a greenness which is associated with autumn rains, night frosts and hot, humid and misty days. Insect pests had left for parts unknown. With the protection of a few evergreen boughs and some mulching with leaves, hay or straw, these green crops were available until they were covered by heavy snow. If the first snow was wet, frozen brussel sprouts, collards, escarolle, chinese cabbage, kale and parsley might be dug from under the snow blanket. At no other season are greens so delicious.

We further extended our growing season by a small sunheated greenhouse in which we wintered many plants and started others for spring planting. The south wall of our tool shed was 18 feet long—just enough to accommodate six cold frame sash, 3 × 6 feet. The tool shed, like all of our buildings, was made of stone. This gave us a south-facing stone wall against which we built a concrete and wood structure that held the six cold frame sash in a semi-horizontal position. On mild, sunny days in winter, with no stove or artificial heating, the temperature inside this sun-heated greenhouse went up to 100° unless we ventilated it.

We designed the place for raising celery, tomato, lettuce and other transplants for the garden. One October, however, we set out oak leaf lettuce plants, six inches apart. The lettuce had been sown outside early in September and transplanted to the pit greenhouse in mid-October; thus it had been hardened by early frosts. We continued to eat this lettuce until January 5th, and felt richly rewarded for our pains. We had almost bridged the winter gap in garden-fresh vegetables. We had not dreamed that lettuce would last so long in an unheated greenhouse under subzero weather conditions.

More surprises were coming, however. In the spring of the same year, following our success in carrying lettuce to January 5th, we discovered in the greenhouse, behind a flat, some of the lettuce plants that we had used for transplanting the previous October. They were hale and sturdy. Oh ho, we said, if these plants can survive the winter in a neglected corner, why not in the back bench of the greenhouse?

The next autumn we tried it. We cleared two inches of soil

from the back bench, replaced it by two inches of good compost, worked it lightly into the under-soil and set out eighty-eight heads of oak leaf lettuce plants from the garden. They were then about two inches high. As the plants grew, we scattered leaves among them to protect the roots against frost. We lost only two of the lettuce plants. The remainder we ate through the winter,—the last of them the following May. On two occasions that winter the thermometer touched 25° below zero.

The next winter we tried Simpson lettuce instead of oak leaf, with no leaves for mulch. Same result: lettuce until May. At the same time we included chives and parsley plants that had been growing all summer in the garden. These were equally successful. We had found an all-winter source of fresh greens. Had the greenhouse been roomy enough, we believe that we could have grown mustard greens, garden cress, leaf chicory and turnip greens all winter with equal success.

For a large part of the winter the top and sides of this unheated greenhouse were covered with snow. With the sun blocked from entering and the temperature down to 25° below zero we often found the lettuce frozen stiff. When cut under these conditions, it wilted immediately upon being brought into the house. Even plunging in cold water failed to revive it. However, if we left it uncut and waited for a warmer day or a bit of sun, the lettuce thawed out itself and stood in the greenhouse crisp and edible.

This discussion of gardening has been written mostly in terms of vegetables. Almost every word is equally applicable to flowers and fruit. To be sure, each flower, like each vegetable, has requirements which must be met if superior results are to be obtained, but the essentials of gardening are the same. Soil building practices result in fine quality vegetation, whether vegetables, fruits or flowers. Flowers and fruit respond to composting and mulching as do other types of plants.

We would like to report here on an experiment with red raspberries which turned out unusually well. We adopted the hill system. A stake two inches in diameter and eight feet long was set every six feet, in rows six feet apart. We put one or two Latham raspberry plants beside each pole. As these plants developed, we cut out the bearing canes in August or September, leaving six or seven new canes close around each stake. These canes we tied to the stake, waist high, with one piece of binder twine. In the spring, before the buds came out, we went over the canes, took out the weakest, reduced the number of canes to three or four, cut them to breast height, and tied them in two or three places to the pole.

Then we encountered the great problem faced by every grower of small fruit,—annual weeds and grass in the patch. If the weeds and grass are left long enough and if they get thick enough they choke out the berry plants. We decided to try a heavy mulch to choke out the weeds, and put about six inches of sawdust on the patch after the old canes were cleared out. The results were magical. Weeds virtually disappeared, except for milkweed, wild morning glory, sorrel and a few others that propagate from roots. Most annual weeds will not start in sawdust. The canes grew thick and high. Blights and pests to which red raspberries are subject did not bother us, though we neither sprayed nor dusted the plants. Fungus and insect damage were slight. Each autumn we added another six inches of sawdust to the patch. Such a mulch in the course of a year is reduced by packing, earthworms and weathering to about an inch in depth. The next year it is further amalgamated with the soil. After eighteen years of this treatment, with no fertilizers or manures, the raspberry patch was hale and hearty, all but weedless, in perfect condition, and had been raised two inches higher than the surrounding garden. The berries were abundant, extra large in size, beautifully colored and of excellent flavor.

We began our experiments with mulch in the raspberry patch. As the years went by we extended the principle to other crops with equal success.

Mulch is material placed on top of the soil in an effort to (1) retain moisture, (2) check weed growth, (3) keep the soil cool for certain crops, (4) prevent water and wind erosion, (5) attract earth worms at or near the surface of the soil, (6) provide additional humus and plant food as the mulch breaks down. Mulching materials range from stones and paper through hay, straw and other stalk growth to leaves, tree branches, wood chips, shavings and sawdust.

We regard the untouched forest floor as the most extensive and most successful experiment in mulching. There, year after year, leaves, branches, tree trunks, the droppings and bodies of living creatures are scattered over the earth's surface. Leaves and twigs from one year are consolidated with other refuse and soon provide nourishment for feeding roots. Year by year the underside of the forest mulch is converted into humus and incorporated into the forest soil.

After years of experience with the mulch in the garden, we are convinced that mulching practices are an indispensable supplement and complement to composting. In the course of our experimenting we have tried many mulching materials on different crops with varying success. Sawdust, especially that from hemlock logs, must be used with discrimination; we tried it on strawberries and potatoes with poor results. Plants like corn, beans and tomatoes prefer warm sunshine around their roots. Mulching these

crops is a questionable practice, in our opinion. On the other
hand, peas and potatoes, which thrive in cool soil, do phenom-
enally well under a mulch. For years we have grown our potatoes
under heavy hay mulch from planting time to harvest, with no
weeds, no hoeing, no bugs, no spraying and, at the end of the
season, almost no digging, as the potatoes lie right under the
mulch. In planting they are laid on top of the soil, covered with
compost and mulch and re-mulched as often as the rains, winds
and the voracious appetite of earth worms reduces the mulch layer
to less than four or five inches.

One of our specialties in gardening was the growing of sweet
peas. Each year we aimed to get in a double row at least fifty feet
long. When we began in Vermont, we could not raise good sweet
peas. The seeds germinated badly; when the seedlings appeared,
they were destroyed by cutworms and stem borers. Plants that
survived were sickly. Blossoms were short-stemmed, small, pale
in color, and not too fragrant.

Once the soil was built up, the entire pattern changed. Young
plants were sturdy; under favorable conditions they grew so high
that the blossoms could be picked only from a stool or a step
ladder. On a number of occasions they measured over eight feet
from the surface of the ground. Flower stems were long. On
many stems we had four to five blossoms, or even six. Flowers
were large, fragrant, and of clear brilliant colors. We were able
to repeat these successes year after year.

Our method of culture was simple. As early as the ground
could be worked in the spring, we spread an inch or two of
compost and worked it lightly into the soil. We made two trenches
about three to four inches deep and eight inches apart, put in the
sweet pea seed with a view to having the plants stand about four
inches apart, filled the trenches with compost and firmed the

earth by walking on it. As soon as the seedlings showed above ground we put a line of pea brush between the two rows and packed six or eight inches of hay or straw close up to the seedlings and across the intervening space to the next row. As the season wore on and the sweet peas grew taller, we renewed this mulch as often as necessary to maintain a depth of six or eight inches. Picking sweet peas involves much daily tramping back and forth with a corresponding consolidation of the mulch.

When the sweet pea vines were 24 to 30 inches high they began to bear flowers. Year after year they kept on bearing until heavy frost. Our flowers were better, in both size and color than those of neighboring professional growers. On one occasion we took a bushel basket full of sweet peas to an organic gardeners' conference which we were attending in early September. An expert, William Eyster, who spoke at the conference, was surprised and delighted that we had been able to grow such flowers and keep them going so late in the season. He said to us, "When you get back home, please send a bunch of those sweet peas to Mr David Burpee. His seed company built its reputation on sweet peas and at one time sold large quantities of their seed. Today this department is languishing because they say gardeners no longer have luck with sweet peas." We sent the flowers and received a friendly note of commendation and thanks.

Sweet peas grow while garden soils are well supplied with humus. Erosion, soil exhaustion and chemical fertilizers lower soil vitality to a point at which the production of good sweet peas is difficult or impossible. Composting and mulching, with the aid of earthworms, had brought our depleted soil back to a level of fertility which produced good flowers, as well as good fruits and vegetables.

Top soil like every other aspect of nature, can be plundered and depleted by wrong practices until it is all but sterile. Reverse these practices, build a living soil, and vegetation flourishes as it is reported to have done in the garden of Eden.

There is an old saying that we reap what we sow. Nowhere is this more evident than in the treatment of the good earth.

"Good dyet is a perfect way of curing:
 And worthy much regard and health assuring.
 A King that cannot rule him in his dyet,
 Will hardly rule his Realme in peace and quiet."
                    Regimen Sanitatis Salernitanum, *11th century*

"Go, tell them what thou bringst exceeds the wealth
 Of al these Countries, for thou bringst them health."
                    John Helme, The Englishman's Doctor, *1608*

"If you shall weigh with yourselfe your Estate and manner of living,
you will easily confesse with me and lay the blame upon your selfe for
such mischiefes. I do not direct my speech only to those who are already
affected with sicknes, but to them rather which yet inioy their good
and perfect health, to the end they may serve themselves with meanes
proper to maintaine the same. For how pretious and deare a treasure it is
to be of good health."
                    John Ghesel, The Rule of Health, *1631*

"Were it in my Power, I would recall the World, if not altogether to their
Pristine Diet, yet to a much more wholsome and temperate than is now
in Fashion."
                    John Evelyn, Acetaria, A Discourse of Sallets, *1699*

"Fly the rank city, shun its turbid air . . .
 While yet you breathe, away; the rural wild
 Invite; the mountains call you, and the vales;
 The woods, the streams, and each ambrosial breeze
 That fans the ever undulating sky—
 A kindly sky! whose fostering power regales
 Man, beast, and all the vegetable reign . . .
 Here spread your gardens wide; and let the cool,
 The moist relaxing vegetable store
 Prevail in each repast."
                    John Armstrong, The Art of Preserving Health, *1838*

"I learned from my two year's experiment that it would cost incredibly
little trouble to obtain one's necessary food, even in this latitude; that
many a man may use as simple a diet as the animals, and yet retain
health and strength."
                    Henry Thoreau, Walden, *1854*

CHAPTER 5

EATING FOR HEALTH

What is health?—Nutrition—Whole food—Seeds—Processed food—Food profiteering—The milling industry—Food poisoning—Drugs—Malnutrition and physical degeneration—A personal and universal problem—Fresh foods all year—Winter storage of foods—Canning—Types of foods—Vegetarians and vegans—Our diet outlined—Meatless meals—Simplifying the feeding process

HEALTH is one of the most important elements in the good life. The better the health, the more adequate and satisfying the life. A design for living, a house-building program and an effective means of producing wholesome food are more or less meaningless unless they promote good health for the designers, builders and gardeners. It is one thing to produce quality foods on the land. It is quite another matter to incorporate these values into the human organism.

When we left the city and its environs to live in Vermont, we were in better than average health. Had we necessarily improved our chances for good health by moving from New York City to Pikes Falls, Vermont? Geographically, the answer must be in the negative. Vital statistics do not show any notable difference between the health of Vermonters and of New Yorkers. Personal observations in our valley and its neighborhood revealed numerous cases of digestive troubles, heart ailments, arthritis, cancer, goiter, tooth decay and mental deficiency. The people in Vermont were subject to about the same climatic conditions, ate much the same food and lived under many of the same pressures as the people in the city. If we wanted health in Vermont, or anywhere else, we would have to tackle the problem deliberately, as in all phases of the good life, and assemble the factors which produced it.

What is health? We have asked many doctors for a definition. The usual reply is "normal, balanced function" or "freedom from disease". When we asked what disease was, the answer came: "absence of health". So we were back where we started. The frankest answer we ever had came from an American doctor who had practised medicine for sixty years. To our question "Do you know what health is?" he answered without hesitation "Of course not". We believe we are correct in stating that no medical school in the United States offers a course on health.

The *Encyclopedia Britannica* has an article on the subject. We reproduce it in its entirety: "Health. A condition of physical soundness or well-being, in which an organism discharges its functions efficiently; also in a transferred sense a state of moral or intellectual well being". Thumbing through the *Britannica* volumes we have found lengthy articles dealing with scores of different diseases; health is given five lines. Medical journals and medical libraries abound in material on disease. It is rare to find in their pages any extensive treatment of health.

One such rarity is a book by an English medical doctor, *The Wheel of Health,* by G. T. Wrench. Instead of spending his time on the subject of sickness, Dr. Wrench asked, "What is health? Why are people well? Where can I find the healthiest people to study?" After much inquiry and research, Wrench concluded that the Hunzas, a tribe occupying a small valley in the border area between India and Tibet are the world's healthiest. Much of his book is devoted to an examination of the reasons for their state of well-being. He concluded that "Diseases only attack those whose outer circumstances, particularly food, are faulty . . . The prevention and banishment of disease are primarily matters of food; secondarily, of suitable conditions of environment. Antiseptics, medicaments, inoculations, and extirpating operations evade the real problem. Disease is the censor pointing out the humans, animals and plants who are imperfectly nourished."[1]

Wrench's wheel of health is a cycle from whole soil to whole, healthy vegetation, to the whole, healthy animals which consume the whole vegetation, and from the vegetation and animal back to the soil; where the cycle begins all over again, on a higher or lower level, depending upon whether the soil has been enriched or impoverished in the process.

"Health is wealth" is an old and a true saying. Health, wholth or wholeness is a primary and positive principle, which applies to human well-being as it does to other aspects of the universe. Health is attained and preserved by taking into the human organism solids and liquids (food and drink), air, light, sunshine and various more or less obscure sources of electro-magnetic, cosmic energy.

Human bodies are composed chiefly of water. Beside water they contain some twenty elements which are derived from the earth, mainly in the form of food. Ceaselessly the cells composing the human body are wearing themselves out through the functioning of tissues and organs, and the blood stream is busy carrying the waste products of body function to the lungs, the pores of the skin and other excretive agencies. Just as ceaselessly the food which enters the alimentary canal is being converted into

[1] London: C. W. Daniel 1938 p. 130

substances which can be used in rebuilding cells, tissues, organs.

Where food intake is low, in quantity or quality, the materials for repair and rebuilding the human organism are low in volume or in excellence. The nature of the materials carried by the blood stream to the cells, tissues and organs determines the character of the resulting bone, muscle and nerve structure. In that sense a man's body is composed of the materials entering it through the digestive tract and the blood stream, just as a building is composed of the materials reaching it over the railways and highways.

Normal bodily growth and function are dependent on the supply of nutrition through the blood stream. The nutritional elements which pass from the alimentary canal via the blood stream to the cells, tissues and organs supply the materials out of which the body is built and repaired. In this sense, we are what we eat. The human intake of solid and liquid food, water, air, sunshine and the other less tangible forms of matter and energy are the substances upon which human beings depend for their sustenance and their physical survival. Among these sustaining elements solid and liquid food occupy an important position. Each day vital organs like heart and lungs wear themselves out by their ceaseless action. In the course of a few years the more important parts of the body are broken down and the refuse is carried out of the body. Worn-out tissue is replaced by solid and liquid food, by air, by sunlight. Food plays a principal part in this process.

Each cell, tissue and organ has a mineral balance,—a workable relation between its component chemical elements. The balance varies in different cells and different body parts. Nutrition, supplied by the blood stream, must maintain that working mineral balance if the body is to be in good health.

Rebuilding in the body, as everywhere else, depends for its

success upon the quantity, variety and quality of materials supplied. A contractor needs stone, cement, lumber, glass and hardware in house construction. The body needs, among other things, more than twenty minerals beside certain combinations of proteins, fats, carbohydrates and vitamins. The absence of a single ingredient such as calcium, cobalt or vitamin A may throw the organs of the entire body into painful disorder. Quantity and quality alone are not enough; the food ingredients must be in proper balance.

Each food contains a differing grouping of nutritional essentials. Only by combining the proper foods in a proper diet can the health-balance be maintained. A food market displays dozens or even hundreds of different foods. An uninformed shopper, influenced either by whim, the colorful label, the radio or magazine ads or the bargain price, may upset the health of an entire household by buying the wrong foods.

We noted, in the previous chapter, that most of the food consumed by human beings comes directly or indirectly from the upper few inches of top soil. A whole soil is one that contains the ingredients necessary to produce sturdy healthy vegetation of the required variety and species. Different plants have different nutritional needs and offer various combinations of minerals, vitamins and enzymes to the animals and humans who consume them. Soil wholeness may be upset by erosion, by cropping, by improper fertilizers. Until the soil balance is restored, the products of an unbalanced soil will be unbalanced vegetation. If such vegetation is consumed, it may transfer its unbalance to the user, causing a person who eats "good food" by ordinary standards, to be far from well.

Good food should be grown on whole soil, be eaten whole,

unprocessed, and garden fresh.[2] Even the best products of the
best soils lose more or less of their nutritive value if they are
processed. Any modification at all is likely to reduce the nutritive
value of a whole food. Peeling potatoes, scraping carrots, milling
wheat, cooking green peas, removes essential parts of the food,
causes chemical changes, or drives off vitamins. Allowing foods
to become stale or wilted has similar effects.

Whole foods are health-giving. They have another important
virtue,—they are flavorsome. A whole raw apple or cherry, raw
peas or corn, a whole raw carrot, beet, radish or turnip, a raw
asparagus shoot, a leaf of lettuce, cress, spinach, endive, chicory,
a ripe raspberry or tomato is more delectable to the unperverted
taste than any product of the most elaborate food processing. We
might remind our readers in passing that compost-grown fruits
and vegetables taste better than the same products grown with
commercial fertilizers or fresh animal manures. The latter have
a sharp, strong, almost bitter taste in comparison with the bland,
nutty flavor of the former.

A bean, pea, corn kernel or other seed, is a whole food. Each
contains a life germ, a complete source of nutriment. All seeds,
including grains, contain protein, oil, vitamins and the other
potent life-giving sources designed by nature to nourish the germ
until the new plant gets down roots and sends up shoots which
will enable it to secure nourishment on its own behalf. Each
type of seed is provided with a covering or skin, containing certain protective materials that will safeguard the germ until it gets

[2] "There is something in the freshness of food, especially vegetable food—
some form of energy perhaps; it may be certain rays of light or electrical
property—which gives to it a health-promoting influence. Certain it is that
no synthetic diet that I have been able to devise has equalled in health-
sustaining qualities one composed of the fresh foodstuffs as nature provides
them." Sir Robert McCarrison, *Nutrition and National Health*, Lon.: Faber
& Faber 1944 p. 11

a start on the life cycle. Each has a mineral balance adapted to the peculiar needs of the plant into which it will develop. Sunflower seeds, for example, contain a calcium-fluorine ratio well-adapted to preserve and maintain the calcium-fluorine content of the human body. The people of East Europe, who are noted for their good teeth, consume an enormous amount of sunflower and squash seeds, cracking the shells with their teeth, and thus presumably getting some of the minerals contained in the shells as well as in the kernels. Whole, entire, raw seeds, with the protein of the germ, the fat in the oil, the starch in the kernel and the minerals distributed through the protective covering, will provide a fairly rounded diet on which animal life can be sustained for a long time.

There was a period in the history of human nutrition during which men took food where they found it and consumed it on the spot, as birds eat seeds, or insects and rabbits and deer eat grasses and green-shoots and then move on. Under such conditions the animal living on vegetation secured whole food.

Western man seldom gets his food in its natural state. Such food gathering is almost non-existent in a modern commercial or industrial city where human beings seldom or never see their food in its natural habitat, but get it, by way of the market, in various stages of preparation, processing and aging. The classic story of the children from the City and Country School illustrates this point. In order to contact the realities of life, this progressive school in downtown New York sent a group of children on a nature study tour of the wholesale vegetable market around Washington Market. When the students had sufficiently admired the piles of bright beets, carrots, celery, cabbages, lettuce and tomatoes displayed on the sidewalks and moving in and out on trucks, the teacher asked, "And where do you think all these lovely fruits and vegetables come from?" The answer came back, "From the A & P of course."

City dwellers suffer from a double liability: the foods which they eat are seldom garden fresh; in addition, most of them are processed. Go through any modern super-market; the majority of goods on the shelves are in cans or packages. Food processing, canning and distribution has become one of the largest industries in the United States. Modern markets are selling everything from baby food to dog and cat food in cans,—pre-cooked, mixed, prepared. Even people who have open land at their disposal find it easier to pick up these products in cans and packages than it is to raise them in a home garden. One lazy gesture with an automatic can opener; spoon the stuff into a pan; heat it, and the meal is ready. Thus an entire generation of humans is being raised, from infancy to maturity, chiefly on processed, prepared, canned and packaged factory foods. Most of such foods have been cooked, peeled, shelled, ground, sliced, minced, tenderized, pasteurized, or in some other manner deprived of their wholeness before they went into the cans or packages. The consumer does not have the entire food put before him, but only such portions as the food processers decide to include in the finished product.

The main factor in commerce which determines what parts of the food under consideration shall be eliminated and what portions shall be retained is profitableness. In order to make a profit, foods must have eye and taste appeal; otherwise there will be no mass sales. At the same time the product in question must have keeping qualities to reach the mass market and stay there in prime condition for an indefinite period. Not merely hours or days, but weeks and often months must elapse between the preparation of food and its consumption. Exceedingly high or low temperatures are necessary to preserve foods while they travel the tortuous road from producer to consumer. Any portion of the food which is specially perishable or might detract from its marketability is removed, even though it may be important from the health point of view. Marketability is the criterion, not the health of the consumer.

The milling of grain is a case in point. For a long time, humans stored their grains whole, as they came from the threshing floor. The grain, if dry, kept indefinitely, and because of the hard shell which covered each kernel, lost little of its nutritive value. Wholemeal flour, however, will not keep. Oxidation alters its chemical character. The oil in the kernel becomes rancid or evaporates. In a comparatively short time wholegrain flour becomes sour and mouldy. Therefore, under ideal conditions, when bread is to be baked, the whole grain should be ground. Dr. D. T. Quigley, in his book *The National Malnutrition,* says "The law in regard to milling and baking should provide that none but whole-grain flour be used and the whole-grain flour used in any bakery should be ground by suitable millers in that same bakery on the morning of the same day in which the baking takes place . . . For home use the fresh flour could be delivered daily as milk is distributed."[3]

When big business corporations moved into the milling industry they took steps to ensure the profitableness of their investments. Their first step was to find ways to cut costs,—in the apt words of the *Senate Report on Utilization of Farm Crops,* "to make a cheaper product resemble a better one".[4]

Two, they undertook to "refine" the flour, "to impart properties of softness and sales appeal",[5] to reduce it to smaller particles so that it could be swallowed with less chewing and would make

[3] Milwaukee, Wis.: Lee Foundation for Nutritional Research 1948 p. 90
[4] *Report 604 of the Committee on Agriculture and Forestry,* Wash. D.C., U.S. Gov. Printing Office 1951 p. 7
[5] *Ibid.,* p. 7

lighter breads and pastries. The germ and outer covering from the grain kernels were removed; with them went the oil, the protein and the minerals.

Three, they whitened flour, on the assumption that what is whiter is cleaner and otherwise superior. This had the added advantage of removing every vestige of livingness from the flour, which became inert and could no longer spoil. Flour was bleached by using one of the caustic chemicals such as chlorine, which sterilizes and reduces to a dead white color.

Four, modern milling involved processing in high speed metal machines which heated the flour and deprived it of any possible remaining nutritional elements.

Five, flours are now "enriched" by putting back substitutes, "synthetic chemicals",[6] for the essential ingredients removed in the course of processing. To quote again from the government report, "Many of the flours and breads contain phosphorus, flourine, silicon, alum, nicotinic acid, potassium bromate, and a score of other poisonous drugs . . . Bakery products, like so many of the processed foods, apparently offer those who would resort to chemicals and substitutes, a great opportunity for profit at the expense not only of the consumer financially but of the actual health of the consumer."[7]

Milling may sound like a horrible example of food processing. It is only one among many. We refer to it in some detail because the colorless, flavorless and lifeless white flour of the present day in the form of bread, crackers, noodles, cakes and pastries forms so large a part of the diet of western man. "Devitaminized wheat flour products imported into the city of New York constitute around 55 per cent of the whole food intake."[8]

[6] *Ibid.,* p. 7
[7] *Ibid.,* p. 11
[8] D. T. Quigley, *The National Malnutrition,* Milwaukee, Wis.: Lee Foundation for Nutritional Research 1948 p. 38

Among the vested interests who have come to the fore in the modern world there are those who deliberately devitalize, drug and poison the population for profit. Perhaps it may seem absurd, in this day and age, to write about deliberate poisoning. Most people associate the poisoning of food with family feuds in the Middle Ages, with primitive warfare or with an occasional bit of spite-work perpetrated in a fit of anger or jealousy. Research shows that the words are more applicable today than they were in the days of the Borgias.

Poison, says the dictionary, is "any substance which by reason of an inherent deleterious property tends to destroy life or impair health when taken into the system". Any food product which tends to destroy life or to impair health therefore may be listed as a poison. With this definition in mind let us refer briefly to bodies of fact concerning foods produced and sold in the United States.

1. Certain processed foods such as bleached white flour, white sugar and polished rice undermine health. White flour products lower intestinal health and harm lower nerve centers. White sugars impair teeth. Polished rice produces beri-beri and other deficiency disease. Pies, cakes, pastries, cookies, crackers, other products of white flour and of white sugar and white rice must be classed as poisons under the dictionary definition. Baking sodas, baking powders and common salt would come under the definition; so would irritating spices and sauces.

2. Food processors and packers in the United States are using several hundred chemicals to color, flavor and preserve foods. A study of the labels on the various food packages available in food markets will give a good idea of the prevalence of this practice. We walked recently through a supermarket and found a dozen products such as bread, pastries, oleomargarine, canned goods,

breakfast foods, puddings, cheeses, candies and carbonated beverages marked with the following chemical ingredients "to prevent spoilage": sodium diacetate, mycoban, benzoate of soda, di-sodium phosphate and citrates, cyclamate calcium, calcium chloride, polyoxyethylene and glyceryl monostearate, calcium propionate, acid phosphate, calcium sulphate, cyclamate calcium, niacinamide, sodium benzoate, pyrophosphate, carboxymethyl, sulphur dioxide, sorbitol, propylene glycol. Do we know what these formidable names are or will do to the product and to us? No. Do you? Probably not. Do the processors? Also probably not. They may be comparatively harmless or they may be extremely poisonous. "The inadequacy of existing laws to furnish safeguards is exemplified by the testimony of representatives of the United States Food and Drug Administration that, of 704 chemicals employed in food use today, only 428 are definitely known to be safe . . . The Federal Food, Drug and Cosmetic Act is not effective to prevent unsafe chemical additions to food before its sale to consumers. For it only applies to food after its introduction into interstate commerce; it may only reach the injury to a consumer thus sought to be avoided, after it has occurred; and it does not require an indicated advance scientific determination whether a chemical addition to food is safe, which alone can prevent that injury."[9] Apparently, in the case of at least 200 chemicals, no adequate study has been made of their effect on the human system. If they improve the looks of foods, increase flavor or postpone spoilage, they are used to the profit of the chemical manufacturer, the processor and the retailer. The eventual result on health and well-being is left as a concern of the customer. Well may the government report say "The increasing use of chemical

[9] House of Rep. *Report 2356, Investigation of the Use of Chemicals in Foods and Cosmetics,* Wash., D. C.: U.S. Gov. Printing Office 1952 p. 20

additives in the production, processing, preservation, and packaging of food has created a serious public-health problem".[10]

3. Foods are being poisoned in yet another way. Most fruits and many leafy vegetables such as lettuce, celery and members of the cabbage family are sprayed and dusted with arsenic, mercury, copper, sulphur and other materials intended to check fungus and insect pests. Even when taken in small quantities these materials poison the human system; in large quantities or over long periods they will cause sickness or death. Those of us who are increasingly aware of this danger cannot hope to wash away the poison with anything short of muriatic acid. These poisons are produced precisely for their lasting qualities. Read the advertisements of "the amazing residual effect of DDT"; "It Gets 'Em and Kills 'Em". "The new insecticides and fungicides are highly toxic, and they persist: that is why they are good."[11]

A government statement again warns us: "The public often feels that because something can be bought over the counter it must be safe".[12] "The housewife frequently fails to realize that insecticide such as DDT, chlordane, selenium, and many others in combinations, which can be bought over the counter, are deadly poison and must be used with extreme caution."[13] "Selenium is an elemental metal which in the form of selenium compounds is used as an insecticide . . . Animal experimentation has shown that three parts per million in the diet, as selenium, will produce cirrhosis of the liver and that, if feeding is continued, the animals may develop cancer of the liver. The residue remaining on fruits or vegetables sprayed with selenium compounds is rather high. For example, on an unwashed apple it

[10] *Ibid.*, p. 25
[11] Eric Hodgins, *Fortune*, Nov. 1953
[12] *Report 2356*, p. 32
[13] *Ibid.*, p. 31

may be as much as one part per million, and since it can penetrate the skin of the apple, it may accumulate in the apple in amounts up to three parts per million."[14]

"Phenyl mercury compounds are used quite extensively on fruit and vegetable crops as fungicides. Investigation of these compounds shows that they accumulate in the kidney and are very poisonous."[15] "Toxicity tests showed that a level of five parts per million (of DDT) in the diet of rats produced slight but definite liver injury. Later it was shown that cows sprayed with DDT, or fed silage sprayed with it, or even housed in a barn in which it was sprayed, would accumulate DDT in the fat and eventually secrete it in the milk. In a carefully controlled experiment, a dairy barn was sprayed in the same manner as would ordinarily be done by a dairy farmer. Nothing was sprayed on the cattle. Within 24 hours DDT showed up in the milk of the cows, reaching a maximum of two parts per million in about 48 hours."[16] "Chlordane is another of the chlorinated hydrocarbon insecticides which has been recommended and used in the household and on a large variety of fruit and vegetable crops . . . The Director of the Division of Pharmacology of the Food and Drug Administration testified that chlordane is four to five times more poisonous than DDT and that he would hesitate to eat food that had any chlordane residue on it whatsoever."[17]

An article in *The Scientific American* for August, 1953, mentions Hydrazine, which has a "toxic drug action". "Maleic Hydrazide is rapidly being adapted as a spray to stop the sprouting of onions and potatoes in storage; to retard the blossoming of fruit

---

[14] *Report 3254, Investigation of the Use of Chemicals in Food Production*, Wash., D. C.: U.S. Gov. Printing Office 1951 p. 4

[15] *Ibid.*

[16] *Ibid.*, pp. 3-4

[17] *Ibid.*, p. 4

trees until threat of frost is past." So now two of the most widely used winter vegetables may be contaminated with yet another poisonous drug.

4. Beside processed, chemicalized and poisoned foods, the food industry, through nationwide advertising campaigns, is selling a wide variety of consumable articles containing such habit-forming drugs as caffein, cola nut extract, nicotine and alcohol. All of these drugs are more or less deleterious or poisonous to the human system and bode ill for the health and well-being of future generations. In the United States alone more than ten billion dollars a year is being spent by the consuming public for products containing nicotine and alcohol.

Poisoned, processed and chemicalized foods result in malnutrition, since deficient foods, even when consumed in large quantities, upset the nutritional balance. Faulty nourishment has immediate effects, on body health, emotional stability and mental efficiency. Such effects extend all the way from a feeling of heaviness and drowsiness, through headaches, constipation and stomach aches to more acute conditions resulting from taking poisons into the system. This is one side of the picture and a serious side in view of the millions of American women and men who are constantly drugging and doping themselves instead of discovering the cause of the disorders.

Long-term effects of faulty nourishment which are far more important appear in the figures concerning sickness and death. A recent report of the Surgeon General estimated that 28 million United States adults are more or less handicapped by disease and its accompaniments. Of these diseased persons, a quarter were suffering from arthritis. The Public Health Service reports that in 1949 half of the deaths in the United States were due to heart disease and a seventh to cancer. Out of a total of 1,443,607 deaths, 720,497 were from diseases of the cardio-vascular system, 206,325 from malignant neoplasms, 49,774 from diseases of the circulatory system, 25,089 from diabetes. Contagious and infectious diseases were minor factors: influenza and pneumonia accounted for 44,640 deaths; tuberculosis for 39,100; poliomychitiz for 2,720; dysentery for 1,440 and typhoid for 161 deaths. In a word, people in the United States are suffering from breakdown of the vital tissues and organs. There is every reason to suppose that this breakdown is related to inadequacies in the food intake.

There is much debate concerning the connection between food processing and poisoning and the increase in the use of habit-forming drugs on one hand, and the extension of degenerative diseases over wider age groups on the other. It is only a few years since cancer was looked upon as a disease of old people. Today it is making inroads among infants.

Other evidence supports the assumption that faulty nutrition is causing physical breakdown. Pre-civilized peoples who have never used western processed, poisoned foods are free from the degenerative diseases which afflict western man. Wrench's study of "the healthiest people on earth", the Hunzas of the Kulu Valley, Kashmir, India, in his previously mentioned *Wheel of Health*, J. I. Rodale's *The Healthy Hunzas*[18] and W. A. Price's *Nutrition and Physical Degeneration*[19] show that when such peoples are fed western foods, they developed our diseases. Dr. D. T. Quigley, in *The National Malnutrition*, writes of the Indians of northwestern Canada who enjoyed good health and long life until they traded for the white man's food. They "took to this with as great enthusiasm as they did to alcohol; resulting in

[18] Emmaus, Pa.: Rodale Press 1948
[19] Los Angeles: American Academy of Applied Nutrition 1945

many cases of arthritis, tuberculosis, and tooth decay, with a shortened life period, and with lessened ability to work. The Indians in the back country who did not have access to the white man's food kept their good health; had no tuberculosis or any of the other diseases mentioned."[20]

Food processing, poisoning and drugging is undermining the health of the American people as well as yielding large profits to the individuals and corporations engaged in processing, poisoning and drugging. City dwellers, no matter how large their incomes and how much they can afford to pay for quantity and quality of foods, can escape the resulting dangers only by taking extreme precautions in regard to what and how they eat. Even country folk will fall a prey to this health menace unless they are able to raise their own food organically and reduce processing and poisoning to a minimum, or else find a means of securing fresh, whole foods, free from chemical poisons.

The reader may feel that we have taken liberties with his time and patience by this relatively long discussion of present-day nutrition in the United States and elsewhere in the West. We believe, as we have stated earlier in this chapter, that nutrition is one of the primary factors in determining the health, happiness and usefulness of every human being. We are equally convinced that the immense sums spent by the food processors, drug manufacturers and pharmaceutical houses for advertising, propaganda, lobbying and other types of "public relations" are having a deleterious effect on the well being of the American and other Western peoples. One of the chief factors that took us out of the city into the country was an awareness of the menace to health arising out of food processing and poisoning and a determination to safeguard ourselves against it.

[20] Milwaukee, Wis.: Lee Foundation for Nutritional Research 1948 p. 3

We admit that our solution of the problem,—raising our own food,—is a personal one since it leaves millions of people in the United States more or less helpless victims of the food industry. We should like to make two points in answer to this contention. The first is that each time even one individual or family wakes up to the situation and takes steps to ameliorate it, an advance is made if only a tiny one for the family or person in question, and for those they influence through precept or example. The second point is even more important. While it is true, at the moment, that all too few individuals and families in the United States are doing anything practical to meet the menace of processed, poisoned foods, we hold that at least half of them, if they so decided, could (1) produce part of their own food scientifically and organically on land that they own or could rent; (2) by creating an organized demand for whole organic food, greatly extend its production and availability; (3) purchase whole foods and prepare them at home instead of buying processed, packaged, chemicalized foods on the market.[21] In a word, our answer to faulty nutrition is not merely a personal one. In the coming growing

[21] J. I. Rodale in "*Prevention*", a magazine devoted to the conservation of human health, has a further suggestion for those who are aware of the dangers lurking in the supermarkets: "If because of family pressure or some circumstance you cannot control, you must buy foods that have perhaps been treated with chemicals, dyes, preservatives or flavoring matter, write to the manufacturer or processor asking him whether such and such a product contains these substances. Tell him courteously but firmly that you do not wish to eat products that contain added chemicals, remind him that the Delaney bills are even now on the Congressional docket for discussion, and suggest that he be one progressive food processor who undertakes to remove chemicals from his products *before* the legislation is passed. Tell him quite simply that you would prefer bread that will mold, rather than bread to which a preservative has been added to keep it from molding. Tell him you prefer oranges with their natural color rather than oranges which have been dyed. Tell him that, regardless of flavor or color, you prefer to eat foods to which no artificial flavoring or coloring has been added." April, 1954, p. 119

season, if they were so minded, millions of United States families could begin to provide themselves with a considerable supply of whole, fresh, unpoisoned food and thus establish and preserve better health.

The food we produced organically during the regular May to October growing season kept us in good health. Then came the next question, how to make this fresh, delicious, health-giving food available throughout the year. Vermont winters froze our ground from November to April. If we wanted to eat our own organically grown products during that period we had to find a way to keep them. Our pattern for the simple life did not include icebox, refrigerator or freezing unit. We aimed to work out alternatives which would provide us with the foods we wanted, at the time we wanted them, and still leave us comparatively free of the power interests and merchandizers of large-scale gadgets. To winter our vegetables we tried vegetable pits or caches, dug in the ground and covered with branches, leaves and straw, with a breather-vent for circulation. In winters of steady cold, they worked well. In a winter of alternative freezing and thawing they were less successful. The vegetables tended to rot.

We finally decided upon root-cellar storage. In the course of our building, we made three cellars. The first one was under the kitchen of the main house. We dug it as we built the house, and designed it to hold maple syrup, preserves, juices and the fruits and vegetables in current use. It was never cold enough for permanent storage because it was separated from the kitchen by nothing more than a double wooden floor.

Our permanent vegetable storage unit was the cellar under the workshop, which later became the guesthouse. Fires were lighted in the room above this cellar only occasionally. The temperature there went to 20° Fahrenheit or lower during the frostiest nights of winter. The cellar had a spring which flowed from under a ledge. This running water helped to keep the temperature equable and the air moist. The floor we made of coarse gravel, allowing free flow of water and yet complete drainage. We equipped this cellar with shelves and storage bins, a foot deep and about three feet wide. Into these storage bins we dumped quantities of maple leaves, gathered when they first fell in the autumn before they became dry and dirty. Root vegetables and fruit were packed away in these leaves—first a generous layer of leaves, then a layer of vegetables, then more leaves and more vegetables until the bins were filled. On the top layer we put several inches of leaves.

The plan worked well. Whenever we wanted potatoes, carrots, beets, turnips, celery root or apples, we brushed away the top leaves and picked out the firm, crisp garden products. The leaves held off frost and at the same time kept the air from evaporating the juices from the vegetables and fruit. Almost every year we ate carrots, beets, onions, turnips, rutabagas, potatoes and apples from this cellar up to the July following the autumn in which they were stored. Many of these garden products lasted over into August.

Noah Webster, in *The Massachusetts Agricultural Repository* says, "I have fresh fruit, of my own raising, the whole year." For those who cannot get quantities of autumn leaves, he then gives his method of preserving for spring use. He recommends using layer upon layer of dry sand. "The singular advantages of this mode of treatment are these—1. The sand keeps the apples from the air. 2. The sand checks the evaporation or perspiration of the apples, thus preserving in them their full flavor—at the same time any moisture yielded by the apples (and some there will be) is absorbed by the sand—so that the apples are kept dry and all mustiness is prevented. My pippins in May and June, are as fresh as when first picked. Even the ends of the stems look as if just separated from the twigs. 3. The sand is equally a preservative from frost, rots, etc."[22]

Having found that our root cellar was too damp for cabbage, we built another type of storage cellar on higher land and with an earth floor, under the toolshed and back of the greenhouse. We strung a scaffolding of boards around the inside of this concrete cellar, drove in nails at intervals of a foot, pulled our cabbage up by the roots and hung them with strings, upside down, around the cellar walls,—no two cabbages touching. With that arrangement we managed to keep cabbage until the following May.

We also used this cellar for storing celery, celery root and parsley root,—pulling them on a wet September or October day before heavy frost, when plenty of earth would cling to the roots, placing four or five heads in an old sap bucket with a leaky bottom (for air circulation) and packed the buckets side by side on the earth floor of the cellar. Under fair conditions the celery would last for two months. If we took it from the garden just before the first heavy frost we had our own celery on the table at Christmas and New Year's. Curly endive, escarolle and chinese cabbage, similarly treated, kept fresh and good up to eight weeks. Witloof chicory roots we put in old sap buckets, covered them with earth and had chicory greens growing through the winter. With a little care, chives and parsley plants were kept growing until spring. Winter squash also kept in this cellar, though a dry, not too cool—not too warm attic is superior for the purpose.

By these various methods of storage we provided a year-round supply of fresh food. To be sure, during the depths of the Vermont winter it was not garden fresh, but, supplemented by greens

[22] 1804, p. 46

from our sunheated greenhouse, it gave us a satisfying and dependable supply of whole unprocessed foods. In most parts of the United States, weather conditions are less severe than they are in the Green Mountains, consequently such procedures could be made even more effective.

The reader, unaccustomed to such practices, may ask whether we did not tire of cabbage, potatoes, parsnips and the like "all winter long". We answer, no. We divided our garden produce into summer crops which we ate at once: peas, corn, lettuce and the like; summer crops which might be carried over winter by drying (peas and beans) or by canning (berries and tomatoes); and autumn crops such as cabbage, potatoes, turnips, squash. These autumn crops we almost never ate in summer. Take the case of cabbage. We never even planted summer or early cabbage. Our cabbage seed went in around the end of May or the beginning of June, in some row from which radishes or mustard greens had already been pulled. It was ripe for picking in late October or early November, when it was harvested and stored. We continued to eat cos lettuce, celery, collards, kale, brussels sprouts and broccoli, mustard greens, cress, escarolle and chinese cabbage (all of which are frost resistant) until heavy snows came in late November or early December. This gave us garden fresh greens almost to the end of the calendar year. Only then did we turn to cabbage, turnips, winter squash, potatoes and onions. Like everything else from the garden, we used them for an appropriate season, and it was so comparatively short that we never tired of our winter greens from the storage cellar.[23]

[23] "There is nothing which doth more agreeably concern the Senses, than in the depth of Winter to behold the Fruits so fair, and so good, yea better, than when you first did gather them . . . You will taste your fruit with infinite more gust and contentment, than in the Summer itself, when their great abundance, and variety, rather cloy you than become agreeable. For this

Another source of winter greens should be mentioned in passing, and a very important one, sprouted seeds. Asians have used sprouted mung beans successfully. Poultry growers sprout oats for their flocks. We sprouted mung beans, soy beans, peas and wheat successfully. The sprouts may be eaten in salads, thrown raw into soups, Chinese fashion, or prepared in any other desired way for the table.

We dried aromatic herbs from our garden,—basil, sage, thyme, summer savory, marjoram, parsley and celery leaves, all of which go well with winter salads and soups. Chamomile, peppermint, spearmint, raspberry and strawberry leaves we dried for tea. We hung the sprays in small bundles over our kitchen stove and when dead dry, crumbled the leaves and stored away in jars.

These methods of storage took care of the solider vegetables and fruits. What of the perishable foods? Was canning, that midsummer bogey of the housewife, completely done away with? Actually we did some canning, but a very little: fruit juices (raspberry, blackberry, strawberry, blueberry and grape), tomato juice, soup stock, and applesauce from our poorer apples (the "non-keepers"), to tide us over a possible "no apple" period in the late spring and early summer.

The fruit juice was put up so simply that it might be worthwhile describing the exceedingly easy and speedy process. The glass jars were sterilized on the stove. A kettle or two of boiling water was at hand. We poured an inch of boiling water into a jar on which the rubber had already been put, stirred in a cup of sugar until it had dissolved (we used brown or maple sugar, or hot maple syrup), poured in a cup and a half of fruit, filled the

reason therefore it is, that we essay to teach you the most expedite, and certain means how to conserve them all the Winter, even so long, as till the New shall incite you to quit the Old." John Evelyn, *The French Gardiner*, Lon.: Tooke 1675 pp. 263-4

jar to brimming with boiling water, screwed on the cap and that
was all. No boiling and no processing. The raspberries, for example, retained their rich red color. When the jars were opened
their flavor and fragrance were like the raw fruit in season. The
grapejuice made thus was as delicious and tasty as that produced
by the time-honored, laborious method of cooking, hanging in a
jelly bag, draining, and boiling the juice before bottling. Our
only losses in keeping these juices came from imperfect jars, caps
or rubber. We found that two people could put up 15 quart jars
in twenty minutes.

We made applesauce by an equally simple method,—the "open
kettle" way. We had syrup boiling in several kettles on the stove
(half maple syrup and half water). Into about an inch of rapidly
boiling syrup we dropped sixths or eighths of washed, cored, un-
peeled apples. We covered and cooked till a fork could pierce the
pieces and they looked slightly glazed (the less cooking the better
the flavor), packed solidly in sterilized jars, sealed and put away.

Our tomato juice and soup stock were made almost as easily.
We filled two-thirds of a large 16 quart kettle with quarters of
washed tomatoes. Then we cut and stirred in about a dozen fair-
sized onions, a half-dozen bunches of celery (the green leaves as
well as the stalks), a large bouquet of parsley, a handful of herbs
(marjoram, basil, savory, sage or thyme) and a few peppers—all
cut fine. No water was added. The mass was covered and cooked
slowly till the celery was tender. Then the whole mass was worked
through a coarse sieve. The juice we reheated to boiling, added
a bit of sugar (maple), a touch of sea or vegetable salt, and the
liquid was ready to bottle, with no further processing.

We made a soup stock with the remaining pulp in the sieve
or collander. This was divided amongst several small kettles on
the stove, with only sufficient water added to prevent scorching.

With constant stirring we brought the mass to a rolling boil, packed it into glass jars, and worked the contents down with a silver knife to eliminate air bubbles. To each half-full jar we added a tablespoon of salt, filled the sterilized jar brimfull, sealed it and put it away. This soup stock gave a zest and flavor to all our winter soups, and was more tasty than soups made daily during the winter from foods stored in the cellar. This was probably because the vegetables were picked and preserved at the top of their form and season.

"But to return again to Health and Long Life, and the Wholesomness of the Herby Diet"[24] . . . The foods we chose to live on were those that had the simplest, closest and most natural relationship to the soil. Jared Eliot called them "the clean productions of the Earth." All foods, animal as well as vegetable, come from the land, but raw fruits, nuts and vegetables are the simplest, come most directly and in the closest connection. They appeal to the taste with no adulterants, with no added flavoring or condiments, come crammed with vitamins and minerals and involve the least care and no cooking. We might call them primary foods.

Dairy products are foods at second or third-hand, reaching humans through the bodies of animals which feed on the produce of the soil. Milk is the secretion of the mammary glands of cows, goats or sheep. Cheese is a coagulation of the curd of this liquid. Eggs are the reproductive media of birds. Milk is a highly concentrated infant food, especially designed to stimulate rapid growth in the early stages of development. Human milk should normally be for baby humans, cow's milk for calves, etc. A calf doubles its weight in a month, a human baby in six months. Food intended by nature for one is not necessarily a desirable

[24] John Evelyn, *Acetaria*, Lon.: Tooke 1699 p. 127

food for the other. Adults of any breed should have been weaned and past the milk stage of feeding.

Humans eat another type of food which is the furthest removed from the soil,—the cooked carcasses of beasts, birds and fish. These animals have lived on vegetation or preyed on creatures which lived on vegetation. The human practice of eating the dead bodies of fellow creatures has gone on for so long a time that it is regarded generally as normal. In a recent study, *The Recovery of Culture*,[25] Henry Bailey Stevens attempts to show that this "blood culture", with which he also associates war, dates back in human history for only a very brief period. Before the blood culture, which began with the domestication of animals, there was a tree culture based on a diet of fruit, nuts, seeds, shoots and roots.[26] If this approach is factually correct, carnivorism is a recent phase in the history of the human diet.

Carnivorism involves (1) holding animals in bondage, (2) turning them into machines for breeding and milking, (3) slaughtering them for food, (4) preserving and processing their dead bodies for human consumption.

We were looking for a kindly, decent, clean and simple way of life. Long ago we decided to live in the vegetarian way, without killing or eating animals; and lately we have largely ceased to use dairy products and have allied ourselves with the vegans, who use and eat no animal products, butter, cheese, eggs or milk. This is all in line with our philosophy of the least harm to the least number and the greatest good to the greatest number of life forms.[27]

[25] N.Y.: Harpers 1949
[26] "Primitive humanity was, no doubt, like the anthropoids, mainly frugivorous." R. Briffault, *The Mothers*, Lon.: Allen & Unwin 1927 Vol. I p. 441
[27] "The use of Plants is all our Life long of that universal Importance and Concern, that we can neither live nor subsist in any Plenty with Decency, or

We aimed to keep our diet at fifty percent fruit, thirty-five percent vegetables, ten percent protein and starch, and five percent fat. The kind of fruits varied with the season. Its proportion of the total diet remained substantially the same. Of the vegetables we tried to have one-third green and leafy, one-third yellow and one-third juicy. This ensured us a rounded quota of essential nutritives. In the summer, fruits and succulent vegetables were at least three-quarters of our dietary,—in winter perhaps a third to a half. Our protein came from nuts, beans, olives and the proteins contained in vegetables and in cereal grains and seeds. We believe that a far smaller amount of protein is necessary and healthful than usually advocated. The craving for concentrated protein foods is an acquired and a dangerous habit, in that it over-energizes the human organism and overloads the system with acid-forming elements. Our fats were derived from vegetable oils,—olive, soy, corn, peanut or sunflower. We have a high opinion of the efficacy of olive oil. Avocado pears are also an important source of vegetable fat for people living on the vegetarian diet.

Our search for simplicity led us away from elaborate variety and in the direction of a mono-diet.[28] To eat little and of few

---

Conveniency or be said to live indeed at all without them: whatsoever Food is necessary to sustain us, whatsoever contributes to delight and refresh us, are supply'd and brought forth out of that plentiful and abundant store: and ah, how much more innocent, sweet and healthful is a Table cover'd with these, than with all the reeking Flesh of butcher'd and slaughter'd Animals! Certainly Man by Nature was never made to be a Carnivorous Creature; nor is he arm'd at all for Prey and Rapin, with gag'd and pointed Teeth and crooked Claws, sharpened to rend and tear: But with gentle Hands to gather Fruit and Vegetables, and with Teeth to chew and eat them." John Ray, *Historia Plantarum*, Lon.: Faithorne 1686 p. 46

[28] "It neither entices men to eat till they be unable for their affairs, nor brings it sickness; it affords strength, and prolongs life." Sir George Mackenzie, *A Moral Essay, preferring Solitude to Publick Employment*, Lon.: Sawbridge 1685 p. 123

things is a good guide for health and for simplicity. There are primitive peoples, for instance the island inhabitants of Tristan de Cunha, whose health and teeth are reportedly superb, who "never eat more than one kind of food at a time".[29] There are individuals in the West who do not mix vegetables with fruits, nor proteins and starches and acids, on the assumption that this facilitates digestion. These points need not be argued here. As a matter of fact, we are still experimenting on them ourselves. We do assert, however, that the closer one gets to a mono diet, the easier is the process not only of digestion, but of food preparation. Whole foods, raw foods and few of a kind make little work for the housewife.

Apply to vegetables and fruit the principles of wholeness, rawness, garden freshness, and one or few things at a meal, and you have the theory of our simple diet. In practice, the theory gave us a formulated regime: fruit for breakfast; soup and cereal for lunch; salad and vegetables for supper.

This fruit breakfast did not include the usual small glass of orange juice, a spoonful or two of berries or prunes or a dab of applesauce in a bowl with cornflakes or puffed wheat followed by toast and coffee. Our breakfast was fruit; fruit alone and plenty of it. It might be strawberry, raspberry, blackberry or blueberry season; we picked the berries in the woods or garden and ate them, perhaps half a quart to a person. Melons and peaches were eaten when in season. Bananas, raisins, oranges and dates were bought in the periods our local fruit gave out. Apples were the perennial staple as we had plenty of them on the place and they kept well all winter. Apples are a fine food, highly alkaline and extremely rich in iron and other important minerals. We often had a one-day exclusive apple diet to revivify and cleanse

[29] London *Times* 2/22/32

the system. Oranges we did not juice, but cut in sixths, longways, and ate like watermelons, down to the peel. Gourmets amongst us dipped whole bananas in honey and then in wheat-germ. Quarter sections of apples were dipped the same way, or spread with peanut butter. Nuts were often cracked and eaten with the apples. Berries were served with maple syrup or honey, or eaten dry. Breakfast was rounded out by a handful of sun-flower seeds, herb tea sweetened with honey, or a tablespoon of blackstrap molasses in hot water.

Another fruit-derived breakfast item which deserves more than passing mention is rose-hip or rose-apple extract, which we often added to our molasses or our mint tea. Rose-hips are an important source of vitamin C, containing on the average thirty times as much as fresh orange juice. "Some species", says Adelle Davis, "have been found to contain 96 times the vitamin-C content of citrus juices."[30] Her cookbook gives methods (which we used) of drying and preserving the rose fruit. Our attention was first called to rose-hip juice when a neighbor, Lois Smith, prepared a supply one autumn and fed a tablespoon per day to Marshall and the youngsters. It cleared up their colds like magic.

People may feel that such a "light" breakfast would not stand by a working-man or woman till noon. That is largely a matter of habit. We have gone for months at a time with no breakfast at all and maintained health and suffered no discomfort though carrying on a full program of work. For ten years we have eaten fruit for our first meal of the day, and yet put in four solid hours at hard physical or mental work until lunch. We felt better, worked better and lived better on it than after a stuffy starch, protein-rich breakfast.

Lunch was ever the same and ever different: a soup and some

[30] *Let's Cook It Right*, N.Y.: Harcourt, Brace 1947 p. 488

sort of cereal. The soup was always vegetable but the ingredients
varied from day to day, one vegetable usually predominating:
potatoes, cabbage, carrots, tomatoes, onion, parsley, celery, beans,
peas, beets or corn. We added dried herbs and sea salt for seasoning. Occasionally barley, soy bean meal, oats or rice were included. At this mealtime we ate all the cereal for the day: wheat
seed, buckwheat or millet. These we bought in bulk (anywhere
up to a hundred pound bag from local feed stores) and stored in
tin ash cans. We soaked a few handfuls of seeds overnight, and
the next day either baked them in the oven with occasional bast-
ing of water, or cooked them slowly on top of the stove in a
double boiler. The grains swelled to double their original size and
were delicious and nutty eaten either hot or cold, with oil or
butter and vegetable salt, with home-made jam or syrup, or with
a peanut-butter-honey emulsion. Two bowls of soup and all the
whole grain one wanted was a man's meal and lasted well till
suppertime.

Raised bread we never baked and seldom bought.[31] We got
the same or better nourishment (and far cheaper) from the whole
seed grain unprocessed. Occasionally we made corn-cob shaped
"journey cakes" with coarsely-ground whole grains, corn meal,
rolled wheat and oats, sweetened with maple syrup or molasses
and moistened with soup stock and peanut butter or oil. After
making carrot juice, the remaining pulp sometimes formed the

---

[31] "Bread on the whole is not a very satisfactory food, because it is very
acid and on this account is apt to ferment and cause flatulence, especially
when eaten with fruit; so in those inclined to flatulence the amount of bread
in the day should be limited to small quantities. I have often seen flatulence
disappear after cutting down bread and fluids. Bread is not only acid because
of the acid salts of the wheat, but acid phosphate and calcium sulphate are
often added in baking powders. This leads to retention and so bread is bad
for rheumatism." K. G. Haig, *Health Through Diet*, Lon.: Methuen 1913
pp. 23-4

base for these tiny loaves, which were baked to a brown crustiness and eaten with our noon meal or taken on trips.

The main dish for supper was a really large salad, enough to provide at least one over-flowing bowl for each person. This salad was fruit or vegetable, depending on the garden resources. In a big wooden bowl we emulsified lemon or lime juice with rose-hip juice and olive oil, and into that cut peppers, celery, onion, radish, parsley, tomatoes, cucumbers, lettuce,—whatever was growing in the garden at the time. Sometimes we shredded raw beet, carrot, squash, celery root, turnip and made that a complete salad, with celery, nuts and raisins, lemon and oil. In winter, white or red cabbage was the bulk item instead of lettuce. To this we added cut up apples, nuts, oranges or grapefruit and celery. In summer we could add raw young peas, tips of asparagus, or fresh raw corn. We picked these salads just before making, and made them just before eating them. Thus the full vitamin content was retained. Supper could be planned and picked half an hour before meal-time, bespeaking "the infinite conveniences of what a well-stocked garden affords".[32] This "vernal pottage" was "ready at hand and easily dress'd; requiring neither Fire, Cost, or Attendance, to boil, roast, and prepare them as did Flesh and other provisions".[33] "The Huswife was never surpriz'd, had all at hand, and could in a Trice set forth an handsome Sallet."[34]

Some suppertimes we merely cleaned and washed the vegetables; then put them, whole, in bowls on the center of the table and let folk serve themselves. There were many possibilities: lettuce hearts; escarolle, endive, dandelion and spinach leaves; cauliflower buds, brussels sprouts, sprigs of broccoli and parsley;

[32] John Evelyn, *Acetaria*, Lon.; Tooke 1699, p. 795
[33] *Ibid.*, p. 3
[34] *Ibid.*, p. 185

whole carrots, radishes, tomatoes and cucumbers; celery and asparagus stalks; young sweet corn, green peas and peppers. In fact, anything that would go into a salad could also be served completely uncut. The people at the table helped themselves and combined whatever specially appealed.

In winter before washing and cutting up the salad materials at suppertime, we put on potatoes or squash to bake. Squash, as well as potatoes, we baked whole, in the skin. The steam generated inside the skin tenderized the vegetables in record time and helped retain all the natural food values. When corn, asparagus, peas or beans were ripe in the garden we added them to our evening meal, cooking as short a time as possible, in as little water as possible. Years ago we got rid of all our aluminum kitchen ware, as we believe aluminum is more soluble than most metals and leaves a deposit in the pan which affects food adversely and probably acts as a slow poison in the human system. What little cooking we did was done in stainless steel or enamel or pottery or glass vessels.

All of our meals were eaten at a wooden plank table, in wooden bowls, the same bowl right through the meal. This practically eliminated the dish-washing problem. With no sauces, no frying and the like, there were few dishes to wash and pans to scrub. Our salad we ate with chop sticks, as we found the "nimble boys" (Chinese "fai-tze") more selective and discriminating in picking up food than the shovel-like fork. We also felt that wooden eating utensils were more neutral and modified the flavor less than the metallic table tools.

These food habits of ours we found simple, economical and practicable, though they were perhaps not usual for 20th century Americans. With advancing civilization, the American diet pattern, like everything else, has undergone a thorough-going change. The business of procuring the necessities of life has been shifted from the wood lot, the garden, the kitchen and the family to the factory and the large-scale enterprise. In our case, we moved our center back to the land. There we raised the food we ate. We found it sufficient, delicious and nourishing. On this diet we maintained a rugged health and patronized no doctors. Our "apothecary shop was the woods and fields".[35] "By attention to Diet, many diseases may be prevented, and others mitigated. It is a just observation that he who lives by rule and wholesome diet, is a physician to himself."[36] With vegetables, fruits, nuts and cereals we proved that one could maintain a healthy body as an operating base for a sane mind and a purposeful harmless life.

[35] Samuel Thomson, *New Guide to Health*, Boston: Adams 1835 p. 9
[36] Anon., *Concise Directions on the Nature of our Common Food so far as it tends to Promote or Injure Health*, Lon.: Swords 1790, p. 7

"It is true that to obtain money by trade is sometimes more profitable, were it not so hazardous; and likewise lending money at interest, if it were an honorable occupation."

Marcus Porcius Cato, De Agri Cultura, 149 B.C.

"The countrey-man hath a provident and gainfull familie, not one whose necessities must be alwaies furnished out of the shop, nor their table out of the market. His provision is alwaies out of his own store, and agreeable with the season of the yeare."

Don Antonio de Guevara, The Praise and Happiness of the Countrie-Life, 1539

"There is no man alive that affects a country life more than myself; no man it may be, who has more experienc'd the delices of it; but even those, without action, were intollerable."

John Evelyn, Public Employment Prefer'd to Solitude, 1667

"He certainly is worthy great Praise and Honour, who, possessing a large and barren Demesne, constrains it, by his Industry and Labour, to produce extra ordinary Plenty, not only to his own Profit, but that of the Public also."

Sir Richard Weston, Legacy to his Sons, 1759

"In our present imperfect condition, a beneficent Providence has not reserved a moderate success in Agriculture exclusively to the exercise of a high degree of intelligence. His laws have been so kindly framed, that the hand even of uninstructed toil may receive some requital in remunerating harvests; while their utmost fulness can be anticipated only where corporeal efforts are directed by the highest intelligence."

R. L. Allen, The American Farmers Book, 1849

"Who ever knew a good farmer, of prudent habits, to fail?"

John L. Blake, Farmer's Every-Day Book, 1850

"If a man would enter upon country life in earnest and test thoroughly its aptitudes and royalties, he must not toy with it at a town distance; he must brush the dews away with his own feet. He must bring the front of his head to the business, and not the back of it."

D. G. Mitchell, My Farm of Edgewood, 1863

CHAPTER 6

ROUNDING OUT A LIVELIHOOD

Livelihood needs—Stability and security—The basis of our consumer economy—Liberation from city markets—The craftsman's competence—A no-money economy—Personal responsibility and foresight necessary for a livelihood

LIVELIHOOD is the central core around which most people build their lives. There are exceptions, of course. But the majority of human beings, notably in industrial communities, dedicate their best hours and their best years to getting an income and exchanging it for the necessaries and decencies of physical and social existence. Children, old people, the crippled, the sick, the voluntarily parasitic are at least partially freed from livelihood preoccupations. Able-bodied adults have little choice. They must meet the demands of livelihood or pay a heavy penalty in social disapproval, insecurity, anxiety and finally in physical hardship.

Livelihood needs, particularly for the necessities, are continuous, operating every day, of every month, of every year. An interruption in the supply of necessary goods and services, even for a short time, results in hardship and creates an atmosphere of uncertainty, insecurity, anxiety and fear. By what means are the stability and security of livelihood to be safeguarded?

Without going into a long discussion, we would suggest seven procedures which will maximize the stability and security of livelihood.

First, regulating the sources of livelihood in such a manner that all able-bodied adults will render a service in exchange for income, thus eliminating the social divisions which develop when a part of the community lives on unearned income while the remainder exchanges labor power for its livelihood.

Second, avoid gross and glaring inequalities in livelihood status.

Third, budget and plan the community economy.

Fourth, keep community books, and open the accounts to public inspection.

Fifth, pay as you go, either in labor or materials, thus avoiding inflation.

Sixth, practice economy, conserving resources, producing and consuming as little as necessary rather than as much as possible.

Seventh, provide a wide range of social services based upon specialization and cooperation.

All seven of these propositions deserve the careful attention of any one interested in rounding out a livelihood. Since livelihood is the subject matter of a previous book, *Economics for the Power Age,*[1] we have outlined its ingredients here only that we might have a background against which to discuss the methods which we followed in meeting the livelihood problem which faced us in Vermont.

It would have been quite possible to live in the Vermont hills as one did in the suburbs of New York or Boston, by going frequently to market in nearby towns, buying to meet all one's needs in shops, using fruits and vegetables loaded with poisonous

[1] Scott Nearing, N.Y.: John Day 1952

sprays and dusts and far removed from their production source, plus the processed and canned output of the food industry. Such a procedure was followed by several families in the valley, as long as they could afford it. Meanwhile they paid the usual price in lowered vitality and ill health.

We were not at all pulled in this direction, partly because we believed in fresh, vital food, organically produced, and partly because our economy was planned on the assumption that we would produce and use everything possible, relying upon cash-spending for the smallest residue of goods and services procured outside the circle of our household establishment.

The basis of our consumer economy was the garden. By raising and using garden products as outlined in the two previous chapters we were able to provide ourselves with around 80% of our food.[2] Shelter, which ranks next to food in the budget of the low-income household,[3] we provided by the system of construction described in the chapter on building a home. For fuel we used wood, cut on the place. Some of our neighbors heated with coal, oil, gas or electricity. We enjoyed work in the forest, which needed continual cleaning and weeding. And wood cut and used on the place necessitated no cash outlay, but represented a direct return for our labor. Thoreau said on cutting one's own fuel: "It warms us twice, and the first warmth is the most wholesome and memorable, compared with which the other is mere coke . . . The greatest value is received before the wood is teamed home."[4]

Our Vermont economy provided food, shelter and fuel, the big

[2] "Food represents nearly 40% of the budget of the average urban family." Ralph Borsodi, in *The Interpreter*, March 1, 1946, p. 2
[3] "Shelter represents, on the average, 25% of the total budget of those who pay rent in cities," *Ibid.*, p. 1
[4] *Journal*, 10/22/1853

items among necessaries,[5] mainly or entirely on a use basis. With rather wide limitations, we could have a supply of these things in direct proportion to the amount of labor time that we were willing to put into their production. Our purpose in going to Vermont however, was not to multiply food, housing, fuel and the other necessaries, but to get only enough of these things to meet the requirements of a living standard that would maintain our physical efficiency and at the same time provide us with sufficient leisure to pursue our chosen avocations. Livelihood was no end in itself,—rather it was a vestibule into an abundant and rewarding life. Therefore we produced the necessaries only to a point which would provide for efficiency. When we reached that point, we turned our attention and energies from bread labor to avocations or to social pursuits.

Current practice in United States economy called upon the person who had met his needs for necessaries to turn his attention forthwith to procuring comforts and conveniences, and after that to luxuries and superfluities. Only by such procedures could an economy based on profit accumulation hope to achieve the expansion needed to absorb additional profits and pay a return to those investing in the new industries.

Our practice was almost the exact opposite of the current one. Our consumer necessaries came mostly from the place, on a use basis. Comforts and conveniences came from outside the farm and had to be procured either by barter or through cash outlays. We bartered for some products,—chiefly food which we could not raise in a New England climate. Cash outlay meant earning additional cash income. Consequently, we endeavored to do as

---

[5] "A proper program of country living would, by providing food and shelter alone, make the average family secure with regard to approximately 60% of their needs." Borsodi, *Ibid.*, p. 2

Robert Louis Stevenson advised in his Christmas Sermon, "earn a little and spend a little less". Food from the garden and wood from the forest were the product of our own time and labor. We paid no rent. Taxes were reasonable. We bought no candy, pastries, meats, soft drinks, alcohol, tea, coffee or tobacco. These seemingly minor items mount up and occupy a large place in the ordinary family's budget. We spent little on clothes and knick-knacks. We lighted for fifteen years with kerosene and candles. We never had a telephone or radio. Most of our furniture was built in and hand made. We did our trading in town not more than twice in a month, and then our purchases were scanty.

"Civilization," said Mark Twain, "is a limitless multiplication of unnecessary necessaries." A market economy seeks by bally-hoo to bamboozle consumers into buying things they neither need nor want, thus compelling them to sell their labor power as a means of paying for their purchases. Since our aim was liberation from the exploitation accompanying the sale of labor power, we were as wary of market lures as a wise mouse is wary of other traps.

Readers may label such a policy as painfully austere, renuncia-tory or bordering on deliberate self-punishment. We had no such feeling. Coming from New York City, with its extravagant dis-plays of non-essentials and its extensive wastes of everything from food and capital goods to time and energy, we were surprised and delighted to find how much of the city clutter and waste we could toss overboard. We felt as free, in this respect, as a caged wild bird who finds himself once more on the wing. The demands and requirements which weigh upon city consumers no longer restricted us. To the extent that we were able to meet our con-sumer needs in our own way and in our own good time, we had freed ourselves from dependence upon the market economy.

Vermont life liberated us as consumers from the limitations, restrictions and compulsions of the city market. It had an even more profound effect upon us as producers. A household economy based on a maximum of self-sufficiency gives the householder a maximum of responsibility.

Householders living under a use economy must provide their own goods and services, not only in sufficient amount, but at the proper time. Dwellers in a remote valley cannot send or phone to the corner grocery an hour before supper. They must plan and prepare during the previous season. If radishes are to be ready for the table on the first of June, they must be planted not later than the first week in May. If seeds are to yield the best results, the soil must be prepared before the planting day. Soil preparation with us, necessitated compost. Compost piles, to be available in the Spring, had to be set up by mid-summer of the previous year. To enjoy fresh radishes on June 1, we began to get ready ten or twelve months in advance.

Similarly with the fuel supply. It is possible to burn green wood by putting it in the oven or under the stove and drying the outside fibres before the sticks go into the fire-box. They will not burn really well, but neither will they put the fire out. Best results are obtained by splitting the wood in the open, leaving it in a heap until sun and wind have seared over the outside, then piling it in an open-sided woodshed for six months. This means, in practice, that the winter's wood supply should be under cover by the previous spring. If the wood can be cut one year in advance, put under cover and burned the following year, so much the better.

Another example of necessary foresight can be taken from our building. There was a place in the lumber shed where cement was kept. Before taking a trip to town (fifteen miles to Man-

chester in one direction or thirty miles to Brattleboro in the other)
we always looked at the cement stock, and if it was below five
bags, we brought back another five or ten. In this way we usually
had cement when it was needed. Otherwise the job would have
been held up while we put in time and motion and money
making a special trip to either town. Incidentally, by buying in
ton lots, paying cash in advance and doing our own hauling from
the lumber yard, we saved from five to ten cents on every bag of
cement we used. By such devices much of our cement cost us as
little as sixty cents a bag, and it was always ready at hand.

Isolated self-contained households meet their needs for current
repairs and upkeep as they meet the requirements for capital
installation, by keeping on hand a modest supply of lumber,
hardware and simple tools and dealing with repairs and replacements at appropriate times. Such jobs, when completed, might
not look professional, but they use the ingenuity and stretch the
imagination of the householder and provide excellent training.
After all is said and done, it is foolish and wasteful to let the
professional building tradesman think out, plan, construct and
at the end of the job thrill with the joy of work well done. "Shall
we," asks Thoreau, "forever resign the pleasure of construction
to the carpenter?"[6]

Power age economy has substituted the specialized machine
and the assembly line for the craftsman, and has transformed
many a skilled worker into a machine tender, with a resulting
concentration, not upon excellence, but upon volume of product.
The average city worker is asked to accept a wage or salary as a
substitute for pride in workmanship and the satisfaction of
mastery over tools and materials.

Our self-contained Vermont economy, with its dependence

[6] *Walden*, Boston: Ticknor & Fields 1854 p. 51

upon our own productive efforts, reopened for us a great variety of competences of which the average city dweller knows little. The most important group of these competences was associated with the use of the soil and the production and preparation of food. Building, equipping and repairing dwelling units, and the making and repairing of tools and implements presented us with a second sphere of productive functioning. Cutting logs and firewood and the clearing of woodland brought us into contact with forestry and its associated practices. In all of these fields we were compelled to think, plan, assemble materials and tools, and practice the techniques required to obtain the results we had in view.

City dwellers, accustomed to a wide variety of services, get to a point at which they believe that the essential questions of day to day living can be settled by arrangement, chiefly over a telephone. A customer with a ten dollar bill can get wonderful results in a department store. But put the same person in the backwoods with a problem to be solved and an inadequate supply of materials and tools. There money is useless. Instead, ingenuity, skill, patience and persistence are the coin current. The store customer, who comes home with a package under his arm has learned nothing, except that a ten dollar bill is a source of power in the market place. The man or woman who has converted material into needed products via tools and skills has matured in the process. A telephone call and a charge account get results in a market center. Very different requirements are called into play in a household aiming at maximum self-sufficiency.

The school of hard knocks is merciless. One can argue with a storekeeper, a taxi driver or even with a traffic officer. A square, a level, a bit of knotty pine, a badly mixed batch of concrete, a leaky pipe or a short circuit are implacable. There they stand, pointing the finger of accusation at the careless or the ignorant or clumsy worker. If, under such conditions, one knows good work and wants it, there is only one thing to do,—tear out the job and begin all over again.

Self-contained rural economies require a certain amount of cash with which to pay taxes, to buy hardware and tools, and in our case to purchase clothing, which we never attempted to produce during our stay in Vermont. The city man who has learned to depend on a wage or salary feels a sense of uncertainty, bordering on terror, when he contemplates weeks, months and years minus a pay check. Where, he asks, is the money coming from?

George Breen, when he came into the valley from Connecticut, had been a salesman for so many years that he could not imagine what it would be like to live a week without a pay check. He stepped into the situation warily, as a man approaches any unknown country, filled with misgivings and a sense of real insecurity. We felt a bit the same way when we plunged from the whirlpool of New York life into the tranquillity of hills and forests. Money was the coin of the urban realm from which we came,—the open sesame to the satisfaction of needs and wants. When we left the city, we felt we had left cash payment behind. When it reared its ugly head even in the Vermont wilderness, we kept it in its place and made it our business to see only that there was a surplus of receipts over expenditures. William Cooper, in his *Guide in the Wilderness* said wisely, "It is not large funds that are wanted, but a constant supply, like a small stream that never dies. To have a great capital is not so necessary as to know how to manage a small one and never to be without a little."[7]

[7] Dublin: Gilbert & Hodges 1810 pp. 53-6

Aside from public education, poor relief, old age pensions and the social security taxes and payments which gradually entered the life of rural Vermont between 1932 and 1952, the stability and security of a household depended upon its internal balance, upon the health of its members and their willingness to work or otherwise contribute toward the goods and services upon which household survival depended.

Houses in our section were well kept or disorderly, neat or squalid and run down, in proportion to the willingness of the adult family members to put time and energy into the multiple tasks that must be performed before neatness and order can be established and maintained. "Many a farm of ample acreage is left to the rheumatic labor of advancing decrepitude. . . There is no strength for repairs, no ambition for improvement, and no expectation of more than a bare subsistence . . . It only requires courage, a cold shoulder to croakers, energy, skill and application."[8]

Virtually every family in the valley had some kind of garden, which was planted in the spring, tended perfunctorily during the summer, and neglected and abandoned to weeds by the fall.

The valley bordered The Wilderness of which Stratton Mountain was the center. Wild life abounded. Deer were so numerous that at times they made gardening all but impossible, yet throughout the valley there were few garden fences. The natives preferred to have their gardens near the house, keep dogs and cats, and take chances.

Rainfall was around 45 inches per year, fairly well distributed through the seasons, but almost every summer there were minor

[8] "Farming in New England", *Report of Commissioner of Agriculture*, Wash. D.C.: Gov. Printing Office 1871 p. 255

droughts, and periodically rainless spells dried cultivated fields to powder. The valley abounded in springs and streams; there were stones everywhere and sand and gravel for the taking. Yet no family built an irrigation tank or the beginnings of an irrigation system.

Garden land sloped, much of it steeply, yet the valley was terraceless. During our two decades in the valley we never saw an example of contour farming, ridging or drainage.

Buildings throughout the valley were poor, many being roofed with wood shingles, involving a high fire risk. Most places did not have water running into the house, nor did they have so much as a rain barrel of water stored against fire during a dry period. To be sure, in the last twenty years, only one house burned down in the valley, but chimney fires were frequent and an adequate fire department miles away.

Of paper work,—planning, budgeting, book-keeping, there was little. Most families spent what they had, ran into debt and hoped for the best. "There is not a single step in the life of a farmer that does not prove the advantage of his keeping regular accounts; and yet there is not one in a thousand who does it."[9]

We never expected to devote more than half of our time to bread labor, but during that time we took the livelihood problem seriously. We had some training in agriculture and forestry, in civil, mechanical and social engineering. We dealt with the entire livelihood problem in the same way that we faced problems in any of these fields. There are accepted techniques, in science as well as in technology. We attempted to apply the principles and practices of science and technology to the problems we encountered in rounding out a semi-subsistence livelihood. We surveyed the problem at hand, thought about it, discussed it,

[9] Arthur Young, *The Farmer's Calendar*, Lon.: Phillips 1805 p. 569

made plans, assembled the needed materials and tools, and then proceeded to work out solutions, in terms of the particular situation. Hence, we fenced, irrigated, terraced, planned, constructed, marking ourselves as odd, queer, over-ambitious and perhaps even a trifle un-neighborly by setting up standards of performance which were far removed from those accepted and followed by the neighborhood.

"That every Man should imploy him self not only for the advancing of his own Interest, but likewise that he may propogate the Wellfare of others will, I suppose, be sooner granted than practised. . . . It is necessary, that some be imployed one way, and some another, So that each may attain to some Competent Degree of Knowledge of, and Dexterity in the Vocation or imployment he Professes, So that every One may be Useful and Assisting to another, And by a mutual Good Correspondence with one another, all may live Comfortable together."

James Donaldson, The Undoubted Art of Thriving, 1700

"Oh, knew he but his happiness, of men
The happiest he! who far from public rage,
Deep in the vale, with a choice few retir'd,
Drinks the pure pleasures of the Rural Life."

James Thomson, The Seasons, 1730

"These countrymen in general are a very happy people; they enjoy many of the necessities of life upon their own farms, and what they do not so gain, they have from the sale of their surplus products: it is remarkable to see such numbers of these men in a state of great ease and content, possessing all the necessaries of life, but few of the luxuries of it. Their farms yield food—much of cloathing—most of the articles of building— with a surplus sufficient to buy such foreign luxuries as are necessary to make life passably comfortable: there is very little elegance among them —but more of necessaries."

Anonymous, American Husbandry, 1775

"Thrice happy days! In rural business passed:
Blest winter nights! when, as the genial fire
Cheers the wide hall, his cordial family
With soft domestic arts and hours beguilt . . .
Sometimes, at eve,
His neighbors lift the latch, and bless unbid
His festal roof; while, o'er the light repast,
And sprightly cups, they mix in social joy;
And, through the maze of conversation, trace
Whate'er amuses or improves the mind."

John Armstrong, The Art of Preserving Health, 1838

"My most serene irresponsible neighbors, let us see that we have the whole advantage of each other; we will be useful, at least, if not admirable, to one another."

Henry Thoreau, A Week on the Concord and Merrimack Rivers, 1849

"We have learned to be chary of roads; they mean people, and commotion, and lack of peace."

Herbert Jacobs, We Chose the Country, 1948

CHAPTER 7

LIVING IN A COMMUNITY

The neighbors look us over—We prefer cooperation to wage labor—Successful and unsuccessful neighborhood group effort—With cooperative effort the valley could have thrived—Insufficient interest and enthusiasm—Community social affairs—The Community House—Individualism rampant—A musical hour—One successful communal effort

WE WENT to Vermont as outsiders. Natives in those parts frequently use the word "foreigners" to describe newcomers. In view of the suspicion they feel and their reluctance to admit outsiders into their neighborhood circle they should call them "interlopers."

Every community demands conformity to its laws, expects the acceptance of its customs and folkways, and prefers to have none but native sons at its firesides. In small remote communities this preference tends to take precedence over all other considerations. In 1932, depression hardship was felt even in our Green Mountain wilderness. Vernet Slason, a native of Londonderry, five miles north of Bondville, married a Bondville girl, Eva Crowninshield, and settled down there. He was handy at carpenter work and painting; fixed up a saw-rig and cut cordwood for neighbors, and quickly made himself a place in the work life of the town. One of the old Bondvillites reacted to this incursion with the comment, "I don't see why these outsiders should come in here and take work away from our boys."

If a native-born Vermonter elicited such a response by moving across some hills and settling down in a nearby valley, imagine the reception given to people born in other states, who emigrated to the town of Winhall, Vermont, direct from New York City. Here was an immense barrier to surmount. We looked upon association with the community as a necessary aspect of the good life. How were we to be accepted? We were law-abiding citizens for the most part, but we did not conform to the folkways and we were not native sons.

When we first arrived, the neighbors looked us over. In less than no time they knew the minutest details about us,—where we came from, what we had been doing there, how old we were, what kind of a car we drove, its condition and performance, the kind of clothes we wore, the food we ate and a hundred other items.

One of our first steps in Vermont was to ask the Lightfoots, who were our nearest neighbors and lived less than a quarter of a mile away, whether they would supply us with milk. They agreed, and one or another of the Lightfoot girls would come over each day and deliver it. Sometimes all three brought it over. There was a much-worn woodbox with a big hinged cover, in the kitchen of our house. There the three little girls would perch like birds in a row—Minnie, the oldest, with her feet just reaching the floor; Mary, with her legs dangling, and Gladys, who must have been about four or five, with her legs sticking straight out in front of her. With their big solemn eyes, they saw everything, remembered everything and doubtless gave their reports to playmates and home-folks.

Our ways amused the neighbors, baffled them or annoyed them. Perhaps the most consistent and emphatic disapproval was directed against our diet. We could more easily have been accepted if we had eaten in the approved way. We ate from wooden bowls, with chopsticks, not from china plates, with forks and spoons; we ate food raw that, according to Vermont practices, should have been cooked, and we cooked weeds and outlandish things that never should be eaten at all. That we ate no meat was in itself strange; but during our entire twenty years in Vermont we never baked a pie, we seldom ate cake or cookies and almost never doughnuts. In a community which serves pie, cake and doughnuts for two if not three meals a day, conduct such as ours was not only unbelievable but reprehensible. We simply failed to live up to the accepted Vermont pattern.

To the credit of Vermont conservatism it must be said that during the two decades of our stay, after innumerable discussions and long-drawn-out arguments on the subject of white flour, white bread, white sugar, pies and pastries, the necessity for eating raw vegetables, and the revolting practice of consuming decaying animal carcasses, no native Vermont family of our acquaintance made any noticeable change in its food habits.

We desired to get on with our neighbors, but we were not willing to conform to their patterns of living and they would not adopt ours. So we agreed to differ and made allowances for each other's idiosyncrasies. They abode by their traditions and we planned and lived our lives un-Vermontishly.

We had much to learn, and some of our ideas were not well adapted to Vermont.[1] For instance, when it came to culverts, which clog up with leaves and brush during the wet season and

[1] "It would seem that the gentleman ought to serve an apprenticeship with some dirt farmer, before he embarked on his own account, in a business with which he is entirely unacquainted." John Lorain, *The Practise of Husbandry*, Phil.: Carey 1825 p. 404

make no end of trouble,—we put in stone-paved, open fords such as we had seen in Washington's Rock Creek Park. The neighbors assured us that these fords would not work in winter because the water would take out the snow at the center of the ford, leaving two high snow banks on either side which would have to be broken down before the road could be used. We persisted in building several of the fords and the neighbors turned out to be right. Furthermore, some of the stones at the edge of the fords were heaved by frost and made additional trouble. We gave up ford building, and the neighbors snorted with satisfaction: "We told you so."

On the issue of concrete stacks, however, we made our point. Vermont sap houses are equipped with galvanized iron stacks. Our evaporator called for a stack 22 inches in diameter and 28 feet high. It came in six foot sections which were bulky and about all one man cared to handle, even on the ground. Traditionally, the stack was erected at the beginning of the sap season. It took several adults to handle the job. The lower sections were easy; the higher ones difficult and dangerous. At the end of the sap season, careful operators took the stack down and stored it, careless folk left it up to rust until the next season.

After mounting and dismounting the stack for two or three years we decided to put up a permanent one. We discussed brick, but finally chose concrete, using our old galvanized stack as the inside form and constructing a square outside form in sections, bolted in place, and moved up as we built. The sap house was already constructed, with concrete foundations and a concrete floor, so we put the stack outside the sap house and connected it through an opening in the galvanized wall. After some minor obstacles had been overcome, we completed the stack and the next sap season, tried it out. It drew well. So far as we know, this was the first concrete stack attached to a Vermont sugarhouse. It has stood in place, without repairs of any kind, for some fifteen years. Instead of laboriously and dangerously erecting a galvanized stack every spring, two men working twenty minutes, inserted a galvanized section between the stack and the evaporator, and we were ready to boil sap.

Building a concrete stack led to plenty of neighborhood comment. Ruth Hamilton, one of the neighbors, who would be rated even by Vermonters as a conservative, came up to have a look at the stack in operation. She had made syrup for years and knew all the techniques. After watching for a time she turned to a by-stander with the approving remark: "Well, they may be socialists but they do have good ideas."

That qualified endorsement was one of the warmest that we got in the neighborhood. Many other comments were far less flattering. Even the neighbors who liked us were sceptical about most of our queer ways.

We were cooperators in theory and were anxious to put the theory into practice. From the beginning we worked with our neighbors, sometimes on their side of the fence, sometimes on our side. We disapprove of the wage relation on principle and if we could avoid it by cooperative exchange of labor we would never enter into it in practice. The purchase and sale of labor power is not a healthy social relationship and we far prefer a fair and equal exchange of time or of products. On every possible occasion we turned to cooperation and mutual aid. When necessary, we compromised on wage labor, but we held it to a minimum, and always on the neighbor's terms. In any such transaction we discussed the work to be done and then said: "How much will you expect for that job?" Or else, after the job was completed, we asked "How much do we owe you?" Never once did we have any reason to question or hesitate to pay what was asked.

The relationships which we enjoy most can be illustrated by the deal we made with one neighboring family who wanted a fireplace. Alice and Chuck Vaughan had bought an old farmhouse, a dozen miles from our place, and were turning it into a ski lodge. The local masons wanted $600 to build a brick fireplace and chimney. We suggested that the Vaughans build it themselves but they had never tackled such a job and were a bit wary. At that time we were building a set of stone steps up a boulder-face to a cabin in the woods. It was heavy work and we could use help. We talked the matter over with them and made the following arrangement. They would put in their fireplace foundation to floor level. We would work with them on the fireplace and carry the chimney to the peak of the roof. We figured this would take us six working days. They, in exchange, would put in six working days on our stone steps, and on some canning.

The plan worked out nicely. At the cost of twelve days harmonious sociable work (plus their work on the foundation) they got a fireplace, with no cash outlay except for materials, which they would have had to buy in any case. We, on our side, got an equivalent amount of help with our heavy stone steps and our canning.

Such relationships are sound economically,—an exchange from which both parties gain, without exploitation on either side. Socially, they are based on the equalitarian principle of exchanging labor time. Each puts in an equal number of hours and does his best according to his abilities. Thoreau says in *Walden:* "If a man has faith, he will cooperate with equal faith everywhere; if he has not faith, he will continue to live like the rest of the world, whatever company he is joined to. To cooperate in the highest as well as the lowest sense, means to get our living together."[2]

A few other of our neighbors were cooperators in theory. Most of them were indifferent, or actively hostile to it. When the theoretical cooperators found that cooperation began with planning, and succeeded only in so far as the cooperators stuck to the plans, assumed responsibility for their fulfilment, and then lived up to their obligations, most of them thought better of it and went back to the individualistic pattern of "everyone for himself and on his own."[3]

The attitude is well illustrated by Harold Field's reaction to our rationalized methods of syrup production. Harold is an amiable, ingenious inventor and a painstaking workman when he once gets going. In theory he believes in cooperation; in practice he likes to go to bed when he makes up his mind to it and to get up and work when he feels like it. He sugared with us one year and found there were disadvantages. During the syrup making season we were extra careful to keep on schedule because so much depended on picking up the sap as soon as it was in the buckets and getting it into the evaporator before it began to ferment.

Harold had a sugar grove of sorts, but his trees were fairly small and many of them were soft maple, not superior producers. He had no sugarhouse. So we made an arrangement whereby Harold would sugar with us, contribute his own time and that of his team, some sap buckets and other tools, in exchange for a specified percentage of the syrup crop, to be shared with him on

[2] Boston: Ticknor & Fields 1854 p. 78

[3] "There are some People that care for none of these Things, that will enter into no new Scheme, not take up any other Business than what they have been enured to, unless you can promise Mountains of Gold." Jared Eliot, *Essays*, Boston: Edes & Gill 1760 p. 135

a day-to-day basis. The season was a good one and Harold ended it with around 150 gallons of syrup in exchange for about six weeks of work.

Harold was more than satisfied by the amount of syrup he got, but he felt that the work routine was too rigid. Besides, he reasoned, if that much syrup could be made with such a small outlay of effort, why should he not use his own trees, set up his own sugarhouses and have all the proceeds for himself? The next sap season therefore found Harold setting up his own sugar establishment and trying to do the job virtually single-handed. Syrup-making asks for division of labor and a considerable degree of coordination of effort. The most efficient tapping team, for instance, consists of three or four people. Gathering sap is one occupation, and boiling it down another. These operations should be performed at the same time, especially in mild weather, so that the sap does not stand around and sour. Harold had some difficult, harried seasons before he gave up syrup making on the argument that it did not pay him the going rate of day wages for the time he put in on it.

Zoe and Floyd Hurd were the people who first taught us how to make maple syrup. From 1933 to 1940 we sugared with them. Floyd and his family were Seventh Day Adventists. Believing that Saturday and not Sunday was the divinely ordained day of rest, neighborhood Adventists refused to work on Saturday or to do business that day. They would milk and water their cattle on Saturday and perform other urgent chores. If a neighbor insisted, they would let him have the necessaries of life, such as milk or eggs. Frequently, however, they would not take the money for these supplies until another day.

Walter Twing, one of the Seventh Day leaders in our neighborhood, had a pit in which there was clean and evenly-graded building sand. He was accommodating and always went out of his way to be friendly, but he would not let us take sand from his place on Saturday. Walter was one of the best sugar makers in the valley. He began extra early in the spring, emptied his buckets more frequently than most, made extra fine quality syrup and sugar, and always aimed to have the first sugar to carry to town meeting day, early in March. There is a tradition in the valley that at the height of his religious zeal Walter went among his maples on Friday at sundown, emptied the sap buckets, set them upside down and left them thus until Saturday's sunset, so that he would not use the sap which might drop on the Lord's day.

Zoe and Floyd were not so strict as Walter Twing. When we first worked with them they were willing to gather sap any day it ran. Later, however, they had some misfortunes which they attributed to their failure to observe the Sabbath. Both decided that, come what may, they would go to church Saturdays and would do no work. This decision, made early in the sap season, was followed by a series of week-ends in which sap started Friday, ran like mad all Saturday, and by Saturday night was overflowing the buckets.

Zoe and Floyd stuck to their principles and let the sap run and went to church. We had no such inhibitions, so we gathered the sap and boiled it down, on Saturday. Then came the crucial question: did the Hurds want to take their share of the syrup which had been made on the Sabbath, from sap that had run and been gathered that day? After debating the issue earnestly, they took their share of the syrup.

Had efforts to establish cooperation and mutual aid succeeded, a collective economy would have been a significant aspect of community activity. While several members of the valley population believed in the theory of cooperation, there was no deep concern to cooperate and no common push in that direction.

The valley in which we lived was designed by nature as an isolated, self-contained economic and social unit and would have thriven on collective undertakings. Five miles west of Jamaica, on the Pikes Falls road, the steep-sided canyon which carried a branch of the West River opened out into a valley half a mile wide by two miles long, running roughly from east to west. On the south loomed Stratton Mountain. On the north was Pinnacle Mountain. Access east and west was blocked by high hills, with half a dozen streams running through steep defiles across the bottom land and down to the West River. The entire valley of perhaps a thousand acres, plus wooded upland of another three or four thousand, did not contain enough good land for one first-class dairy farm. It was too high (1500 to 2000 feet above sea level) for most fruit. Three times in twenty years, July and August frosts trimmed squash, tomatoes, corn and even potato tops. Aside from the bottom land, flooded with every run-off of rain or melting snow, there was hardly a five acre piece that could be plowed without danger of severe erosion damage. The grazing season was short. Often snow lay from Thanksgiving to Easter.

On the other hand, there were eleven sugar groves in the valley, besides thousands of hard maples which had never been tapped. The surrounding hills carried millions of board feet of spruce, fir, hemlock, hard maple, yellow birch, white ash, bass-wood, beech, soft maple and poplar. Forest reproduction was automatic and forest growth was rapid. Given this set-up, it would have been possible (1) to erect a community saw-mill, saw out the necessary lumber and build or rebuild fifteen to twenty houses on appropriate pieces of land; (2) provide each dwelling unit with land for garden, fruit and outbuildings; (3) set up a central dairy unit to serve the entire valley; (4) maintain a central machine shop, carpenter shop, greenhouse unit and garage; (5) attach to the sawmill a wood-working plant which would convert the output of the scientifically forested timberland into toys or some other marketable wood product; (6) make maple syrup cooperatively, build a central packing house, put maple syrup and sugar into fancy packs and market them as opportunity offered; (7) supplement valley cash income by making hooked or braided rugs, carving wood, blacksmithing, making furniture, setting up a local school, a library and reading room, a social center and all facilities and activities necessary for a rounded life in the local community. Such an organization, well managed, and supported by the enthusiasm and idealism of the inhabitants, would have provided a livelihood and a reasonably satisfactory social life for 75 to 100 people. This would have been possible only on the basis of a common purpose, coordination, strong discipline and an iron will to see the project through over a period of at least a decade.

Plenty of young idealists drifted through the valley, staying for days, weeks, months and even years. To none did these ideas appeal sufficiently so that they were willing to take a hand and do something about it. Despite much talk and many meetings and discussions, no such cooperative unit was established. A few sporadic starts were made but no scheme was ever carried out to a successful conclusion.

The result was that an occasional itinerate saw mill, brought in for brief periods by professional lumbermen, made away with the standing timber. During our years in the valley we saw millions of feet of logs and lumber trucked out to Londonderry, Jamaica and Newfane. On the average, less than half of the

sugar groves were tapped in any given year. Most of the syrup
went in barrels to wholesale buyers, for a small return. Several
attempts were made to do local bread-baking, but they were
neither systematic nor long-lived. Almost equally unsuccessful
were the efforts to organize a nursery school and kindergarten.

Literally scores of families, many with quite young children,
visited the valley with the idea of locating there. A few of these
tried it out for longer or shorter periods. At the end of twenty
years, the valley population totalled a little less than it did at the
beginning of our sojourn, and the degree of cooperation was
limited to random swaps of products and services, with occasional
examples of mutual aid in the handling of sickness or the care
of young children, which would go on in any ordinary community in any part of the world.

The valley was inhabited by Vermonters and outsiders trained
to private enterprise and, for the most part, rejects from private
enterprise economy. Most of these men and women treasured
their freedom as individuals and looked upon cooperative enterprise as the first step toward super-imposed discipline and coercion. They were suspicious of organized methods and planning.
They would have none of it. Consequently, most community
projects dealt only with leisure-time activities,—diversion or
recreation.

These social affairs played an important part in the life of the
valley. Despite the absence of a common economy, there was a
persistent endeavor to organize neighborhood get-togethers at
several different levels. "As Recreation is most necessary, so to
none is it more due than to the Husbandman; . . . every toyl
exacting some time for Recreation."[4]

In the early days, community affairs were held outdoors during

[4] Gervase Markham, Country Contentments, Lon.: Sawbridge 1675 p. 2

the summer and early autumn. There were picnics at Pikes Falls and at different homes, marshmallow roasts, husking bees, house-raising bees, dancing parties. Outdoor meetings were fine in daylight or warm weather but some other arrangements obviously had to be made to meet storms and cold. Our stone-floored pine-panelled livingroom could accommodate almost forty people on couches, chairs and cushions, before a crackling fire. For several years it was used as an assembly point for discussions on world affairs and philosophical and other questions. These meetings usually took place on Saturday or Sunday evenings.

There was also a forum group in West Townshend, about 15 miles to the east of us, which held meetings on Wednesday evenings. The valley meetings seldom attracted more than thirty people. Attendance at the West Townshend Forum ran as high as a hundred on special occasions. Sometimes people from West Townshend came up to our meetings; frequently a dozen or more from our valley went down to theirs.

War tension in the early years, associated with the war of 1939–45, and later the passions roused by the cold war and the Korean war, put obstacles in the way of effective meetings. With few exceptions native Vermonters refused to attend the discussions both in our valley and in West Townshend on the ground that they were too radical. This was not surprising in view of the fact that the Vermonters, Republicans almost to a man, looked upon Democrats as way to the left. During the early years of the West Townshend Forum, high school students were encouraged by the local liberal principal to come from Leland and Grey Academy, five miles distant. Students also came from the nearby Newton School in Windham. As tension increased, students ceased attending the forums. In centers of population and with competent, experienced leaders, discussion groups are difficult to maintain over long periods even in peacetime. Discussion groups in wartime, in small, isolated communities, present still graver problems.

There were two main interest groups in the valley. One was concerned with world affairs and the meaning and purpose of life. The other wished to deal with strictly local matters and recreation,—the care of children, the organization of a nursery school, square dancing and the construction of a community house adequate to house these and similar undertakings. Attempts were made to alternate meetings on world affairs, local problems and recreation. Increased war tensions were reflected in the conflicting attitudes of valley folks. Eventually discussions were dropped and entertainment held the field.

Early in the development of valley community affairs, suggestions were made that a community center be established. Attempts to secure a local schoolhouse, belonging to the Jamaica School authorities, were unsuccessful. Norman Williams met the situation by buying an abandoned lumber camp, standing on forty acres of accessible land, and turning it over, under a deed of trust, to be used as a community center. After the place had been cleaned up and repaired, it was available for recreation and social gatherings.

From the time he came into the valley, Norm stood for a high degree of equalitarianism. He was disturbed because the local people remained aloof from community activities. Norm believed that "true community" was impossible unless all of the neighbors joined. In order to secure their participation, he argued, it was necessary to carry on activities in which all would be glad and willing to participate. In other words, activities were to be levelled down to the lowest common denominator.

Since experience had proved that the native Vermonters would not attend discussion groups, it was necessary to develop other more inclusive community undertakings. Norm believed that picnics, suppers and dances would fill the bill. The refitted community house was used for these purposes. With accordions and phonograph records and some amateur assistance, square dancing and folk dancing were developed to such a point that teams of dancers from the valley were invited to surrounding towns to give exhibitions. Square dances were held Saturday nights. So successful were they that people came for miles to take part in them. Still, everyone in the valley did not attend the Saturday night affairs. Furthermore, a new complication arose,—the use of liquor.

Soft drinks had been served or sold at the dances from the beginning in the community center. As attendance at the dances increased, people came who had been drinking. Others brought liquor and drank on the premises during the dances. There was brawling in one instance. Richard Gregg, Orpha Collie and Nelson Rawson, who were trustees of the community center at that time, posted a notice forbidding the use of liquor in the center. This brought the issue to a head. A community meeting was held. The trustees resigned. As their successors, three men were elected, all of whom favored the use of liquor on community house premises during dances. The trustees who had resigned were all at or past middle age. The new trustees were all members of the younger pre-middle age generation.

The liquor issue shook the community to its foundations. The decision to permit the use of liquor in the community center was thoroughly threshed out. There was no question but that the majority of the community favored freedom for drinkers and drinking. The anti-liquor minority refused to attend functions at the center if liquor was permitted.

Several issues involving morals and ethics had faced the community and had been settled or laid on the table without serious disruptive results except for the individuals concerned. The liquor question divided the community and proved so divisive that it caused the ultimate liquidation of the whole community house project. At one point there had been much talk of rebuilding the community house, so that it would include a craft center, school facilities and room for enlarged recreational activities. The controversy over alcohol drinking knocked the plans into a cocked hat.

This experience underlined the oft-repeated generalization that ideological agreement is an indispensable pre-requisite for the establishment of a successful cooperative group. Unity on objectives and on techniques is not enough, and even that was not in evidence in our valley. The community which desires to survive must have an ideology which is accepted by all of its members. The community house might have been a unifying factor of considerable importance in the life of the valley. Instead, almost through inadvertence, it underscored an element of discord which has played havoc with many an individual life and many a social group.

Throughout the entire effort to achieve valley-wide cooperation, each household remained an independent economic and social unit, with minor features of give and take maintained by special arrangement between the families involved. When the cycle was completed and the community house was abandoned, the valley stood about where it had been a decade earlier. There were recreational get-togethers now and again, but instead of valley-wide cooperation, animosities, family feuds and ideological antagonisms threaded through the entire life of the community.

Certainly this is not a pretty picture, nor does it offer hope to the many individuals and groups that have been looking and working toward the establishment in North America of cooperative communes or intentional communities of work. Perhaps the most significant lesson of the experience is that human beings, conditioned from birth by the professions and practices of a private enterprise, individualistic pattern have little more chance to cooperate effectively than a leopard has to change his spots.

War-time pressures and the sharp differences of viewpoint which were frequently expressed during our discussions of public questions, plus our own inclinations, led us to try out another experiment looking to community integration,—a musical hour each Sunday morning. During the open season, weather permitting, we held the musical session on a back terrace of the house, under the trees; in rough weather, before the fire in our livingroom.

The affair was very informal. At 10:30 whoever was on hand began taking part. The program itself was put together in terms of the interests and capacities of those present. Because of the wide diversity of religious and anti-religious views in the valley, it was necessary not to stress nor yet to avoid musical compositions of a religious nature. With minor exceptions we crossed this hurdle successfully. Rounds and folktunes were always possible. Singers who could tackle more ambitious part-songs were not always present but were eagerly sought. If no one came from outside the immediate household, which was occasionally the case in bad weather, the phonograph or organ was played.

For regularly attended sessions the music period was divided roughly into two parts,—*amateur* singing or instrument performances, and *professional* music from records,—unless we were fortunate enough to have present professional vocalists or instrumentalists. If people came who could perform musically or

who had pronounced musical tastes, the program shifted ac,
cordingly. At one time a good violinist dropped in and played
for us to organ accompaniment; a guitarist came who picked out
Bach themes on his strings; at another time a woman with an
out-standing voice happened by who delighted us with her deep,
full tones. We took advantage of any talent. One notable Sunday
a professional flautist and two recorder players appeared from
nowhere, a quintet was organized and put in four solid hours
working through a pile of ensemble music. Time was barely
taken out to eat and then back to the music. These artists dropped
in by chance and we never saw them again.

The music hour proved to be a community success. More
people came to it than attended discussions of public questions.
When the music was over, they visited together, looked over
our garden or the house and usually departed with arms or boxes
filled with vegetables or flowers. As far as we could judge, they
got more from music than from discussions. Certainly antagon-
ism and bitterness were almost entirely absent from our musical
sessions.

One notable event did bring the valley together,—the cancellation of the mail route in 1945. The war was on and gasoline
was rationed. We were deep in the snows of a heavy winter.
Cars were few and the young men to drive them were mostly
overseas. Old folks particularly were hard put to it to get to
town, and Wallace Crowninshield, the local mailman, kept them
in touch with the outer world by bringing and taking the mail
three times a week, plus occasional help with needed groceries
and other provisions. At this critical juncture, with only a week's
notice, the Post Office Department in Washington ordered the
rural mail route discontinued, on the ground that the service did
not pay its way.

People in the valley were shocked and stunned, and then, as the full import of this decision dawned on them—angry. Talk back and forth crystallized almost immediately into action. A volunteer committee secured the use of the local schoolhouse, contacted all who depended on the mail route, and called a meeting to decide on a course of action. The meeting was held on a snowy night in February. The valley people struggled through the drifts. Several groups came in from nearby Jamaica and Bondville. By meeting-time, the schoolhouse was crowded with forty-odd men, women and children. The stove was cherry red; the two school oil lamps and several lanterns dimly lighted up the faces of natives and newcomers alike. During our whole time in the valley we never saw so representative a gathering,— not even at a funeral. Uncle Sam's abrupt cancellation of the mail route had brought the entire community together in a move to get back the R.F.D.

The meeting elected Charles McCurdy chairman; Helen Nearing, secretary, with Jack Lightfoot, Raymond Styles and Scott Nearing to act as advisers of "The Pikes Falls Citizens Committee." Strategy was discussed and provision was made for rounding up all possible help and sympathy in getting the cancellation order rescinded. Our program was simple. All present were asked to write to the Postmaster General first of all, protesting the unfairness of his decision, next to our Senators and Representatives, notifying them of the situation and of our ire, and demanding their help. Letters were to be sent to the boys at the front, telling them to protest this cutting off of mail to and from their folks.

We planned letters to the local newspapers, but before we got them written, came a body blow from the *Brattleboro Reformer*, which said editorially that Pikes Falls was a nice little place to go fishing in the spring and summer but that the government was hardly justified in running a mail route for a mere fourteen families. This raised a howl from our little valley and some indignant letters to the paper. After printing them, the *Reformer* reversed its stand and said that instead of our puny Tuesday, Thursday, Saturday mail delivery we should be given daily service, with trolley car service and electric lights to boot. From then on, the *Brattleboro Reformer* was on our side in the fight and printed some twenty notices, letters and articles on the Pikes Falls mail route issue.

Another nearby paper, the *Bennington Banner,* started off with an editorial scoffing at the pretensions of a handful of little people back in the hills. Why, said the Editor, these folks have much greater advantages today than their like had a hundred years ago; the trouble with them is they've been educated to expect that by turning a spigot plenty of what they want will gush forth. That was going a little far. Both Brattleboro and Bennington had city water supplies; the comparison was offensive to people who carried their own water, from well or spring. These towns were our shopping towns and they were sneering at the countryside which brought them their business. We wrote our opinion of such tactics.

We came across a timely clipping from the *New York Times* which was brought to the attention of all and sundry. The issue of February 22, 1945 reported that the Post Office Department "expects an operating surplus of $265,214,280 in the next fiscal year." The gross annual cost of our mail route was less than $800. The big boys in Washington were saving dollars by taking pennies away from little people whose sons were at the front, fighting democracy's battles.

What a situation,—a handful of hill folk, isolated in a remote valley by a New England winter, their provincial need overshadowed by war, and their young men at the front,—entering a contest with the Government of the United States of North America. It was a case of David versus Goliath; a mouse attacking an elephant. The odds were against us, but we know who won in the Bible story and we had heard of mice putting elephants to flight.

We hired the Jamaica Town Hall and put on a well-attended meeting. Minutes were read of the first meeting, telling how the whole situation arose. Speeches from the floor were made, by children, by farm women whose sons were in the Pacific, by a soldier, John Stark, home on leave, by Frederick Van de Water, representing Freeman, Inc., who were currently engaged in a drive to prevent the Army engineers from constructing a dam that would flood the West River Valley. Resolutions were adopted and sent to the Postmaster General, to the Governor and to our Congressman and Senators. The meeting was lively and spontaneous. It was many a year since the neighborhood had been so stirred up and excited.

Response to this meeting was immediate. The Rutland and Burlington papers came to our support with articles. Headlines flared: "Pikes Falls Asks Senate Inquiry"; "Restoration of Mail Service Demanded at Mass Meeting". The Hon. Charles A. Plumley, member of Congress from Vermont, made a statement in the House of Representatives on Feb. 21st dealing with the rural service throughout the nation. After saying that he noticed that the Post Office Department was doing business at a profit and had accumulated a surplus of millions, he stated that its motto should be "service" not "profit". "The fact is the Department by rule of thumb is consolidating rural free delivery routes, suspending them, abolishing them all over the country to save money when they have a surplus, and at a time when the patrons

anxiously await the arrival of a letter from their boys and girls
in the service, which letter is never delivered." (Apparently
Representatives do read the letters from their constituents.)

During the first week of the mail-route discontinuance a photo-
grapher and a reporter from the *Boston Globe* told the David-
Goliath story to New England ("Vermont Hamlet Aroused by
R.F.D. Discontinuance"). The second week, the story was in the
New York Times ("Fight to Restore Rural Mail Route: 16 Vermont Families, with 4 Cars on Rationed Gas, Ask Washington
for Justice"). We had enlisted the *New England Homestead*,
the *Rural New Yorker* and other farm papers in the battle. We
were just getting up steam on the third week of our campaign,
when the Post Office Department announced the restoration of
the valley's mail service.

Although this rather took the wind out of our sails, we at least
could have a bang-up celebration. We got in touch with Mortimer Proctor, who was then Governor of Vermont, secured his
consent to come to Jamaica, and arranged a victory party in the
Jamaica Town Hall. "What? You've asked the Governor to come
to Jamaica?" the townsfolk gasped. "Surely," the Committee
answered, "Isn't he the Governor of Jamaica as well as other
parts of Vermont?" The meeting was a great success. The hall
was decorated; refreshments were served; the Governor and his
wife attended, and a fine time was had by all. "It pays to holler,"
said one townsman; another shrewdly commented, "The wheel
that squeaks the loudest gets the grease."

The theme of the celebration was the importance of building
up rural areas. "The spirit that is in this room tonight," Governor
Proctor said, "is the spirit of the Green Mountain Boys. You
have the courage and perseverance and determination that the
Green Mountain Boys had when they went down to the Con-

tinental Congress and presented the case for Vermont. When you presented your case in Washington, Washington recognized the kind of thunder that rolls out of Vermont when its spirit is aroused."

For the first and only time during our twenty years in the valley, the whole population, from "natives" to "outsiders," really worked together with a will. Cliques and animosities were forgotten. The episode provided a splendid example of the kind of community cooperation that was possible if people really made up their minds to do a job together.

"Now pause with yourselfe, and view the end of all your Labours . . . unspeakable Pleasure and infinite Commodity."

Gervase Markham, A New Orchard, 1648

"The ground is locked up, the farmer's exertions must relent, and now for him is the time to indulge in thinking and speculating upon what is passed and what is likely to come."

J. M. Gourgas, New England Farmer, January 25, 1828

"I went to the woods because I wished to live life deliberately, to front only the essential facts of life, and see if I could not learn what it had to teach, and not, when I came to die, discover that I had not lived. I did not wish to live what was not life, living is so dear; nor did I wish to practise resignation, unless it was quite necessary. I wanted to live deep and suck out all the marrow of life, to live so sturdily and spartan-like as to put to rout all that was not life, to cut a broad swath and shave close, to drive life into a corner, and reduce it to its lowest terms, and, if it proved to be mean, why then to get the whole and genuine meanness of it, and publish its meanness to the world; or if it were sublime, to know it by experience, and be able to give a true account of it in my next excursion."

Henry Thoreau, Walden, 1854

"He who digs a well, constructs a stone fountain, plants a grove of trees by the roadside, plants an orchard, builds a durable house, reclaims a swamp, or so much as puts a stone seat by the wayside, makes the land so far lovely and desirable, makes a fortune which he cannot carry away with him, but which is useful to his country long afterwards."

Ralph Waldo Emerson, Society and Solitude, 1870

"I do not think that any civilization can be called complete until it has progressed from sophistication to unsophistication, and made a conscious return to simplicity of thinking and living."

Lin Yutang, The Importance of Living, 1938

"When humanity gets tired enough of being hounded from pillar to post, when the powerful have sufficiently persecuted the weak and the envious weak have sufficiently obstructed the strong, perhaps our way of life will come to seem the true one, the good one; and people everywhere will awake in astonishment at having for so long neglected its simple wisdom."

Louise Dickinson Rich, My Neck of the Woods, 1950

CHAPTER 8

A BALANCE SHEET
OF THE VERMONT PROJECT

Social service, not escapism—Unified theory and practice
—Communal possibilities—Economic success—Visitors observe us—The valley's social inadequacy—Patternless living
the norm—Everyone for himself—Our individual stand

AGAIN and again people have asked us: "Why did you escape to
this idyllic spot? Why not stay in the noise, dirt and turmoil of
one of the great urban centers, sharing the misery and anguish of
your fellow humans?" We recognize the relevance of this question. Indeed, it extends to the social foundations upon which
those not satisfied with western civilization must strive to build
an alternative culture pattern. We would go further and agree
that this question reaches beyond sociology into the realm of
ethics. In several respects, it is the question of questions. Like
any basic social or ethical issue, it cannot be answered easily, nor
can it be met with a categorical reply. Any attempt at an inclusive
answer must contain exceptions and limitations.

Suppose we begin our answer to this perennial question by
admitting that in a remote Green Mountain valley one is not in

daily contact with the labor struggle, nor is he subject to the pressures of those who live, work, travel and recreate in New York, Chicago or San Francisco. The life in Vermont is different in texture from that of a metropolis. Is it "better" or "worse"? That depends upon the way in which the words are used. For us the life in Vermont was definitely better because it permitted frequent contacts with nature, because it afforded an opportunity to master and direct nature forces, because manual skills were still practiced and because the routine of living was less exacting. Instead of spending early and late hours in dirty, noisy, subway or train, we stayed on our own grounds week in and week out. Travelling to and from work, for us, meant walking two hundred yards from kitchen to saphouse. If snow was deep, the trip might require snowshoes or skis, but that was an advantage because it called for another skill.

This answer does not meet fully our central question: "Why should you avail yourself of these many advantages when fellow humans are deprived of them in city slums?" If we were compelled to answer this question categorically, we would say that under any and all conditions one is responsible for living as well as possible within the complex of circumstances which constitutes the day-to-day environment. Where there is a choice, with the evidence all recorded and the circumstances all considered, one chooses the better part rather than the worse.

Living is a business in which we all engage. In the course of the day, there are certain things we must do,—for example, breathe. There are also things we may do or may decide not to do,—such as, stay home and bake a cake, or go out and visit a friend. The center of life routine is surrounded by a circumference of choice. There is the vocation which provides livelihood, and the avocations which thrive on leisure and surplus energy.

A professional actor or musician must live close enough to his job to get there every working day. A poet or painter has a wider range from which to choose his living place. Under what obligation are these individuals to stay in the congested centers of population?

We would put the matter affirmatively. Since congestion is a social disadvantage, these individuals are in duty bound to avoid congested areas unless for some reason business or duty calls them there. If they go into the centers of population, instead of improving matters they make congestion worse.

We may state the issue in another way,—whatever the nature of one's beliefs, one's personal conduct may either follow the belief pattern or diverge from it. In so far as it diverges, it helps produce unwanted results. At the same time, it splits practice away from theory and divides the personality against itself. The most harmonious life is one in which theory and practice are unified.

From this it follows that each moment, hour, day, week and year should be treated as an occasion,—another opportunity to live as well as possible, in accordance with the old saying "Tomorrow is a new day" or the new Mexican greeting "Siempre mejor" (always better) in place of the conventional "Buenos dias" (good day). With body in health, emotions in balance, mind in tune and vision fixed on a better life and a better world, life, individually and collectively, is already better.

On this point we differ emphatically with many of our friends and acquaintances who say, in effect, "Never mind how we live today; we are in this dog-eat-dog social system and we may as well get what we can out of it. But tomorrow, in a wiser, more social and more humane world, we will live more rationally, more economically, more efficiently, more socially". Such talk is nonsense.

As we live in the present, so is our future shaped, channeled and largely determined.

Apply this thinking to our problem of living in the Green Mountains and believing in and working for a cooperative, peaceful, social order. Our life in Vermont may be justified, or can justify itself,—(1) as an instance and an example of sane living in an insane world; (2) as a means of contacting nature, a contact in many ways more important than contacting society; (3) as a desirable, limited alternative to one segment of the existing social order; (4) as a refuge for political deviants; (5) as a milieu in which heretofore active people can spend their riper years (in accordance with the Eastern conception of life stages: the sage or anchorite following the stage of householder); (6) as an opportunity for the sage or mature person to follow his profession and avocations.

Action has its advocates. Contemplation also has its adherents. The former tends to be exterior, peripheral or centrifugal; while the latter, by comparison, more inner, central and vital.

Perhaps we can summarize our point of view in this way. We are opposed to the theories of a competitive, acquisitive, aggressive, war-making social order, which butchers for food and murders for sport and for power. The closer we have to come to this social order the more completely are we a part of it. Since we reject it in theory, we should, as far as possible, reject it also in practice. On no other basis can theory and practice be unified. At the same time, and to the utmost extent, we should live as decently, kindly, justly, orderly and efficiently as possible. Human beings, under any set of circumstances, can behave well or badly. Whatever the circumstances, it is better to love, create and construct than to hate, undermine and destroy, or, what may be even worse at times, ignore and *laissez passer*. We believed that we could make our contribution to the good life more effectively in a pre-industrial, rural community than in one of the great urban centers.

During several decades we have been in close contact with like-minded men and women all through the United States who have tried the rural alternative and with others who have tried the urban alternative. We feel that both groups have made and are making a contribution. We still feel, however, as we did in 1932, that the rural alternative (the "small community" of Arthur E. Morgan, Baker Brownell and Ralph Borsodi) offers greater individual and collective constructive possibilities than the urban.

We are far from assuming that the ruralists will be able to set up a social communal alternative to capitalist urbanism. In the face of centuries of experience we did not assume that in 1932. We are surer now than we were then that these communities are confined rigidly to the few, rarely endowed and super-normally equipped men and women who are willing and able to live as altruists after being trained, conditioned and coerced by an acquisitive, competitive, ego-centric social system.[1]

What we did feel and what we still assert is that it is worthwhile for the individual who is rejected by a disintegrating urban community to formulate a theory of conduct and to put into practise a program of action which will enable him or her to live as decently as possible under existing circumstances.

Viewed in a long perspective, our Vermont project was a personal stop-gap, an emergency expedient. But in the short view it was a way of preserving self-respect and of demonstrating to the few who were willing to observe, listen and participate, that life in a dying acquisitive culture can be individually and socially

[1] For examples of attempts at organizing communal centers in the U.S., read V. F. Calverton's *Where Angels Dared To Tread*, N.Y.: Bobbs-Merrill 1941

purposeful, creative, constructive and deeply rewarding, provided
that economic solvency and psychological balance are preserved.

Economically the successes achieved in the working out of the
Vermont project far outweighed the failures. First and foremost,
our idea of a subsistence homestead economy proved easy of
realization. In exchange for a few months per year of carefully
planned bread labor, we were able to provide ourselves with the
bulk of our year's food. A few weeks of work furnished our house
fuel. Another few weeks provided the needed repairs and replacements on buildings, tools and equipment. Capital replacement of
housing (new stone buildings for old wooden ones) was a more
extensive task, involving considerable outlays of planning, time,
energy, persistence, materials and capital. Once a stone building
was in place, however, the yearly cost of repairs and replacements
fell almost to zero.

With this provision of necessaries went an unbelievable degree
of good health, which is a matter of primary importance to people
aiming at economic self-sufficiency on the one hand and social
reconstruction on the other. Literally, we were always well, and
on the rare occasions when the approaches of a cold appeared
temporarily to lower our vitality, we followed the accepted practice of the cats and dogs of the neighborhood, and stopped eating
until we felt fit. It is unnecessary for us to say that the difference
between good health and bad is the difference between the success and failure of almost any long-term human project.

Life's necessaries are easily come by if people are willing to
adjust their consumption to the quantity and variety of their
products. Difficulties begin when the subsistence advocate enters
the market with its lures and wiles for separating the unwary
and the dullwitted from their medium of exchange. Never forget
that from the private ownership of the means of production,

through the monopoly of natural resources and patents, the control over money, the imposition of the tribute called "interest", the gambling centers which trade in commodities and "securities", to price control and the domination by the wealthlords of the agencies which shape men's minds and the machinery of government, the entire apparatus of a competitive, acquisitive, exploitive, coercive social order is rigged and manipulated for the rich and the powerful and against the poor and the weak. Keep out of the system's clutches and you have a chance of subsistence, even if the oligarchs disapprove of what you think and say and do. Accept the system, with its implications and ramifications, and you become a helpless cog in an impersonal, implacable, merciless machine operated to make rich men richer and powerful men more powerful.

As a means of providing a subsistence household with the cash necessary to buy out the market, to shop from one end of a mail order catalog to another or to provide the family with endless comforts, conveniences, labor-saving gadgets, trinkets and habit-forming drugs, our project was a dismal failure. It could not compete with the big show in the big tent of western culture. But if treated as a venture in economic self-containment and an experiment in economy, frugality, self-discipline and day-to-day training for a new way of life, our project was a real success. In that respect, we dare say that during the twenty years we spent on our Vermont enterprise we learned more things and more important things than we could have found out during twenty years in Harvard, Columbia and the University of California all rolled into one.

Among the many questions which were asked us while in Vermont, perhaps the most crucial one was: "If you were back in 1932, but knowing what you know today, would you do the whole thing over again?" Our answer to that question in an emphatic affirmative: "Most certainly we would!" We consider the time and energy put into the adventure as well spent. We do not know how we would go about spending them to better advantage under the circumstances prevailing in the United States from 1932 to 1952. For us, the two Vermont decades were an exciting, engrossing, enlightening, rewarding twenty years, which we were glad to share with our Vermont neighbors and the ceaseless stream of relatives, friends, acquaintances and utter strangers who knocked at our door.

Our early years in the valley brought few visitors. We were only newly established, and our address was not known. As folk began to find us out and travel up the dirt road to our door, they met a welcome, but accommodations were limited. The Ellonen house was not built for company. We put up all over-nighters in the nearby schoolhouse, furnished with only bare necessities.

When building our new house we included a guesthouse in the plans. With this and the rented schoolhouse we could, and did, accommodate a large shifting population of visitors all summer long. The existence of this surplus housing had magical drawing power. Lone wanderers, and families with dogs, cats and baggage arrived from nowhere and kept the rooms occupied. The doors were never locked. Anyone was welcome to occupy the guesthouse, and no one ever paid for room or board. It was, as some friends dubbed it, a "free inn". Many a morning, at breakfast, a whole family would stroll into our kitchen, "Good morning, we slept in your guesthouse last night." Then they would sit down for breakfast.

Ah, there came the rub. Most of them were in for a shock. No coffee, no cereal, no bacon, no eggs, no toast, no pancakes or maple syrup. Just apples, and sunflower seeds, and a black molasses drink. Such a fare sent many a traveller on his way soon enough.

M. G. Kains, in his well-deserved best-seller, *Five Acres and Independence,* describes his experiences with itinerate visitors. "After they have taken up farming, many a city man and his wife—particularly his wife!—have run the gamut of emotions through all the descending scale of delight, gratification, pleasure, surprise, perplexity, annoyance, disgust and exasperation (a full octave!) to discover how popular they have become since moving to the country. Not only do their intimate friends drop in un-announced on fine Sundays, but less and less intimate ones even down to people who just happened to live around the block, arrive in auto loads and all expect to remain for dinner, perhaps supper also! . . . As you will probably have to solve the same problem, let me tell you the answer: For Sunday dinners have corned beef and cabbage, beef stew or hash! Good luck to you!"[2] They came to us all days of the week and we served them raw cauliflower and boiled wheat! However, there were those of our way of living and eating who said they had with us some of the best meals of their lives.

There was another fact which tempered the felicity of our easy hospitality. "The busy Man has few idle Visitors; to the boil-ing Pot the Flies come not." We had certain things to do every day and we aimed to do them, come who would. We went about our jobs as usual and let guests fend for themselves, or come and help, if they wished. We served no iced tea on the terrace while telling or listening to life histories. By some we were thought uncordial, but we did not aim to entertain.

We learned to distinguish the drone from the worker. There were those who were hammock-liers (although we provided no

[2] N.Y.: Greenberg 1942 p. 9

hammocks), out for a vacation and a good time. They never stayed long. Our mattresses were not foam-rubber nor our coffee Maxwell House. Then there were those good souls, forever under foot, who were willing to help but incapable or too feeble. We liked them, but had to leave them, and unless they had inner resources they too left soon. A few—a very few, took hold and really fitted into our life pattern. They usually were in demand somewhere else and could not stay long enough. They were welcome again and again.

From all our guests we asked a minimum of consideration for ourselves and others, which included cooperation on household maintenance. We came to hope for very little in the way of assistance with bread labor, and perhaps it was too much to ask of worn-out, frazzled city-dwellers on vacation. We also came to realize that we should warn people before they arrived, entertaining false notions concerning our forest farmhouse. And so we evolved a form letter which we sent to inquirers who wrote and asked if they could come and stay a few days, a week or a month and more. It ran something like this:

"We are a small family working out a way of living, and at the same time earning a living. Our accommodations are built for that purpose only and we do not conduct an inn or a sanatarium or a vacation center. We work at bread labor at least four hours a day, plus the short time needed to get our simple, vegetarian meals. We all follow this daily routine and expect those who happen to stay here for a time to fit in. Meat, tobacco and alcohol are taboo on the place. Our living is simple and austere; some would say hard and comfortless. If you are ever passing this way, you are welcome to stop in. We are always glad to see people of our way of thinking and living, and to share with them whatever we have, do, feel and think."

More than nine-tenths of the hundreds of visitors who stopped at Forest Farms went away with the oral remark or the mental note: "Its a nice way to live if you can take it. Maybe such a life pattern is alright for them, but preserve me from having to endure it for any length of time". They admitted that we ate more wholesomely, and cheaper, than they did; our health was far better than most; we were adequately clothed and comfortably housed; we had time for leisure in beautiful surroundings; but as for themselves, they could not or would not discipline themselves; nor go without the excitement, the rush, the glamour, the gadgets and the soporifics of civilization. If they had stayed, they would have had to face the fact that subsistence living allows only a narrow margin of purchasing power for new cash capital outlays. This is one of the most drastic limitations in a society which insists upon changing and replacing tawdry, temporary capital goods with each invention or discovery or each new advertising campaign.

There was another matter of great importance, especially to young couples. Our set-up contained no small children and did not have to take into consideration their support or higher education. We believe that small children could have been accommodated in the economic and social apparatus of our project, without too much rearrangement and reorganization. But we are sure that as set up, it would not have permitted a parent to send a child to an expensive private school or finance his way through a professional course such as medicine. Such enterprises are possible for the well-to-do in urban centers. They are out of reach of the subsistence homesteader unless scholarships or outside work are possible for the would-be student.

If it were the place in this book, we would glady argue out the entire educational question, especially in its technical and professional phases, which, in the past few years, have been taken over so largely by the United States military authorities. Suffice it here to note that it is a high hurdle for those who wish to fit their offspring to succeed in the get-ahead-grab-and-keep competition of contemporary North America.

Considered in terms of individual health and happiness, our project was an emphatic success. Viewed socially, however, even on its economic side, it left much to be desired. Our household group, for instance, was relatively small,—never more than four or five adults, with a stream of visitors from the outside world who did not stay for long. When it came to planning, therefore, we suffered from the absence of varied viewpoints and varied experience. In the execution of plans the group lacked emulation and the stimulus that accompanies friendly rivalry. It suffered from the absence of diverse skills of many individuals. It also suffered from its small numbers when it came to doing big jobs of construction, wood cutting and the like. On such big jobs, teams of experienced people, accustomed to working together, can run circles around small groups of amateurs.

In the absence of effective neighborhood cooperation, the small size of the group deprived us of an opportunity for specialization and division of labor and placed an undue burden of varied chores and tasks upon each participant in the experiment. When two or more of the tasks demanded attention at the same time, the result might well have been strain, tension and dissipation of energy to no constructive purpose. Had our group consisted of a dozen or a score of capable adults, animated by the same purposes and willing to follow out agreed plans, along lines of well-established practice, our standard of living could have been attained and maintained with far less expenditure of energy and labor time, leaving much more time and energy for leisure and avocational interests.

The social inadequacy of our Vermont project is characteristic of all rural America, where separatism and individualism have subdivided the community almost to the point of sterility. We have said that there were too few of us to be economically effective, even in a simple economy based chiefly on hand tool agriculture and hand crafts. The social or sociological inadequacy of our group was even more pronounced.

Had we been able to integrate fifteen or twenty families of the immediate neighborhood into a well-knit unit, based economically on cooperation and mutual aid and socially on the principles of live and help live, not "mine for me" but "ours for us", the resulting community still would have been woefully deficient in a variety of complementary skills, talents and social relationships.

For example,—there would not have been enough good voices to make up a choir, not enough passable musicians to man a local orchestra or enough actors to set up an effective dramatic troupe or dance team. Or, viewed from another angle, there would not have been enough babies to warrant the organization of a nursery school or kindergarten, nor would there have been enough six-year olders for a first grade or enough teen-agers to establish and maintain a reasonable balanced social group at that difficult, unbalanced age.

Had the community undertaken to set up a dramatic club, a kindergarten or a teen-age group, it would have been compelled to augment its members by bringing in outsiders who were either indifferent or hostile to the ideological standards and social purposes of the community. Once the inflow of outsiders began, it would have been a matter of time before the life of the community would have been diluted or disrupted by unfriendly outside influences. This is exactly what did happen in the community center.

Skinner, in his *Walden Two*,[3] correctly stated the minimum social requirements for an intentional commune,—(1) enough people to provide variety, diversity and specialization; (2) sufficient control over ingress and egress to preserve ideological purity, group identity and group purpose. Our valley in southern Vermont, like virtually all rural America, was lacking in these minimum requirements for a balanced, autonomous community existence.

In one sense Vermont offered less rather than more opportunity for collective experiments than most other parts of rural America. Vermonters were strong individualists; the percentage of home ownership and farm ownership was unusually high; the population was thin and widely scattered, and all the major Vermont traditions emphasized the individualism of the Green Mountain folk. Inhabitants of our valley, like other rural Americans, were organized in autonomous households. "Autonomous" is hardly the word. "Sovereign" would be a more exact descriptive term.

Vermont life was "free" in the sense that it placed before the individual and the household a wide range of choices. There was no set pattern. The State of Vermont was scarcely in evidence. During the entire twenty years of our sojourn we never saw a uniformed policeman pass along the dirt road in front of our house. Once a year the town listers assessed property, but their visits were brief and perfunctory. From day to day and year to year we did as we pleased. Aside from our own thinking and direction, our lives need not have been planned or patterned.

There was a degree of neighborhood pressure toward social

[3] B. F. Skinner, N. Y.: Macmillan 1948

conformity. Otherwise we were our own masters so long as we paid our taxes and obeyed traffic laws on the state highways. The only management or discipline to which we were subject was self-imposed. In fact, the word "discipline" was in such disrepute among the families in the valley, that its mention aroused sharp opposition.

With minor exceptions every household group in the valley owned land, buildings and tools in fee simple. Each household was, to that extent, economically self-contained. Each was socially self-regulating. In a word, each household was a law unto itself and was based upon a solid economic foundation,—a piece of the earth from which, at a pinch, it could dig its own livelihood. Only the tax collector, the truant officer and the recruiting sergeant could break into the domestic castles. In extreme cases, the police, the sheriff and the game warden could invade the premises, but only on complaint or suspicion of flagrant law violation. In such cases, law enforcement personnel went in groups and armed, since practically every rural Vermonter kept firearms and a stock of ammunition.

There is no positive force, in rural Vermont or in rural America, drawing communities together for well-defined social purposes. Churches, parent-teacher associations, farm unions, granges, farm bureaus, cooperatives and improvement associations cover specified fields, and perform particular functions. No one of these groups deal with general rural welfare, even to the extent that the service clubs in trading towns and small cities deal with general urban welfare.

Someone may suggest that general welfare is the business of government, under the constitutions of Vermont and the United States. To a degree that is true, and the New England town meeting plays such a role in a restricted sense. Outside of New

England and a few border states, however, the town meeting has not existed, and in New England its functions have been sharply circumscribed by its infrequent, formal meetings and by the organization of rural life into sovereign households, each with its economic base in land ownership and each with its arsenal prepared to defend its individualism to the death.

Atomism, separatism and consequent isolation have increasingly played havoc with rural life in the United States as the family has decreased in size while the household has shed some of its most essential functions. Meanwhile rural mail routes, mail order houses, travelling markets and salesmen have joined hands with rural telephone lines, rural electrification, school consolidation, radio and television, mass auto production and good roads to link the rural communities to urban markets and urban shopping and recreation centers. The resulting absence of group spirit and neighborhood discipline, the chaos and confusion of perpetual movement to and from work, to and from school, to and from the shows and the dances, has destroyed the remnants of rural solidarity and left a shattered, purposeless, functionless, ineffective, unworkable community.

Against this all-pervasive decline and dissolution of the fragile, tenuous structure of America's rural community life we attempted to make a stand in the Pikes Falls valley, in Vermont. Our chances of success were about equal to those of an Alpinist who throws himself against an avalanche.

We are not writing this by way of self defense or self justification. Rather we are attempting to explain and to understand the determined, stubborn resistance of Green Mountain dwellers, in and near our valley, to every attempt at community integration and collective action. Socially our experiment was a failure because the social set-up doomed such an experiment before it was born.

Were we aware of these facts when me moved to Vermont in 1932? Certainly. We knew the social history of the United States; we had heard the issues discussed a hundred times. We did not know the detail as we encountered it in our efforts to build a local community in a disintegrating society. But had we known all and more, we would have persevered, because the value of doing something does not lie in the ease or difficulty, the probability or improbability of its achievement, but in the vision, the plan, the determination and the perseverance, the effort and the struggle which go into the project. Life is enriched by aspiration and effort, rather than by acquisition and accumulation. Knowing this, and despite the odds against success, if we had it to do over again we would attempt the Vermont project in its social as well as in its economic aspects.

"Thus gentle Reader I have (I trust) fully satisfied thy desire in as many things as are needful to be knowne: wherefore I commit my little Booke to thy gentle judgement. If thou maist receive any profit or commodities thereby, I shalbe glad to it: and if not, yet favorably let it pass from thee to others, whose knowledge and experience is lesse than thine therein, that they may gather such things as to them are strange, though to thee well knowne before."

Thomas Hill, The Arte of Gardening, 1608

Continuing

THE GOOD LIFE

"I have written no more than I have seene, nor added a benefit which I have not knowne liberally bestowed upon the industrious; of which, if you will be a partaker, follow their imitation, and to good labours add a good life."

Gervase Markham, Farewell to Husbandry, *1620*

"Let not the Farmer expect Novelties in every Page; let him not wonder if he finds his every-day Practice plainly and concisely related. My Book is not designed to amuse but to instruct, being filled with Truth, not fancies. And Truth is so plain and obvious that in great Measure 'tis known to all in every Age."

John Laurence, A New System of Agriculture, *1726*

"Everything calculated to increase the comforts of the fireside will be found treated in our pages, in so plain and perspicacious a manner, that any individual may practise them without fear of a failure."

A Lady, The Cook's Complete Guide, *1827*

"The author offers no special theory, clothed in visions of fancy; his are the proceedings of a man, who, used to move in a respectable sphere, felt the reverses brought about by political causes, and who, as a true citizen of the world, sought the reinstatement of his former circumstances by seeking a place where his diminished means, his personal labour, and the resources of his mind could be actively employed."

Joseph Pickering, Inquiries of an Emigrant, *1832*

"Since I have given my attention to the cultivation of the soil, I find I have no competition to fear, have nothing to apprehend from the success of my neighbour, and owe no thanks for the purchase of my commodities. Possessing on my land all the necessaries of life, I am under no anxiety regarding my daily subsistence."

John Sillett, A New Practical System of Fork and Spade Husbandry, *1850*

"The case of one wholly inexperienced has been assumed in the present instance, and the information necessary to enable him to meet the different emergencies of the farm carefully yet succinctly given in the following pages, so as to form what it is hoped will be found a useful manual of husbandry on a small scale."

Martin Doyle, Small Farms, *1859*

"If he be by nature indolent, and in temper desponding, easily daunted by difficulties and of a weak frame of body, such a life would not suit him. If his wife be a weakly woman, destitute of mental energy, unable to bear up under the trials of life, she is not fit for a life of hardship—it will be useless cruelty to expose her to it."

C. P. Traill, The Canadian Settler's Guide, *1860*

HOMESTEADING AS A PRODUCTIVE AVOCATION

WE HAVE been experimenting for almost half a century with living a simple life: maintaining health and vigor with a minimum of effort and money and a maximum of satisfaction.

Living the Good Life, a book we originally published in 1954, was based on nineteen years of homesteading in Jamaica, Vermont, seven miles up a dirt road to Pikes Falls. Since 1952 we have been homesteading on another farm, along another dirt road, in Harborside, Maine, on Cape Rosier. This is a report on our Maine experiment and experiences.

Both in Jamaica and in Harborside we took over exhausted, derelict farms. During our time in Vermont the Pikes Falls back road was poorly graveled. At the start and for many years the Harborside-Cape Rosier road was of gravel and came to a dead end, the last of all town roads to be plowed in the snowy spring. Both farms were isolated and remote from towns.

Homesteading in Vermont and in Maine taught us many things about life in general and homesteading in particular. Both were part and parcel of one experience: building and maintaining a solvent family economy amid the wreckage and drift of a society that was disintegrating in accordance with the laws of its own self-destructive being.

209

In Harborside, as in Jamaica, we turned depleted farmland into good soil, enriching it to a point that made raising our own food possible and productive. Both farms eventually provided us with the food, fuel and shelter which are the minimum requirements of life in New England. At the outset in Vermont, the going was a bit rough because we were novices. By the time we reached Maine, we were sufficiently experienced and equipped to make the transition and the new start with a good deal of background.

In our off-seasons (the deep freeze and its approaches) in both homesteads, we busied ourselves by making essential improvements in our housing. Year by year we became better established, through our own efforts and those of friends and chance itinerant helpers.

At the same time we continued to take an active interest in our professions (Helen, in music; Scott, in social science). Both of us have traveled widely. Both have done a considerable amount of reading and study, and taught when and where opportunity offered. Our interests were and are wide and will continue so in the future. An old adage says that change of occupation is as good as a rest. We would say better than a rest, because the changes in our occupations have provided relaxation without any boredom.

One of our sophisticated city visitors asked us: "What do you do with your spare time?" "We have no spare time; we keep busy," was the answer. "As a matter of fact, the days are so short that we run out of time constantly." "But what do you do for pleasure?" our visitor persisted. "Anything and everything we do yields satisfaction. If we didn't enjoy it, we would do something else, or approach our jobs in a way that made more sense."

"Examine any one of our days," we continued to our inquirer, "or any one of the major activities in which we are engaged: food production and storage; the cutting of our wood for fuel;

gardening; building houses; forestry; research; teaching; music making; speaking; writing articles and books; traveling. Each one of these has its own particular advantages and opportunities. When it reaches a climax or leads to a conclusion, we say: That job is done to the best of our ability; now let's see what the next item on the program is and get on with the day's or week's or season's work."

Our lives are not loaded down with sterile repetition or barren routine. Each new project and each new day is a fresh challenge and an exploratory experience, unless we make some stupid blunder and are compelled to rip out the faulty construction and improve on it. If you identify the mistake and find out how and why it was made, you have the satisfaction of doing the job to the best of your ability and avoiding a like mistake in the future.

Does this sound mechanistic and self-satisfied? We don't mean it that way. If you tackle a job that is far beyond your experience and your energy, it may get you down and keep you down. But if you bite off no more than you can chew, and masticate it thoroughly, your chances of success are good.

There is a tendency nowadays to elbow a way through the mazes of a complicated life. Wisely and slowly is good advice. If you are running a relay race, it is not decided in the first few laps. Take your time. Ration your energies. Plan your operation carefully. Take one step at a time. Then prepare carefully for the next step. It pays in the long run.

Is this a repudiation of the Big Leap principle? Far from it. A single step is better than none at all. In a revolutionary situation a big leap may be the obvious and expedient answer for an individual or an entire group. A big leap at the wrong time, or in the wrong direction or with insufficient preparation or insufficient means, may set an individual or a movement back for a generation. With widely scattered forces and a minimum of experience, a step-by-step policy may well be the right tactic.

Actually, what we have been doing during these decades of experiment and construction is to meet a series of challenges, each in its own time and at its own level. Each challenge had its own peculiar character. Some of them dealt with our basic assumptions; others involved minor practical details. Each was interesting in its own way, and each when solved or resolved yielded its own measure of satisfaction. Each challenge met and mastered adds zest to the present moment. Each one opens up interesting prospects for the immediate and the more distant future.

Even at our advanced ages (both of us are far past the point of customary retirement), we have no desire to withdraw from life. On the contrary, we are eager and anxious to live. The past has been replete with zestful experiences. The present opens up interesting prospects for the future. Life for us has been rewarding, even in its details and minor incidents. We have every reason to suppose that it will continue to yield greater satisfactions as we grow wiser and more competent to deal with what the future has in store.

photo: *Richard Garrett*

"The breaking waves dashed high on a stern and rock-bound coast,
And the woods, against a stormy sky, their giant branches tossed....
The ocean-eagle soared from his nest by the white wave's foam,
And the rocking pines of the forest roared; this was their welcome home!"

Felicia Hemans, The Landing of the Pilgrim Fathers, 1830

"Bustle, bustle, clear the way, He moves, we move, they move today;
Pulling, hauling, father's calling, Mother's bawling, children squalling,
Coaxing, teasing, whimpering, prattling, Pots and pans and kettles rattling,
Tumbling bedsteads, flying bedspreads, Broken chairs, and hollow wares
Strew the street—'tis moving day.

Bustle, bustle, stir about, Some moving in—some moving out;
Some move by team, some move by hand, An annual collithumpian band.
Landlords dunning, tenants shunning; Laughing, crying, dancing, sighing—
Spiders dying, feathers flying, Shaking bed rugs, killing bed bugs,
Scampering rats, mewing cats, Whining dogs, grunting hogs,
What's the matter? Moving day!"

Peter Parley's Almanac for 1836

"Moving yet and never stopping, Pioneers! O Pioneers!"

Walt Whitman, Leaves of Grass, 1865

"O fortunate, O happy day,
When a new household takes its birth
And rolls on its harmonious way among the myriad homes of earth."

Henry Wadsworth Longfellow

CHAPTER 1

WE MOVE, BAG AND BAGGAGE, TO MAINE

WE HAD built up our good life in Vermont, improving the soil, clearing out and enlarging the sugar orchard, replacing wooden shacks with concrete and stone buildings, reconstructing the roads and generally converting a sickly, bankrupt farm into a vigorous, healthy enterprise that was paying its own way and more. Several of the friends and visitors who stopped in to see us said quite early: "You have something going here which is very special. When you want to sell the place, let us know before you put it on the market."

We thanked our prospective buyers for the compliment they were paying us, but assured them that we had put much thought, time and energy into the construction and furnishing of our Forest Farm homestead, and selling out was the last item on our list of priorities.

We were overlooking one of the most implacable taskmasters that dog the steps of mankind: the effect of change. We were juvenile and soft-headed enough to believe that we were settled in Pikes Falls, Vermont, forever. We were wrong. There, as elsewhere, change ruled the roost.

We lived at the foot of Stratton Mountain. Like the other Green Mountains of Vermont at that time, Stratton was covered from foot to peak by a forest of evergreen and deciduous trees. Its 24,000 acres were owned by paper interests who had bought up the mountain and were holding it as a forest reserve. The village of Stratton, a one-time prosperous farming community, had been reduced to a few scattered families. Stratton roads had been neglected or abandoned. Once-productive fields had been taken over by a thriving forest with half a century of untended growth. Neighbors in our valley called the place "the wilderness." It provided them with a source of a few random Christmas trees, balsam fir for wreaths and successive crops of ferns which were picked and sold to florists in Boston and more distant cities.

Across the town road that separated our farm from our neighbors to the south, the land sloped upward toward Stratton Mountain, cutting off the sunlight on short winter days by half-past three in the afternoon. North and east of us, lesser mountains, mostly forested but denuded of big timber, stretched for miles along the banks of the West River.

After we had lived in Vermont for about fifteen years, the paper interests started to cut the forest in preparation for developers who planned a new life for Stratton. Clearings were to be made on the north, east and west slopes. Roads were to be constructed and paved. Almost overnight the Stratton wilderness disappeared. Its place was to be taken by the Stratton ski slopes—one of the largest and best-advertised ski developments on the East Coast.

Our Forest Farm nest became less and less desirable to us as these plans of the ski promoters took shape. The Pikes Falls of the early 1930's was to be swallowed up by the forces centering around a ski-town type of life.

The whole tempo of the valley was changing. Our once-isolated farm had become too available to outsiders from the New York City area and Boston. Countless visitors dropped by, and others moved in. These people were less austere and hard-

working than those we had lived with. They were more
interested in having a "good time" than they were in hard work.
They were vacationers at heart, not workers. The outside world
became too much with us. Our seclusion was gone.

Other local circumstances also led us to consider a move from
the valley where we had thought we were settled for life. When
we came in 1932, we settled down quietly among people who
had farmed there for generations. There was little community
life, though there was occasional help among neighbors. There
were certainly local feuds. By and large it was a stable grouping
of families who worked for a living on their own land.

The war changed things. Some of the older folk went to work
in war plants; some of the younger were conscripted. Quite a
number of conscientious objectors refused to become killers and
moved up to our valley. They talked about a good life, about a
living from the land, about arts and crafts and even about hard
work. We saw the possible dawning of an economic basis for
cooperative living. A wholesome, rewarding community life
might be built up, we hoped. We endeavored to do our part, on
our own place and in the neighborhood.

After war's end, in 1946, there came a change locally. People
let down, lowered their ideals, got back to normal. They took
things easier, gossiped, feuded again. The talk of community
died down. There were cliques and little cooperation. People
wanted freedom at all levels—freedom from work, from
discipline, from community responsibility. They were out for a
good time, for fun, for plenty of leisure to gad about.

Community enterprise, such as it was, in the valley became
largely centered around dances and beer parties. There was no
community economic enterprise and little social enterprise.
People wanted to escape thoughts of wars past and impending.
We were told in so many words: "We don't want to hear
anything about politics. We want you just as neighbors. Come to

the dances." Or, "Come to see us. Pay us a social visit. Have some small talk." And, "Beer promotes good fellowship."

In almost every newcomer's house in the valley, dancing and liquored parties were the social enjoyment of the young people. To what purpose? We felt that life was earnest, that it was an opportunity to learn, to serve, to build truth, beauty, justice into the world. If this were not so, dances, gossip-bees and beer parties might be in order, because then life would be futile and meaningless and any form of escape would be preferable to boredom.

To us, life was real, vital, urgent, important. There were many things that needed doing. We preferred to spend our time and energy in places and among people who were similarly concerned and who were prepared to discipline themselves and organize community affairs in such fashion that the issues of the day were met and the difficulties surmounted. In any case we were not happy in surroundings that were becoming a center for trivial activities and purposeless living.

The straw that really broke the camel's back and made us decide to leave Vermont and seek more isolation elsewhere was an episode that brought a group of seventeen uninvited, unknown visitors. They turned up one working day and trooped into our kitchen on a morning when we were boiling maple syrup into sugar on the stove for a rush order. The people were inoffensive enough—sightseers enjoying an off day in the backwoods observing the natives. For them it was an escape from the treadmill of urban existence. Time hung heavy on their hands, and they were killing time.

"What a lovely house! And you did it all yourselves!" they exclaimed. "And is that how you make maple sugar?" "We want to see the sugar bush." "Do tell us something of your lives." "How did you ever find this place?"

We had chores to do and deadlines to meet. We shooed them

upstairs to look at the view from the balcony. After they had gone, Scott burst out to Helen: "This is becoming impossible! How can we get our work done if we are interrupted every twenty minutes by a new bevy of sightseers? We'll have to move!"

Up to this point Helen had borne the chief burden of dealing with such casual drop-ins. She had greeted them and engaged in the necessary conversation. Scott had stayed in his rock-walled study on the big boulder behind the house. Then she began sharing the burdens of tourism, saying to visitors: "Scott is out in his study on the big rock; why not climb the steps and see what he is up to?" Helen's system brought the expected reaction from Scott. We began to think seriously of moving.

When the facts are set down on paper, they seem inoffensive enough. What if a couple of dozen outsiders a week did upset our routine and seventeen or so descended on us one morning? We could put aside our work for the time being and indulge in conversation, sometimes desultory and sometimes very worth while, with a group or two. But the days had passed into weeks and months of it. All summer long, visitors came and went, until both of us agreed that Pikes Falls, Vermont, had become an impossible place for us and our projects and program.

Where to go? When? And how to go about the search for a continuation of our chosen version of the good life? Where should we find another farm as isolated, as productive and as beautiful as our Vermont Forest Farm?

Our requirements were: isolation enough to avoid the hustling and jostling of the city and its suburbs; a minimum of fertile soil on which to grow our food; abundant fresh water; a woodlot to provide our fuel. And this time, instead of in the mountains, we could look for a place on the water. For nineteen years we had homesteaded in the Green Mountains of Vermont. Now, as we pictured our future, why not spend the next twenty years beside the sea? Both of us enjoyed the hills; both of us were equally attracted by large bodies of water.

We had traveled enough to be able to say that we had seen the world. Where should we go? We agreed in avoiding the Arctic and Antarctica. We agreed in avoiding the tropics and semitropics. With the Arctic and the tropics out of bounds for us, where should we turn? To the temperate zone, of course, but on what spot, on which continent? Europe perhaps? Helen loved her mother's land of Holland and we both had enjoyed time spent in Austria's Tirol, but Europe was crowded, and there was the language difficulty. Everything considered, we decided to stay in the United States where we were born. We would try to find another farm in New England, where we had spent the last twenty years under conditions that were satisfactory to both of us.

One important factor in making our decision was that we could afford to live in New England, particularly in its more remote areas, where land was still available at a reasonable price.

New England has another advantage—its climate. We enjoy the change of seasons and relish each one with its infinite variety. Autumn we appreciate the most, with its crisp weather, the leaves' deep coloring and the absence of bugs. The deep freeze of winter months compels a substantial change of occupation, enabling us to follow our professional and avocational interests.

New England also has geological advantages of considerable importance. Between its minor river valleys, it consists of a succession of secondary mountain outcrops that divide the landmass into relatively small areas of well-drained soil and considerably larger areas of rugged slopes that make open cultivation difficult and emphasize the usefulness of hill pastures. Such broken landmasses lend themselves to the homesteading that has played so significant a role in New England's history.

In making our choice of a New England homesite for a second time, we decided to follow the example of a widely publicized Maine citizen, Henry Gross, and use a dowsing rod to find our future farm. At all times in human memory, as set down in folklore and written records, there have been people with the usual five senses plus a sixth or perhaps a seventh or eighth sense which reports the existence of underground water and even indicates its distance from the surface and the volume of its flow. Water diviners sense vibrations more diverse than those reported by the five senses. Helen is one of these people. When we were looking for water on two farms in Vermont, she had been able to detect its presence.

One day we had run across a book, *Henry Gross and His Dowsing Rod,* written by Kenneth Roberts (Garden City: Doubleday, 1951). Henry Gross, besides finding water for his friends and neighbors, had, while still in Maine, taken a map of Bermuda, and, following Kenneth Roberts' directions, secured fresh water in an area where no water had been known to exist. We decided to use the same technique for finding a farm by the waterside.

Taking a detailed map of Maine, Helen went back and forth, fixing her mind on the kind of place that we wanted and asking the pendulum to indicate that place. Consistently the pendulum circled the Penobscot area, at the head of the bay.

We set aside a week, crossed the 350 miles that separated Jamaica, Vermont, from Penobscot Bay, Maine, and began our search by visiting two organic gardeners who lived very close to the point on the map indicated by Helen's pendulum.

Our organic gardener friends received us hospitably but could not think of any parcel of land that met our specifications. We had supper, stayed the night and in the morning continued our search along the tortuous Maine coastline up toward Canada.

We visited real-estate offices, inspected properties. We even took a boat and looked over land on an island.

We spent five days in the search with no tangible results. On the sixth day we headed back toward Vermont. On the way we passed close to the farm operated by our two organic gardener friends. It was getting on toward evening and we were still far from our Vermont Forest Farm. We stopped once more at their David's Folly farm. They welcomed us cordially and asked what luck we'd had in finding the place we wanted. We told them glumly that we had had no luck at all, had given up the search for the moment and were returning empty-handed to Vermont.

"We've been thinking again of the kind of place you want: a fertile farm, isolation and on the water. We think we know just the place for you, but we don't know if it is still on the market." We contacted the owner, Mary Stackhouse, and yes, the place was still for sale. She had found it too lonely for one woman to live way out on the point of Cape Rosier, and on her desk at that moment was an ad she was sending to the *Boston Globe* in an effort to sell the place right away.

We lost no time the next morning in driving down the miles of narrow dirt roads that led to the Cape. The farm in question was overgrown and neglected, with the meadows in poor condition. On one side of the house the soil was predominantly clay, on the other side sandy loam. There was a bubbling spring on the edge of the woods that ran by gravity into the kitchen. That was a great find. Helen went into the house for a few minutes and satisfied herself that it was sunny and roomy.

The farm was certainly isolated, down on a dead-end road with no near neighbors. It was on a lovely little westward-facing cove of its own. The land could be brought back to good tilth. There was good water. In fifteen minutes the decision to buy was made.

These events took place in the fall of 1951. We were already in contact with a hardware salesman from Hartford, Connecticut, who was eager to buy our maple farm and expected to operate the sugar bush as his source of cash income. We arranged to work with him and his wife and show them the ropes of sugaring during the coming 1952 sap season.

During the late winter of 1951 and early spring of 1952, our pickup truck and a friend's ton vehicle made several trips moving our belongings over the long miles that separated Pikes Falls, Vermont, from Harborside, Maine.

In the spring of 1952 we finished out our last sap season. With keen regret we turned our backs on the most enjoyable work we had ever done in Vermont: tapping maple trees, boiling down the sap and making sugar and syrup from the hard maples that studded our Forest Farm. We were also sorry to leave our sturdy, attractive stone buildings that had been such a pleasure to build and to live in. The hills also we had to leave behind, and a few choice friends with whom we had found much in common.

As the snow melted in the late spring, and planting time beckoned to us, we went up to work over the new-plowed land that was to be our Maine garden for the next quarter-century.

"Now, welcome, somer, with thy sonne softe, That hast this wintres weders overshake."

Chaucer, The Parliament of Fowls, *1380*

"What can your eye desire to see, your ears to hear, your mouth to take, or your nose to smell that is not to be had in a garden?"

William Lawson, A New Orchard and Garden, *1618*

"Spring is the most busy and hurrying season of any in the year."

Samuel Deane, in The New England Farmer, *1790*

"In March it is time for winter to depart, but he may be compared to a crocodile, who, having paid you a visit and staid as long as he ought, pretends to go away; but while he puts his head and body out of doors, leaves his huge tail writhing, bending and brandishing behind. Thus, during March, winter's tail is left to annoy us with squalls, gusts, tempests, rain, hail, snow. There often seems to be a strife between the seasons, spring and winter alternately getting the ascendancy. But, after a while, the latter finds his icicles melting away, and to avoid being reduced to a stream of water, he slowly retreats, first to New England, lingering along the Green Mountains, till pursued by the Genius of Flowers, he goes across Hudson's Bay and hides himself behind the hills of Greenland, till he can venture out again with safety."

Peter Parley's Almanac *for 1836*

"Winter having passed away, the time for labor and the singing of birds again returned....It was now the season for me to bustle about, fix up my land, and get in my crops....All my visitors from the city were surprised to see the garden so free from weeds, while they did not fail to notice that most of the vegetables were extremely thrifty. They did not know that in gardens where the weeds thrive undisturbed, the vegetables never do. As to the neighbors, they came in occasionally to see what the women were doing, but shook their heads when they saw they were merely hoeing up weeds. They said that weeds did no harm, and they might as well attempt to kill all the flies. They had been brought up among weeds, knew all about them, and it was no use trying to get rid of them."

Anonymous, Ten Acres Enough, *1864*

"Warm summer sun, shine friendly here;
Warm western wind, blow kindly here."

Richard Richardson, "To Annette," *1890*

CHAPTER 2

SPRING AND SUMMER GARDENING

POETS think of spring as the season of showers and flowers. "It is not raining rain to me, it's raining violets." For us in Vermont, spring had meant the delightful task of sugaring. Now we were to adapt to a new kind of season.

In Maine, spring begins with the disappearance of ice and snow in the first real thaw, which may not come till April. Up to that time, zero and sub-zero temperatures may hold the earth in their iron grip for weeks or months on end. But the sun is moving northward and with the lengthening days temperatures climb steadily. Spring is in the air. Spring sunshine alternates with April showers. Sunshine warms the air. Showers melt the snow.

Our first Maine spring was unusually warm. Ice and snow disappeared. We had had the newly marked-out garden site plowed and harrowed the previous fall—for the first and last time. (Since then we have done all cultivation with hand tools.) We had covered the upturned soil with a heavy mulch of hay which we took off in the spring.

As soon as the ground dried out, we spread compost (brought from Vermont in old sap buckets) and worked it lightly into the soil. Day after day the dry weather provided conditions

seemingly ideal for planting. We began with onion sets, radish
seed, mustard, early lettuce, beets and carrots. In preparing our
soil for planting, we had added a protein meal of our own
contriving: soybean meal, cottonseed meal, sifted wood ashes,
screened peat moss, pulverized phosphate rock and granite dust.

Still the good weather held. We put in our early peas. To our
surprise, the next day some of the pea seeds were on top of the
ground. We poked them back under. Days passed; the soil grew
more dry; nothing much came up. One day our onion sets,
planted more than an inch underground, began to appear, lying
on the surface of the rows in which they had been planted. That
told the story. They had been dug up. No animal that we knew
ate onion sets. Birds had obviously scratched through the
planted land looking for particles of soybean meal, to which
they are very partial. The soil, reduced almost to dust by the dry
weather, was easily scratched away by even the smaller birds,
who tossed peas and onions aside in their search for soybean
fragments or for seeds.

By the time the first showers came, wetting the soil and
helping the seeds to germinate, our carefully planted rows had
disappeared. Germinating seeds were scattered over the entire
garden patch, hither and thither. The bird population in its
scratching frenzy had reduced our carefully laid-out truck garden
to a shambles. We refertilized (without the soybean meal),
reworked and replanted the entire area.

Since that enlightening disaster we have been careful about
early planting whenever the topsoil begins to dry out.
Fortunately, parched earth early in the New England spring is a
rarity. It can happen, however, and when it does occur it will
bear watching.

Whether or not you are starting from scratch (as we did in
more ways than one in this first Maine garden) in your quest for
gardening experience, there are several things that you should
do with a piece of ground that you plan to cultivate. It must be

cleared and drained, the sod broken up, the ground so fertilized that the balance between nitrogen, phosphorus, potash and more than a dozen other soil elements has been established and can be maintained.

It might be well on new land to visit the county agricultural agent, consult his soil maps and have the soil on your proposed garden spot tested. It will cost little or nothing and will give you a good start on your garden. The county agent will make general suggestions which should be followed until your own experience enables you to take over and make your own decisions.

Then you must work the soil. Working the soil in this sense means sifting it, breaking up big lumps, refining it to the point at which each rootlet on the growing plants can readily secure a correctly balanced ration that will enable it to go on growing. If the chemical balance and the texture of the soil are correct; if light, sunshine and moisture are adequate; if temperatures are in the proper range, your seeds should germinate and your plants should grow, flower and bear fruit. The health, vitality and growth of the vegetation in a particular row of plants depends partly upon the variety of the seed or transplant put into the newly prepared topsoil, but mainly on the balance of the fertilizers.

There is a saying that there is nothing sure in life except death and taxes. We would like to add some other certainties. (1) With almost infallible accuracy a beet seed will produce a beet and the onion seed an onion. (2) If you get the right combination of warmth and moisture, seeds will germinate. A botanist can set down—with almost mathematical accuracy in a sequence of stages—the indescribable drive, push and persistence of sprouting seeds. (3) If the soil in which the seeds are lying is properly provided with a balanced ration of nitrogen, phosphorus, potash and the necessary trace elements, the result will be growth, flowering and fruiting.

Our organic garden is fertilized largely by humus from

compost piles of our own making. We have more than a dozen such piles at various stages of maturity, with several tons of compost in all. In Chapter 6 we will describe the process that provides us with the great bulk of the fertilizer we use in growing all our crops.

Significantly enough, the forest does this job for itself. It is a simple process that proceeds uninterruptedly twenty-four hours each day, from season to season, from year to year, from century to century. Leaves, twigs, branches and sometimes entire trees are shaken loose by rain, wind, frost and snow. They fall to the forest floor and lie layer above layer, enriched by animal droppings, sometimes by the bodies of birds and other animals. In reforesting areas of New England, barring fires which reduce the soil cover to ashes, the soil of an undisturbed forest builds up an inch in about three centuries. The process is slow, but as the volume of humus available for its own further growth increases, it pulls itself up by its own bootstraps.

The gardener must do much the same thing for his plants. With planning and direction, making topsoil ceases to be a process and becomes a policy, with limits set by available materials. Each crop, each day, each growing season, the competent gardener deepens and enriches his topsoil. The forest makes its own compost through centuries; we gardeners can make excellent compost in a few weeks.

Long-extended New England springtime, with its misty days and frosty nights, provides a period of ten or a dozen weeks, from late February into early May, with sufficient daylight and sunshine to encourage hardy greens to push their growing centers farther above the earth without danger of frost damage. Our last possible killing frost hit our Vermont gardens in mid-June. It hit our Maine garden only in late May. By June no more serious frosts were to be expected. We could work over our soil, add our compost and other fertilizers, work them thoroughly into the soil and plant the bulk of our summer garden crops, which comprise corn, beans, squashes, cucumbers and tomatoes.

The general layout of the garden necessitates keeping beds for permanent items such as asparagus, rhubarb, berries and perennial herbs in set areas. Otherwise, the entire garden should be systematically rotated so that the same crop does not get back into the same spot without an interval of at least one growing season.

Generally, in laying out a garden, low-growing plants such as spinach, lettuce, carrots and onions are grouped together. Similar groups are made of tall crops such as pole beans, sweet corn, staked tomatoes and brushed peas.

If the rows or beds of the garden run north and south, rather than east-west, a maximum of direct sunlight will get to the roots of the seedbeds or to the roots of plants in the crucial period of their early growth.

The spring-summer garden is not left to chance. We have a loose-leaf notebook in which we keep current and past records of the garden: row by row, bed by bed or section by section for each year. This includes date of plantings, varieties planted and results for the season. The pages for each year are on file so that we know, from year to year, what crops have been planted and harvested in particular parts of the garden.

Each row or bed is numbered as part of the overall garden plan for the current year, with rotation of crops kept strictly in mind. For records of garden developments, garden rows or beds may be marked with numbered stakes. We make our row- and bed-marking stakes of cedar. They are sixteen inches tall, pointed with a hatchet and numbered with a blue or black lumber pencil.

For family-scale gardening, a few tools only are necessary. Any garden of less than a quarter of an acre (100 x 100 feet) can be worked with a shovel or spade, a hoe, rake and garden string, a supply of marking stakes, a hatchet and a watering can. Our favorite garden tool is a Planet Junior hand cultivator. We are not sure this is still on the market, but some form of hand-pushed cultivator is available and very useful.

Success in spring and summer gardening depends on getting seeds into the earth with a moderate soil cover of at least a quarter of an inch, and keeping them in the soil while they germinate; they must then get roots down and their stems or leaves through the soil surface as speedily as possible. Once this growth process is begun, it should go on unchecked, steadily and rapidly, as the plant builds itself into a self-generating part of the life process.

It goes without saying that, other things being equal, the more fertile the soil the more rapid and more extensive the growth of the plants being fertilized. Of course there is an optimum level beyond which increased amounts of fertilizer do not result in increased quantity and quality of produce. One time when we sent in samples of our garden soil to be analyzed by the experts at the University of Maine in Orono, the reply came back: too rich; cut down on your compost spreading.

Many seed houses print on their seed packets a normal life span for each plant. Oak Leaf or Simpson lettuce, for example, should take forty-five days from planting to maturity. Extra fertility may alter this life span or it may not. The gardener who seeks the best and the most in product must experiment in order to determine the possibilities in any particular case. Generally, if the gardener can afford the outlay, extra fertility pays off in both quality and quantity.

Gardens may be planted in rows or beds. They may also be broadcast. Our preference is for rows in general and beds in particular cases. Tall-growing plants such as pole beans are grown on poles or trellises. In these hurry-up days, gardeners tend to plant dwarf or hill crops and avoid trellises, which are more trouble and take time to set up. We may be in a minority, but we are using more trellises and longer poles.

Years ago we decided to bypass bush beans. It is so easy to put in a row of bush beans and so much more effort to get the poles, place them and do the planting around each pole. Nevertheless, we are convinced that, per square yard of soil, the crop yield on poles is much greater than on bushes.

Thirty inches between rows had been most satisfactory for bush beans. With poles, we began with 3 feet between the rows. With 8-foot poles, 4-foot spacing kept the developing vines largely in shadow. We tried 52 inches between the rows of poles. Today we are inclined to make the distance 5 feet, with the poles 5 feet apart in the rows.

Given good growing weather, pole beans reach the top of an 8-foot pole quite early in the season, then continue to put out vines, flowers and additional beans. We asked ourselves what would happen if the poles were 12 feet instead of 8 feet in height. Experience has convinced us that the average pole bean in an average season will cover a 12-foot pole with foliage, producing both flowers and mature beans all the way up. Today we are experimenting with even taller poles, hoping to get more beans per pole, as we have heretofore.

If the beans are to be picked and eaten green, additional pole height is questionable. One would need a stepladder from which to pick. But if the beans are to be matured and allowed to dry on the poles, there is no picking until the first frost. The bean plants can be uprooted when frost threatens. The vines are left on the pole; the bean pods dry out and are easy to shell.

There is a tendency nowadays to grow dwarf peas. We have compared them with high-growing "telephone" varieties. In our experience the tall-growing peas are superior in both flavor and volume of yield to the dwarf version. Certainly the picking season is longer on the tall peas. Until a tall pea vine is blighted or uprooted, and so long as it continues to flower, it will bear edible peas.

Those who grow tall telephone peas tend to put them on galvanized wire fences. As the sun gets higher, the wire gets hot and stays hot so long as the sun shines. The delicate pea vines like cool weather and resent being burned. Under these conditions we have elected to grow 5- to 6-foot telephone-type peas and to grow them on brush from our own woods.

As we go about our forestry and trim or cut trees, we take a look at each trimmed-off branch. If it is flat and fan-shaped, we lay it in a special brush pile. Periodically, we go over this brush, pick out the likeliest limbs, trim them when necessary, point them with a hatchet and store them off the ground on our pea brush rack. Some of our pea brush is 10 feet high, and the pea vines have often climbed up to the very top.

When our young peas are 4 or 6 inches high, we make holes in the soil with a bar, push the brush into the holes and tap them lightly with the bar. When the whole row is brushed, we take a wheelbarrow of rooted sod and pack it around the pea brush. This steadies them against high winds and provides the peas with a mulch.

At the end of the pea season we sort out the pea brush and put the best on a rack, where it stays until the next pea season. The rejected brush is kept until a dry, hot day, sawed with a pruning saw into 16-inch lengths, packed in paper cartons and stored in the woodshed. It makes excellent faggots for kindling fires.

Early in our gardening experience we learned that fast-growing weeds will often overshadow or crowd out the plants chosen by the gardener to occupy a given row or bed. If weeds get a good start, the future of the garden may be at stake. We know that a current theory is to let everything grow and pick out the edible plants when the time comes. We have never followed this practice.

There are three ways to deal with weeds. One preventive, which we have never practiced, is to lay down building paper and cut a hole where a selected plant is wanted. Another is to go over the bed and pick out every perennial weed by hand. What we do is to hand-cultivate lightly after every wetting, from rain to irrigation. If the cultivation is done carefully, the soil surface will be broken except in the planted rows and germinating weed seeds uprooted. This is a form of early birth control. Periodically the gardener can work out each row, thinning where necessary and removing any weed that has found its way into the seed row. Our vegetable garden covers about a quarter of an acre. If this area is gone over periodically, especially after each wetting, the possibility of weed growth is reduced to a minimum.

Incidental to cultivation, but of vital concern to garden growth, is the practice of side-dressing or mulching. A row or bed of lettuce, for instance, is coming close to maturity. It has grown steadily and well through its entire life cycle. Before cultivation or watering, a light dressing of compost spread close to the lettuce plants and worked in by the hand cultivator can provide the stimulation needed to convert excellent lettuce heads into superb specimens. Side-dressing is not a necessity; the crop in question may be doing very well, but an additional bit of attention may cover the slight spread that separates good from better to best.

Mulch is a layer of litter scattered over a piece of land to prevent the growth of unwanted plants, to check evaporation, to keep the soil cool in warm weather and warm in cold weather, to filter sunshine and modify its extremes. Any light loose material may be used as a mulch. We used branches, seaweed, hay, straw, autumn leaves or other litter. In dry weather a dust mulch checks evaporation. In cold weather a dust mulch protects against undue freezing.

Sunshine and fresh, clean air are essentials of most plant growth. A third essential is water. Plants share with animals this common feature: a large part of their bulk consists of water. Young plants and new transplants are peculiarly dependent on an adequate water supply. Gardens that depend on artificial irrigation perish when the water supply is cut off. Plant growth can be retarded by an undersupply or an oversupply of water.

New England gets enough rain and snow to provide an annual precipitation of about 45 inches. Fortunately, this is moderately well distributed through the average year. To be sure, there are dry periods and wet ones, dry years and wet years, but through more than four decades of New England gardening we have never had a general failure of crops due to too much or too little moisture.

photo: Ralph T. Gardner

"Nothing can be more abounding in usefulness or more attractive in appearance than a well-tilled farm."

Cicero, De Senectute, 45 B.C.

"He certainly is worthy great Praise and Honour, who, possessing a large and barren Demesne, constrains it, by his Industry and Labour, to produce extra ordinary Plenty, not only to his own Profit, but that of the Public also."

Sir Richard Weston, in New England Magazine, no. 3, 1759

"In our present imperfect condition, a beneficent Providence has not reserved a moderate success in Agriculture exclusively to the exercise of a high degree of intelligence. His laws have been so kindly framed, that the hand even of uninstructed toil may receive some requital in remunerating harvests; while their utmost fulness can be anticipated only where corporeal efforts are directed by the highest intelligence."

R. L. Allen, The American Farm Book, 1849

"O suns and skies and clouds of June,
And flowers of June together,
Ye cannot rival for one hour
October's bright blue weather."

Helen Hunt Jackson, Verses, 1884

"Such Gardens are not made by singing "Oh, how beautiful!" and sitting in the shade."

Rudyard Kipling, The Glory of the Garden, 1911

"A garden is a work of Art using the materials of Nature."

Anonymous

"The leaves fall early this autumn, in wind. The paired butterflies are already yellow with August."

Ezra Pound, A Letter

CHAPTER 3

THE FALL GARDEN

IN OUR part of New England, the general gardening practice is
to start planting on Decoration Day, which is late in May. Hardy
things are planted first, followed weeks later by the more
perishable crops. This sequence carries the garden to mid-
summer, when planting usually stops. Gardening is considered
ended for the year in August, except for harvesting. When this
is over the land is left fallow, or cover crops are put in or weeds
accumulate. Major gardening is considered over till the next
spring.

Our practice is quite different. It closely approaches the
Japanese way of gardening. Their land is so circumscribed that
they must economize drastically on space. When they take out a
radish, they replant a lettuce or other seed in the vacated spot.
When we take out any section of a bed or row, we do almost the
same as the Japanese until well into September. We plant in the
spring; we plant in the summer; we plant in the fall. As
planting space is opened up by harvesting early summer greens
and roots, we immediately put in some other crop that can be
planted late and will mature before or during light freezing.

Fall days with us are sunny and crisp, closely approximating the days of early spring in temperature. So we plant in the late summer and early fall the same type of vegetable that flourished in the spring and that again will have time to ripen in the fall: radish, lettuce, chard, mustard, spinach, collards, early cabbage for greens. Even carrots when planted late will mature in the fall into little "finger" delicacies. All of the items we have mentioned thus far are frost hardy. Most of them will live and thrive with night temperatures as low as 18 or 20 degrees Fahrenheit. Some of the seeds will lie dormant and fail to germinate; some will break ground and be frozen out. Many will sprout and grow. The results of fall planting have been well worth the effort, time and our small expense for the experimental seeds.

This means that in September and October, when most other gardens are empty or weed-choked, our garden is full of up-and-coming greens. The fall garden can be almost as green as the spring and summer garden. The Decoration Day to Labor Day gardener does not expect this to happen. Visitors to our fall garden often remark on the amount of vegetables still in the ground. Members of a local Garden Club visited our place one day late in September. There was hardly a square foot of garden space empty. They exclaimed: "Your garden is as green as it was in June. It looks like spring, and we are almost in October. How do you do it?" Our answer is simple: continue planting.

Early in the summer, when the first mustard greens, lettuce, spinach and bunch onions are moving from the garden to the kitchen table, we are busy replacing them with root crops such as turnips and beets, which in turn will give way to young greens for fall use. At the same time in the early fall that hardy greens are going into the ground as seeds, it is possible to transplant main-crop lettuce, endive, Chinese cabbage and celery plants from seed flats to the garden beds. Following this system, the fall vegetable garden can supply fresh greens and roots a couple of months after early frosts will have wiped out squash, beans and tomato vines, ending the spring and summer garden.

Foresight and a few seasons of experience will tell the gardener what to expect and when to make the necessary shift of crops coming out and crops going in. Here is an example:

Early smooth peas are harvested and eaten and the vines are ready to be pulled out of the ground early in July. We replace them immediately by the earliest stages of the fall garden. Even though there are still edible green peas and even pea blossoms on the vines, we agree that the occupied space could be more profitably used. We decide on the day that they should come out.

Instead of the ordinary routine of picking individual peas, we pull out the plants, strip them of all pods and divide them into three containers: the over-mature peas to be dried and stored for winter use; the ripe peas that can go into the day's soup; and the few remaining young peas and green pods that can be put raw in the day's salad.

While this operation is in progress, a member of the garden squad, equipped with a light mattock, loosens the soil where the pea vines were and pulls out any chance weeds. Another member of the garden squad follows with a fork, puts weeds and dried vines into a wheelbarrow and moves them to the compost area, returning with enough compost to put an inch on the area from which the peas and weeds have been removed. A hand cultivator works the compost and a sprinkling of nitrogen meal into the former pea row.

The next operation, with a single-pointed hoe attached to the cultivator, opens a trench along the erstwhile pea row. We sow spinach or some other short-term hardy crop into the row that had been occupied by peas a few hours before.

This operation moves smoothly and is soon completed. All members of the team, whether two or ten, understand what is going on; all approve of it in principle though they may differ as to detail. But if the pea season is to be brought to a close and replaced by spinach or some other short crop, the sooner the peas are out the better. The summer garden has left the area and the fall garden has entered it in less than four hours of a single morning.

Similar operations, repeated as each row is removed, mark the end of the summer garden and its replacement by the fall garden, row by row, with not much loss of time and few unproductive motions.

The fall garden, in terms of its preparation, includes part of July and all of August. In terms of harvesting, it begins in the early autumn and extends through two or three months until night frosts are sufficiently severe to check or even prevent effective growth.

Celery and parsley and spinach will survive moderate freezing in the garden. Broccoli, cauliflower, Chinese cabbage and the hardier western cabbages will take hard freezing. Let them thaw out in the ground on their own roots and then harvest them. If cut for the kitchen while frozen, they will be flabby. If the outside leaves of cabbage or Chinese cabbage are frost damaged, remove the frozen outer leaves. Even after a zero night, such plants may be fresh and entirely edible inside *if* they thaw out before being cut. With south winds and sunny days, the plants' condition will be alleviated by fall and winter thaws that sometimes last for days.

A mulch of hay, straw, leaves and/or evergreen branches laid over crops on especially cold autumn nights can provide an effective cover against the cold. Almost anything from a scattering of autumn leaves over a lettuce plantation to a bed blanket will do wonders to offset frost. We keep a pile of birch, beech or other fairly small leaves handy and dry. If they are scattered over a bed of greens early on a frosty night, they may be effective enough to offset even a 10-degree frost.

Sooner or later, as autumn advances toward chill November's wintry blasts, the garden will lose some of its green freshness and begin to look chilled, but the longer this day can be postponed the longer one can get green nourishment from the fall garden. During the latter part of the autumn-winter gardening period, the adroit gardener can snatch a cauliflower or Chinese cabbage and a hardy chard plant here or there. He can also pick fresh spinach and lettuces and radishes, which have not yet given up their efforts to take advantage of the few hours of growing weather between frost-crusted earth in the midmorning and the onset of sunlessness in midafternoon.

Winter gardeners, willing to experiment, will often have the satisfaction of digging out hardy green plants from under a cover of mulch and light snow. Here in Maine we have had entire rows of lettuce, spinach, parsley and broccoli survive the winter and reappear as the snow covering melts. Brussels sprouts, kale, rape, wheat and rye survive New England winters almost as a matter of course, especially if they are helped along with a light covering of hay, straw or autumn leaves.

When our gardening passed from spring through summer into autumn and winter, we faced a problem that most people would consider insoluble. Cold nights certainly discourage plant growth, flowering and fruiting. We knew this when we began our experiments with cold-weather gardens. We take such adversity for granted. Despite setbacks, however, we have made real progress since the days when 32 degrees was accepted as the point at which most gardeners pick up their tools and go home. Experience convinces us that noteworthy successes are possible with certain hardy plants.

Some present-day lettuces will survive sub-zero temperatures and go on growing and heading. Red radishes have at least a fifty-fifty chance to produce edible roots before they are plunged into permanent winter weather by a degree of frost that keeps the earth frozen hard even on a sunny afternoon. Long after these fall-planted seedlings have given up their struggle against the New England winter, parsnips and oyster plant, witloof chicory, celery roots, and Chinese cabbage and brussels sprouts will survive. Once the ground has been deeply frozen, during subsequent thaws, parsnips, oyster plants and witloof chicory can be dug and turned over to the kitchen.

We have continued our outdoor gardening to later and later periods year after year until heavy frost solidified the earth. We intend to continue our experiments with growing hardy plants in Maine's cool falls and into its cold winters, although we can never be absolutely certain what will survive, particularly with variable weather conditions. Only experience will give us reasonable certainty as a result of these operations. But our efforts to date suggest that we can expect at least a modest degree of success. Each time we eat a fresh salad that comes from our fall-into-winter garden, we have one more assurance that we are on the right track.

"The Spring visiteth not these Quarters so timely. Summer imparteth a verie temperate heat, recompencing his slow fostering of the fruits with their kindly ripening. Autumne bringeth a somewhat late harvest. In Winter we cannot say the Frost and Snow come verie seldome and make a speedie departure."

Richard Carew, The Survey of Cornwall, 1602

"I do hold it, in the Royal Ordering of Gardens, there ought to be Gardens for all the months in the Year."

Sir Francis Bacon, Sylva Sylvarum, 1605

"Snow is beneficial to the ground in winter, as it prevents its freezing to so great a depth as it otherwise would. It guards the winter grain and other vegetables in a considerable degree from the violence of sudden frosts, and from piercing and drying winds. The later snow lies on the ground in spring, the more advantage do grasses and other plants receive from it. Where a bank of snow has lain very late, the grass will sprout, and look green earlier, than in parts of the same field which were sooner bare."

Samuel Deane, The New-England Farmer, 1790

"Imagine that to the substantial garden there is added a small green-house, or a flued pit! What a source of amusement and interest does not either of these garden structures hold out to the amateur gardener, during the winter and the spring!"

Jack Loudon, The Suburban Gardener, 1838

"I cannot conceive the Spring of lands that have no Winter. I take my Winter gladly, to get Spring as a keen and fresh experience."

Odd Farmwife, The Old Farmhouse, 1913

"It is said land under glass is fifty times more productive of garden crops than open ground. Glass is certainly the solution of the raw winter greens problem. For with no more than the two-sash hotbed in which we start tomato, pepper and other seedlings, we can eke out the fall lettuce supply until after Christmas."

Henry Tetlow, We Farm for a Hobby and Make It Pay, 1938

"The pleasure of year-round gardening is one of the greatest tranquilizers there is. In a world filled with tension and frustration, you can enter your greenhouse, close the door, and shut yourself away from all the world's problems. There's something soothing about firming seeds in the soil and tending plants under glass while raindrops and snowflakes fall against the panes."

George and Katy Abraham, Organic Gardening Under Glass, 1975

CHAPTER 4

WINTERTIME GARDENING

OUR COMMENTS on fall gardening were written from a homestead that can expect not more than 105 frost-free days per year, with 260 days and nights when frost is possible and/or probable. One of the simplest ways of lengthening the frost-free season for plants is to build a cover with glass or some equally effective transparency, which allows sun rays to enter the area but prevents or retards heat from escaping after sunset.

The problem is complicated by the irregularity of sunlight. If each day were sunny and the gardener had to face only the night chill, the answer would be a simple night covering. New England fall and winter weather includes a minimum of clear sunshine and a maximum of clouds, fog, mist, drizzle, rain and snow. There are periods during the spring and early summer when we do not see the sun once in a week. Such periods may be prolonged in late winter and early spring to weeks when sunshine is a rarity, when day temperatures rise to the thirties and low forties, while night temperatures drop regularly, and often reach the upper twenties. In deep winter, of course, temperatures occasionally fall far below zero.

This need to protect plants from cold weather has produced cold frames (wooden frames glazed by glass or some other transparent material at or near ground level). Using spare time and secondhand materials, any homesteader can provide himself with one or another form of cold frame-greenhouse. Sun-heated glass houses are really just enlarged cold frames. If they are attached to the south or west side of an existing building or wall, in shed form, they are open to the sun, and protected against north winds, and they accumulate whatever warmth the sun is sending. During many days in the winter it gets so warm in our greenhouse between noon and 3 PM that we could take sunbaths there.

Let us begin with the construction of our greenhouse. Our fondness for stonework and the existence in most parts of New England of plenty of fieldstone has made it our choice and custom to build our greenhouses of stone. The present sun-heated greenhouse in Maine is built on a concrete and rock foundation which is 16 inches wide and deep enough to avoid frost-heave. The greenhouse faces south. The north and east walls are stone and concrete from foundation to roof. The south and west walls are made of surplus storm sash. The sloping shed roof is glass, resting on 2 x 4 cedar rafters, and is 9 feet wide and 40 feet long.

The roof is made of double-strength window glass 16 x 24 inches. Both corners of each rafter on one 2-inch side have been replaced by a half-inch groove in which the glass rests. Each pane of glass is lapped one inch on the pane below and held in place by sprigs and glazing compound. The rafters are spaced to allow the glass panes to fit comfortably into the grooves.

The simple shed roof of our Maine greenhouse has a 10-degree slope which is sufficient to drain off water and to be fairly independent of snow and ice. On the outside of the north wall, at a convenient height, we have put a catwalk from which we aim to keep the roof free of snow and ice. During a snowstorm we wait until the internal warmth of the greenhouse has made it possible for the snow to slide easily on the glass;

then with a light wooden pusher we break up the snow cover unit by unit and start the clumps of snow moving toward the low side of the roof. The procedure is possible only when the temperature inside the greenhouse is above freezing.

With concrete foundations and stone and concrete walls that protect on the north and east sides, we find that the daytime temperature inside the greenhouse will be about 20 degrees higher than that of the outside air. On bright sunny days the differential between inside and outside will be much greater—as much as 40 degrees, if no strong wind is blowing. The stones in the north and east walls act as radiators. All day they absorb heat. After sundown they give off this heat as temperatures inside and outside tend to be equalized.

Cloches (small glass enclosures for individual plants), cold frames and formal greenhouses have two disadvantages. First, the initial cost is to be considered. Second, there is always a chance of breakage. Builders of glass houses must take these two items into account when they plan such projects. If plastic greenhouse covers would last for a reasonable number of years, greenhouses could be built far more cheaply. Thus far we ourselves have considered plastic not durable or reliable enough to put into a permanent greenhouse. For the time being, greenhouse builders must shoulder the cost of replacing glass, but with good care and good luck, glass breakage can be held to a minimum, which will more than justify the capital and labor expenses that attend greenhouse construction.

A well-constructed and well-ventilated solar greenhouse will add months to the period during which a New England family can supply itself with greens. Food directly from the garden is unlikely from November to March. This is the period during which the New England garden is least able to furnish fresh vegetables for the family larder and when the greenhouse may be counted on to fill the gap.

The traditional greenhouse provides benches on which pots, flats and other containers can be maintained at waist level, making it more convenient for the gardener. When greenhouse plants are chiefly potted or flatted flowers, the practice may be justified, but in a greenhouse such as ours—which aims to produce many rangy vegetables—it seems desirable to keep the greenhouse floor at ground level, utilizing the full height of the building.

There are three possibilities for the greenhouse floor, presupposing that the greenhouse is a part of the garden area. It may be at the same level as the surface of the garden; it may be above that level; or it may be below it. A pit greenhouse is below garden-surface level. A built-up greenhouse floor is above garden-floor level. Our greenhouse floor is at the same general level as the surrounding garden.

Pit greenhouses have enthusiastic backers who argue that they are warmer and more even in temperature. They cool off more slowly after sundown. It is easier to restore the temperature on each succeeding day because the earth inside the pit is at sub-soil warmth rather than air coolness.

However, dampness and even standing water collects on the pit greenhouse floor unless it is well situated and fully drained. At best a pit greenhouse may be damp. We continue in our opinion that, where there is a choice of greenhouse floor levels, it is easier and more logical to keep the greenhouse floor at about the same level as the surrounding garden than it is to establish and maintain a higher or a lower level.

We go a step further and maintain our sun-heated greenhouse without any assigned walking space. In a 9-foot greenhouse, an 18-inch footway occupies one-sixth of the total floor space. A grower of greenhouse tomatoes, for example, could increase his crop by 16 percent if the path were abolished and gardeners stepped between plants. With us, no part of the greenhouse floor is a regularly trodden path. The roots occupy the entire greenhouse area and with each new crop the footpath shifts.

We built our first glass house in Vermont to give seedlings an early start. Our present glass house in Maine takes care of the seedling problem; it provides us with tomatoes, sweet peppers, eggplants in summer. It also gives us greens during the fall, winter and spring.

Sometime in March, depending on the severity or mildness of the weather, we begin planting seeds in short rows in the greenhouse. Among these seeds may be quick-growing mustard, radish and early cabbage. All of these will be used as salad greens, even when they are quite tiny. Onion, leek and parsley, when well started in the seed rows, are transplanted into garden flats, kept there for a few weeks and, when large enough to transplant again, put directly into the garden.

Flats of young lettuce seedlings will play a leading part in supplying greens in the late winter and early spring. If possible, seeds of the hardiest lettuces should be sowed in September or October in seed flats and be moved into the greenhouse when the weather threatens their further survival outside. These plants, around 2-3 inches high and with sturdy roots, can be set 6 or 7 inches apart in greenhouse flats and/or in greenhouse beds. They should get their start when the greenhouse temperatures are high enough for the plants to get going and become sufficiently accustomed to chilly nights and even chilly days so that they can go on growing when the weather gets colder.

The best lettuces for this purpose are leafy varieties (not head lettuce), with thin central stems and sturdy non-heading leaves. Many lettuces have thick, juicy spines which freeze easily, being moist and fat. We find that the drier the leaf web and stem is, the less damaged by the conversion of water into ice. We tested certain varieties of lettuces that can be expected to survive heavy freezing in an unheated greenhouse from December to March and will begin growing as the sun gets higher and warmer in March-April.

Green Boston, Simpson, Oak Leaf and Buttercrunch lettuce and Celtus (a plant midway between celery and lettuce) suffer comparatively little frost damage. By mid-March, most years, we can start picking individual leaves from all five of these varieties and use them to make salads. We can also strip the outer stems and leaves of parsley and kale plants set in the earth on the greenhouse ground in October. During the coldest parts of winter, growth may be minimal, but the plants survive. We sometimes keep extra garden flats of small plants in the greenhouse all winter to be used as replacements for any transplants in the greenhouse rows that do not make it.

The winter greenhouse also accommodates some adult plants which submit to the humiliating process of heeling. Heeling-in is a procedure whereby the plant is dug up and then replanted with undamaged roots. If carefully done, the plant should remain as upstanding and colorful as any normal plant of its type and age left in the original ground, though there is little further growth.

We might illustrate the process with an example of a bed of giant leeks that were planted in the greenhouse last March, taken out to the garden, and brought back in November, and which we are now eating a year later, in the spring of 1978. They spent a summer of growth during 1977 in the garden and weathered the early frosts of September-October, reaching the first week of November in a state of excellent health, when we decided to bring them under cover.

We picked a cloudy, damp day so that the earth around the leeks would be moist and cling to the roots. We dug a trench 8 inches wide and 6 inches deep in the ground of the greenhouse. Then we went to the outside leek bed with a shovel and used it to pick up a leek plant, being careful to damage its roots as little as possible and to keep an earth ball around the roots. We carried the earth ball containing the leek plant on a shovel into the greenhouse and planted it in the newly dug trench, pulling the earth up around the leek and tramping it in with the heel, pressing the earth firmly.

Then back to the leek bed with the shovel, where we took up a second leek, placing it as close as possible to the first heeled-in leek. We repeated the operation until the trench was filled. With room for a second dozen, we put in more in the same fashion. When the move was completed we watered the leeks moderately. On that day and during the following days and weeks, not a single leek plant wilted or looked or acted any worse for the move. Those that survived our picking through the winter were still green and sturdy in the greenhouse in the middle of April 1978.

We have also dug up and heeled in our parsley plants with hundred-percent survival. We do somewhat less well with lettuce transplanted from garden flats into the greenhouse, but at least half of them survive.

We had even less success with celery. They seemingly cannot take it. During the summer of 1975 we raised from seed several rows of fine celery plants. We had about two dozen summer Pascal plants which had surged to a height of nearly three feet and to great bulk. Some of the plants weighed up to five pounds each. We dug these plants and heeled them into the greenhouse in early November. They took the shift rather badly. Despite plentiful watering, they never fully recovered the upstanding vigor of their celery bed outside, but they did stay alive. Their leaves and stalks were edible until February, when they gave up the fight and collapsed under a fierce bout of sub-zero weather. Meanwhile we had been eating excellent celery from the heeled-in plants for three months.

The fall and winter gardener cannot bother with semi-hardy plants that are rubbed out by temperatures between 20 and 30 degrees Fahrenheit. Experience in each location will show which varieties will survive and which will not survive cold weather. We found that mature chard plants froze after about sixty winter days. Chinese cabbage lasted another month. Parsley and kale plants survived cold winters in the greenhouse, resuming their growth as the outside temperature rose in the spring.

As experiments go forward and hardy new varieties of established plants are developed and introduced by selection and crossing strains, the plants available to fall and winter greenhouse gardeners will increase in both number and hardiness.

For those who have the money and the facilities, the possibility of gardening in heated greenhouses is always present and can be carried forward as long as the electric power is on. Here we are concerning ourselves with fall and winter gardening in solar-heated greenhouses. We are among those homesteaders and small-scale gardeners who prefer to have sun-heated greenhouses, to collaborate with Mother Nature, rather than having to deal with the electric and fossil fuel companies.

"What cost to good husband is any of this?
Good household provision onely it is.
Of other the like, I doo leave out a menie,
That costeth the husbandman never a penie."

Thomas Tusser, Five Hundreth Pointes of Good Husbandrie, *1557*

"In a house where there is plenty, supper is soon cooked."

Miguel de Cervantes, Don Quixote, *1605*

"Gather at the full moone for keeping apples. Let them sweat for ten days on straw. Then pack in bran."

Anonymous, West Country Herbal, *1631*

"The infinite conveniences of what a well-stor'd garden and cellar affords... All so near at hand, readily drest, and of so easie digestion, as neither to offend the brain, or dull the senses."

John Evelyn, Acetaria, *1699*

"There can be no doubt whatever that by far the most economical plan of supplying a household with necessaries for consumption is to lay in a stock for the week or month in lieu of purchasing, as but too many do, from hour to hour."

One Who Makes Ends Meet, Economy for the Single and Married, *1845*

CHAPTER 5

WINTER STORAGE

THE DANGER of frost for food crops in our part of Maine is considerable. For more than half the year commodities subject to frost danger must be stored or otherwise protected. In a very real sense the success of each homesteading year depends upon carrying perishable food from the period of its production to the time of its consumption.

The methods of keeping some vegetables fresh in the winter greenhouse have just been described. An even easier method of food storage is to leave the hardiest of vegetables in the ground. Parsnips and Jerusalem artichokes, for example, winter in that way better than any other we know of. They may be dug and eaten during any winter thaw sufficiently deep to allow the roots to be lifted from the ground. They may also be dug before freeze-up in the early winter; then they are not so sweet. Unfrozen, the parsnip is as bland as the average turnip. Freezing converts their starch into sugar, making the root more tasty. This is true of both Jerusalem artichokes and the parsnip.

Parsnip and artichoke devotees have a period of perhaps a month, beginning with the first spring thaw, during which the main root may be dug and eaten raw or prepared and cooked to taste. As spring advances, the plants begin to send out small feeders from the main root, which gets more fibrous and less sweet. Under ordinary Maine winter conditions, it is best to dig parsnips and artichokes to be eaten promptly if the upper layer of topsoil is frost-free. During winter thaws they may be chewed by rodents or other animals; in very severe winters they may even be frozen out.

Salsify may be left in the ground over winter. Like the parsnip, the salsify root is most edible immediately after winter break-up and before the new crop of feeding roots has begun to put in an appearance.

Almost all of the roots grown in the ordinary home garden, except potatoes, will survive moderate frosts. Some are improved by moderate freezing. Most of them will be seriously damaged by a series of severe frosts unless well mulched.

It behooves the Maine homesteader to get his or her food directly from the garden as late as possible in the autumn and as early as possible in the spring. Under the best of conditions, winter's deep-freeze hiatus of garden-fresh vegetables will last for perhaps three months. During this frozen-up period in Maine, storage of some kind is essential if roots are to be kept in prime condition.

Most family homes in New England are equipped with some sort of cellar. If the cellar contains a furnace or other heat source, the entire area will be too warm for the storage of perishables. Even if the heating unit is separated from the remainder of the cellar by a concrete wall, the cellar tends to be out of bounds for storage purposes.

Professional storage facilities are equipped with air conditioners that maintain an even level of temperature, winter and summer. Like all mechanical sources of assistance, air conditioners cost care and attention to maintain. In the long run they wear out, deteriorate, require professional attention. Eventually they must be repaired or replaced. Short of a professionally built and equipped storage unit, the problem of keeping fruit and vegetables in winter, like so many other problems, looms on the horizon for the homesteader with the oncome of winter.

The house we bought in Harborside had no central heating, but it did have a small cellar, with sturdy stone foundation walls and a cement floor. In this cellar the temperature seldom fell below freezing and seldom went higher than 45 degrees Fahrenheit. In this cellar we have kept vegetables and fruit from the harvest time of October-November until the following July. Only the best specimens could maintain themselves for months after being separated from Mother Earth. On rare occasions, as with the summer crop of 1975, some of our stored potatoes, onions, turnips, beets, celery roots, carrots, apples and rutabagas were still edible when the new crop was harvested in the late summer of 1976.

It goes without saying that freshly harvested roots are more juicy and tasty than those that have lived in storage during an entire winter season. Stored roots are alive and subject to aging and spoilage. Even under professional storage conditions which hold temperatures at exact levels month after month, losses due to rotting and wilting are expected. We go over the boxes of vegetables and fruit stored in the vegetable cellar once every month or six weeks, pick out those that have turned bad and get rid of them, and use up at once those that show signs of incipient decay.

One of our most valuable stored items in Maine, as in Vermont, is apples. At harvest time we sort our apples carefully into two lots: those that are perfect and will keep; and the non-keepers, which have blemishes or bruises. The bulk of the keepers we put away in autumn leaves, while some we eat or give away. The non-keepers go into apple juice or applesauce.

Our simple recipe for applesauce is to wash the apples, cut the smaller ones into quarters, the larger into eighths (taking out the cores and any blemish or rot), put them in kettles with a minimum of water and cook until they soften up. We then pack the fruit in sterilized jars without processing them further. We seal the filled bottles and store them in the cellar. No sugar or other preservative has been added. When the applesauce is eaten, if desired it may be sweetened with a little honey or maple syrup.

This is an "open kettle" method—the simplest of the simple. Only occasionally one jar in perhaps fifty thus treated will ferment or mould and go to the compost pile. If this happens, it is usually due to a cracked top or faulty rubber. At least 95 percent of the canned material thus stored in our cold cellar is perfectly good when used even after two years.

Our canning of other produce is as easy and casual. When tomatoes are plentiful, we pick them by the bushel and make a soup stock, with celery, parsley and onions chopped up and boiled together; no water is added. These are all soft crops that would not last in the garden through the first heavy freeze, or, as to the onions, they are blemished or too small to keep. The four vegetables are boiled together by the same open kettle method as the applesauce. When the celery (the toughest of the vegetables) is forkably tender, it is all put through a sieve, with the resulting juice being brought back to a boil and then canned. The thick residue that does not go through the sieve is put back on the stove with a minimum of hot water, brought back to a rolling boil and canned with a bit of sea salt in quart jars, to be used later as soup stock.

This is about the extent of our canning, except that we put up a few dozen bottles each of blueberries, raspberries and rose hips, in the following manner. We sterilize the quart bottles, pour in a cup or two of boiling water, add a large spoonful of honey, stir to dissolve, drop in a cup and a half of one or another fruit, add boiling water to the top of the jar, seal and put in the cellar.

We were given a freezer and find it very handy for storing overstocks or surpluses from meals or from the garden. We dispose of masses of raw blueberries in cellophane bags. We blanch extra asparagus and eat the icy stalks in the wintertime without further cooking them (they become flabby and less tasty when cooked). We could live happily without electricity for lighting, but we find the freezer of considerable assistance in keeping certain few foods.

In the absence of a reasonably cool and dry house cellar or a freezer, it may be economical to build a root cellar for storage purposes. It must be set high enough and dry enough and cool enough. Like any other storehouse, it must be proof against invading insects such as ants and against rodents such as rats, mice, squirrels, raccoons and skunks.

One of the early means of storage was a pit, lined and covered with hay or straw, and held in place by boards and loose earth and properly ventilated. Located on a knoll to obviate the accumulation of water, such storage pits proved to be reasonably frost-free. Periodically, on warm days, pits could be opened up, a portion of the contents removed for immediate use and the pit reclosed.

An alternative was to pick a side hill location close to the farm buildings, dig a hole into the hill, build a front with a door and ventilator. The side hill location, well chosen, took care of water accumulation. The part of the storage cellar protruding from the hillside should be double boarded or in some way protected against summer, spring and autumn warmth. The chief obstacle to any of these storage structures is the difficulty of making them vermin-proof.

We will never forget one of our winters in Harborside when we had stored twelve lugs of apples in the cellar supposed to be rat- and mouse-proof. The apples were layered with abundant semi-dry autumn leaves below and above the fruit and a good covering of leaves. We closed the door of the cellar and went off on a transcontinental lecture tour. On our return, four months later, we went to the cellar to look over our dozen boxes of carefully stored apples.

The cellar floor was covered with debris, inches deep. We felt in the boxes. Of the hundreds of stored apples, only one apple remained—a fine specimen of Northern Spy. We never saw the marauder (probably a rat or a squirrel), nor could we find out where it got in. It had gone from box to box, chewing up the apples and leaving plenty of the chewed pulp as a token for us latecomers. What a winter it must have had!

Our neighbor, Eliot Coleman, who maintained an organic market garden next door to us for several years, built a carefully planned root cellar as an independent unit. The cellar consisted of two rooms drained and insulated. It was equipped with double doors and was designed to be vermin-proof. The elaborate structure was of double wood with concrete floor and retaining walls, and, so far as we know, functioned well.

Thus far we have discussed winter storage of living objects like carrots, potatoes or apples. Another method of storage is to dry garden produce sufficiently to prevent its decay. In earlier days much fruit—apples, pears, plums, cherries, and various berries—was dried and stored for winter use. We have not done much of this, preferring to eat the fruits as they come along in season, or canning those that are going by.

Many herbs are dried and stored for flavoring, seasoning, preserving, making herb teas or for medicinal purposes. We have grown various species in our herb garden: mint, thyme, chives, lemon balm, lovage, tarragon, summer and winter savory, dill, marjoram, camomile, coriander. These and others are picked by the branch just before ripening, hung on the kitchen rafters to dry, and used for morning teas or put in soups or salads.

It goes without saying that if possible we prefer to grow all our own food and have it garden-fresh, but in our climate this is not possible. We therefore have worked out these various ways to store, dry, freeze, can and otherwise preserve what foods are not eaten straight from the garden.

"Lay durt upon heapes, some profit it reapes."

Thomas Tusser, Five Hundreth Pointes of Good Husbandrie, *1557*

"It were good to trie whether Leaves of Trees swept together, with some Chalke and Dung mixed, to give them more Heart, would not make a good Compost; for there is nothing lost so much as Leaves of Trees."

Francis Bacon, Sylva Sylvarum, *1605*

"Lay your material in a large heap, in some convenient place: A layer of fresh and natural Earth, taken from the Surface, and another of dung, a pretty deal thicker; then a layer of Earth again, and so successively, mingling a load of lime to every ten loads of dung, will make an admirable Compost, somewhat shaded, so as neither the Sun too much draw from it, nor the violent rains too much dilute it."

John Rose, The English Vineyard Vindicated, *1675*

"Have allways ready prepar'd several Composts, mixed with natural pasture earth, a little loamy: skreene the mould, and mingle it discreetely with rotten Cow-dung; not suffering it to abide in heapes too long, but be frequently turning and stirring it, nor let weedes grow on it; and that it may be moist and sweete, and not wash away the salts, it were best kept and prepared in some large pit, or hollow place which has a hard bottom and in the shade."

John Evelyn, Directions for the Gardiner, *1687*

"There being nothing so proper for Sallet Herbs and other Edule Plants, as the Genial and Natural Mould, impregnate, and enrich'd with well-digested Compost."

John Evelyn, Acetaria, *1699*

"The leaf-harvest is one of importance to the farmer if he will but avail himself of it. A calm day or two spent in this business will enable him to put together a large pile of these fallen leaves....Gardeners prize highly a compost made in part of decomposed leaves. The leaf-harvest is the last harvest of the year, and should be thoroughly attended to at the proper time."

Anonymous, Ten Acres Enough, *1864*

"Plants require a well-proportioned quantity of all the necessary mineral elements for their healthy growth, just as much as man and animals do. Sufficiently or wrongly nourished plants, like animals, fall a prey to diseased conditions more quickly than those specimens which are well built, as a result of an adequate supply of the essential mineral elements."

Otto Carque, Vital Facts About Food, *1940*

CHAPTER 6

BUILDING THE SOIL WITH COMPOST

SOIL IS that portion of the earth's crust which supports the growth of vegetation. Soil—plus water, plus air, plus sunshine, plus the magnetic field—provides the medium in which the life forces functioning through plants, men and other self-motivating creatures thrive and multiply.

Plants live on the soil. Animals, including man, live directly or indirectly on plants. Directly or indirectly, the soil (whether topsoil or the lower layers of subsoil) provides the mineral elements of which plant bodies and animal bodies are composed. Sand, gravel and rock particles plus organic matter make up both topsoil and subsoil.

Plant nutrients exist mainly in the topsoil. Through its feeding roots, the plant secures the water and building material which constitute the plant body. Anchor roots penetrate the subsoil sufficiently to provide the anchorage without which the tiny feeding roots would be unable to keep the contacts through which they receive moisture and nutriment.

Left to her own devices, Mother Nature builds topsoil, enriches it with organic material, adds the products of water and wind erosion and thus deepens the layer of topsoil and lays the foundation for grass and later for forest cover. Growing vegetation adds gradually to the means of its own perpetuation and enrichment.

We know that Maine's combination of soil fertility and climate will produce magnificent tree crops. Fine forests were found here by the Europeans when they began prospecting and colonizing the New England area. But colonists who moved from Old England to New England were not concerned with conservation. On the contrary, they felt they had to hustle in order to prevent the forces of nature which dominated life in their newly acquired land from pushing in and obliterating the relatively feeble impact of human handiwork. There was small chance then that man would obliterate nature. It seemed probable that the forces of nature would push man aside and continue with their natural processes.

Maine farmers occupy a segment of the New England countryside that until recent years was practically covered by a mixed stand of softwoods and hardwoods which in its long occupancy of the land had built up a topsoil and subsoil well adapted to provide a livelihood for homesteaders and other would-be occupiers.

In the initial rush to use up and profit by the treasure that nature had wrapped up in Maine's topsoil, the original settlers generally interfered little with basic natural processes. Then, as the population increased and entrepreneurs were looking for a quick profit, they began to slash down the forests wholesale, broke up the grassy covers and opened the way for the grazing, overcropping, erosion and eventual fertility exhaustion that now is so widespread.

With the advances in growing awareness (local, state and national) of the desirability of maintaining present soils and deepening them in the present and future, an entire generation of conservation-conscious Maine youngsters could dedicate itself to building up the Maine topsoil. Every landowner in Maine who has the economic and ecological welfare of the state at heart could follow a policy of putting more humus into the soil each year than is being subtracted by cropping or lost by erosion. Granted, such processes are so slow that a single generation may be unable to observe the losses and measure them against the gains.

Even though quick profits have been made by lumbering, and incidental advantage has been taken of Maine's vacationing possibility, close attention could be devoted to harvesting successive forest crops, and the bulk of Maine's land could be turned to good advantage as arable land.

Certainly Maine homesteaders have little or no hope to "strike it rich" as prospectors did in the early days in California and more recently in Alaska. Instead, they can work out a program that may give them a simple livelihood in exchange for a minimum of consistent and persistent labor. The surest path to success with their land is to increase its fertility.

Homesteaders are often inexperienced and impatient. They are eager for quick returns and will not wait for years to get results. Properly equipped and with a minimum of courage and good health, they can win sure and decisive successes. We know this from our own experience, and some of our neighbor homesteaders know it from experiment and experience.

In Maine an average land-based family of four or five adults and children requires at least a quarter-acre (100 x 100 feet) of moderately fertile garden soil to produce a minimum amount of vegetables, small fruit and greens. The fertility of this garden land can be increased from year to year by deepening the topsoil and adding decaying organic matter (mature compost) and necessary quantities of missing trace fertilizing elements. This land could be used actively for at least eight months out of the year in growing garden edibles. If some glass or other cover was used, a part of the garden space could be used for a full twelve months.

Each year, with proper attention, the topsoil should increase in depth as a result of the application of compost and cultivation. Each year an alkaline balance should be maintained in the soil. Each year any underlying clay bank should be broken up by the addition of compost, sand, sawdust, autumn leaves, wood dirt from the forest floor and peat moss. Each year more nitrogen, phosphorus, potash and trace minerals must be added to the soil than are removed by cropping and erosion, thus adding fertility.

On our Maine farm we are adding our mite to the growth process by increasing the productive capacity of our particular cranny of the earth's surface. Survival and growth depend upon the capacity of the farmer to do a bit more each day and each season. This means a more effective use of the land strip that he has undertaken to cultivate and improve. To do this, the soil must become more productive. As each crop is harvested in our garden, before we replant the area we spread an inch or two of compost and work it into the soil surface; we then plant the next crop. As we are building up our soil, we try to add a bit more than we take out in crops, plus some allowance for erosion.

Compost is decaying organic matter that has reached a stage in its disintegration at which it is ideal food to be built into roots, stems, branches, leaves, flowers and fruits, which make up the physical structure of plants. A good general rule for composting is: utilize any and all available organic materials. Utilize everything that has grown, is growing or will grow. Destroy little or nothing by burning or throwing in the dump.

We visited an organic garden in northern Holland. The husband managed a business; the wife made herself responsible for the garden and did much of the work in it. When we visited their place, one of our first questions was: Where is your compost pile? Our hostess showed us the pile. It was in moderately good order and was made up of kitchen wastes and an abundance of soft annual weeds, with masses of chickweed and purslane.

We asked whether all of the garden wastes went into this pile, as it was rather small for the size of her garden. Our hostess answered: "No indeed! We divide our garden weeds and wastes into two categories: the soft ones that will make compost and the hard ones that will not make compost."

We asked what had happened to the uncompostable materials. "Oh, those," she said, "are down in a heap in the lower end of the garden." In a low-lying corner a place had been used for many years under the direction of this gardener, who year by year had dumped the hard or "uncompostable" weeds in a ridge at least twenty feet long and several feet wide and high.

The ridge was overrun by a jungle of brambles and vines, among which were some nettle plants that were five to six feet high, still at the plant stage but reaching out like embryo trees. We pulled out some of the coarser weeds and dug into the ridge with a shovel. The soil was as black as the proverbial hat. The ten-year accumulation of weeds "too tough to compost" had given our hostess an estimated forty tons of the finest compost that you could hope to see.

Another instance of a real find in organic material happened in Vermont. Our sugar grove had included many weed trees, especially evergreens: spruce, fir and hemlock. Each year in the off-season we cut out these weed trees, limbed them and piled the brush in low spots. As we went back over our clearings, we noticed by the third year after such brush piles had been heaped up and covered by successive layers of autumn leaves, if we turned over the piles of brush and leaves we found feeding roots from the surrounding maple trees working their way up into the rotting brush piles. The same process can be observed in any forest where brush is gathered up and tramped into compact piles. Nature was making compost for the maple trees.

Our chief sources of compostable material are grass clippings and hay cut once a year on our mowings; garden wastes, including weeds, leaves, stems and roots and thinnings; seaweed; grass from salt meadows; sawdust (in small quantities, 5 percent or less of the total pile); and kitchen garbage. We aim to keep reserves of any or all of these materials (except the kitchen wastes) in special heaps or bins near the composting area so that they will be handy for compost making.

Each compost pile should be located so that it can be turned at the proper time with minimum effort. It should be set high enough to avoid standing in water. The compost area should be out of direct sunlight if possible. If the weather is hot and dry, the piles should be watered and covered.

Currently we maintain about a dozen compost piles, 6 feet square, standing in a row and spaced 18 inches apart. Our piles are edged with poles about 2 or 3 inches in diameter and exactly 6 feet long. When we are cutting or thinning in our woodlot and run across a piece that is straight and at least 72 inches long, we say, "That is for a compost pole." We measure it accurately and limb it carefully. Then we put the pole in our reserve pile for later use.

When we get an accumulation of compostable materials and an open space in our compost yard, we take a bar and an axe and start a new pile 18 inches from its neighbors. If there is a grass sod, the area should be desodded so that earthworms can easily enter the pile from below.

We select four good-size, fairly straight poles and lay them in an open square. Across this square at the center we lay four or five slim poles an inch in diameter. They may be left loose or tied in a flexible bundle. This is our horizontal air drain. At the center of the open square we set up four or five vertical poles of the same size, pointed and driven lightly into the ground and tied together with wire or string. This provides for the vertical air drain.

We are now ready for four or five inches of coarse material: weeds, grass, hay, straw, cornstalks—the coarser the material the better, because it allows air and moisture drainage at the bottom of the pile. We spread over it a one-inch layer of good topsoil or compost. This material will contain the insect and bacterial life that plays so important a role in breaking down the cellulose in the pile. There is difference of opinion as to how thick this soil layer should be. We aim to make it one inch.

At this point we cover the earth layer with a thin sprinkling of pulverized limestone or sifted wood ashes if we are making an alkaline pile; for an acid pile we sprinkle ground phosphate rock.

The first layer of the pile is now completed. We next spread three or four inches of seaweed, which we cover with an inch of topsoil, followed by a sprinkling of lime or phosphate rock and then by an inch of sawdust, completing the second layer of the pile.

Each layer of material is held in place by another four compost poles, laid on top of the earlier ones. The poles need not be notched. Early in our composting experience we notched the poles so they would not roll out of place. That made four notches on the end of each pole. In a pile of 40 poles, that was 160 notches. "Why notch?" someone asked. "The poles won't move if other poles are on top of them and if there is composting material to hold the poles apart." We tried the experiment and the poles did not move unless they were pushed by man or animal. From that day on we have done no more notching.

We did encounter another difficulty. If the poles were put in without notches and if the composting materials were spread across the pile and trampled hard, enough expansion was generated by the hard tramping so that, come freezing weather, the composted material expanded to force the poles out of the sides of the compost piles. We stopped tramping and had no further difficulties with this type of expansion.

If garden or kitchen wastes are available, they make the bulk of the third layer. So the pile grows larger, layer by layer, like a layer cake, with an inch of topsoil between each two layers. We go on building as long as it is convenient to reach up and across with hand tools.

If the pile reaches a height of 5½ feet, within three weeks in warm or hot weather fermentation has developed an internal temperature of about 150 degrees Fahrenheit. This heat speeds the breakdown of the pile. At the end of three weeks we cover the pile with four or five inches of hay and let it "cook" for approximately a month.

At the end of the month we remove the hay cover and, with a fork and/or shovel, turn the pile into an adjoining open space, taking off the compost poles as we work down the pile and using them for building the new pile. We turn the corners and edges of the old pile into the center of the new pile and spread the material evenly as it goes in layer by layer. The result will be a heap of semi-decayed organic matter.

We cover the turned pile with hay or straw and let it continue to ripen until the materials can be easily broken up with a shovel. The compost is then ready for use as a fertilizer. Through the years our compost has been the only bulk fertilizer used. We do not touch the bagged commercial fertilizer commonly sold to farmers. Incidently, during this period we have used no animal manures or animal residues such as bone meal or blood meal. As vegetarians, we do not want any part in the raising, exploitation or slaughtering of animals for food.

Given ordinary summer weather, including fogs and rain, the pile should be ready for use in the garden in about two months from the time it was built. On this basis, a six-foot-square pile in the compost yard could produce at least two and often three tons of ripened compost each season.

Our method of composting is a modification of one commonly used by organic gardeners in the United States and Europe. We have been using this method of composting in our present garden for twenty-five years. What began as a tough yellow clay soil that hardened to brick-like consistency if it was worked while the ground was still wet could now pass for a high-level sandy loam soil. Now immediately after a shower we can work the land without having it stick to the tools.

When we started with our garden plot in 1951 it had been a gone-to-seed mowing for years. The chap who gave it the initial and only plowing, our neighbor Russell Redman, commented as he labored over it, "You'll never get a garden on this poor land." He now comes nearly every summer and looks over the garden wall with pride, admiring our produce.

This transformation has been achieved by generous additions of compost, sand, sawdust, and rock powder, plus much tillage and deep spading. Our garden is a living demonstration of the changes that may be brought by using organic materials on a piece of unpromising soil. The time element—twenty-five years of patient work—is also a factor.

"*Whosoever will build a mansion place or house, he must situate and set it there where he must be sure to have both water and wood. For profit and health of his body, he must dwell at elbow room, having water and wood annexed to his place or house; for if he be destitute of any of the principal, that is to say, first, of water for to wash and wring, wood to cooke and brew, it were a great discommodious thing. And better it were to lack wood than water, although that wood is a necessary thing, not only for fuel, but also for other urgent causes, especially concerning building and repairs.*"

Andrew Boorde, A Dyetary of Helth, 1542

"*As to the cituacion and standing of a Garden, the Moste commodious and profitablest placinge of a garden, is (as Paladius sayth) to be near to a playne field, somewhat lyeing a slope, sendyng downe small courses of water, by certayne distances one frome another, through the garden.... Water is a great nourisher to herbes. For of necessity a Garden muste be often watred, for therby it causeth (as Plinie sayth) that the seed which is sowe doth the sooner sprynge up, spread abroad, and wax great.*"

Thomas Hyll, First Garden Book, 1563

"*In the Springtime water in the mornings, in Summer, the evenings; in Winter be sparing of watering; and ever let it be a little warmed. Water gently, not hastily, or in a greate streame, for it only hardens the ground, and not penetrate: therefore imitate the natural showers.*"

Sir John Evelyn, Directions for the Gardiner, 1687

"*They are happy, who have a piece of standing water in their garden, or a rivulet near at hand, from whence the garden may be watered without much labour.*"

Samuel Deane, in The New England Farmer, 1790

"*It is well to have some water in your neighborhood, to give buoyancy to and float the earth.*"

Henry David Thoreau, Walden, 1854

CHAPTER 7

WATER FOR HOUSE, GARDEN, AND A POND

PEOPLE who say, "I would like to buy a farm," usually have in mind land rather than water. Yet land without water is all but useless. Whether they are thinking of themselves and their family, their farm livestock, their growing crops or their own hour-to-hour and day-to-day needs, they must include water among their basic necessaries. In homesteading the two prime requisites are enough land and an abundance of unpolluted water.

On the first visit to our Maine farm we asked about water on the place. Mary Stackhouse, the owner, triumphantly took us up to a bubbling spring in the woods about seven feet higher than the kitchen floor, which meant that spring water ran by gravity from the spring into the house. Flowing water, clear, cold and constant, with gravity feed! What more could we ask.

Still, it would be nice to have a pond, for swimming in summer, for ice skating in winter and as a source of irrigation for the garden. Was there any such possibility on the place? We learned that the westward-sloping hillside on which the farm was located had a number of places in which spring grass or water grass grew, indicating the presence of water near the soil surface. The slope also included a swamp area—a place of low-lying land on which water accumulated and stood for much of the year.

How does one go about converting an acre or so of swampland into an acre of pond? The typical American way is to call up the nearest contractor who has a bulldozer and get him to take on the job, finishing it in a few days (and leaving a mess of unsightly piles of topsoil, subsoil, rocks and roots all mixed up together). We had an alternative method. We proposed to do the job with hand tools.

The pond area had not been mowed or otherwise farmed for a generation at least. Filled at the outset with black alder, pin cherry, poplar and willow, the land was rapidly developing a stand of white birch, balsam fir, some spruce and swamp growth. Our first job was to get rid of this adolescent jungle, beginning with the trees. A bulldozer would have taken care of the young trees in short order. We had another way.

The subsoil of our pond area was yellow clay—in places, several feet of it. Such a subsoil repels the anchor roots of trees, so instead of growing down into the clay and hardpan, the anchor roots radiate horizontally on top of the clay bed. We therefore began operations by stripping the sod around a sizable tree and with a grubbing axe chopped through all the side roots. Small trees could then be pushed over by hand, the root cut off and the trunk converted into small wood for the kitchen stove.

Larger trees were treated differently. With a mattock and a grubbing axe we dug a small circular ditch around each tree, cutting off the horizontal roots a foot or so from the base. We then cut the tree about two feet above ground level, pushed a crowbar under the stump at the clay level and lifted the bar vigorously. Three times out of four the tree stump was pulled loose from its clay subsoil and could be tossed into our brush pile.

In an operation of this kind, instead of burning brush and stumps, we moved them into a low spot and filled it well above the level of the surrounding land. In the course of a few years, rot, gravitation and the pressure of winter snow and ice pushed the forest refuse down to the surrounding ground level, and a few wheelbarrow loads of clay or other subsoil held them in place. Thus a single operation disposed of the forest wastes without burning them and raised low-lying land areas above swamp level.

In the deeper parts of the pond we were removing at least two or three feet of soil. When this job was completed the trees or tree stumps were standing high and dry on pedestals that could be removed by mattocks and shovels without serious trouble.

We excavated the pond bed with contractors' wheelbarrows with 16-inch wheels and pneumatic rubber tires. When the area was wet we used loose, movable planks for wheelways. When it was dry we could wheel on the clay.

Our first cargo from the pond area would be sods—not polite, neat lawn sods but masses of vegetation—roots, leaves and branches. Coarse vegetation, root and leafage, went into sod piles built, like our compost piles, log-cabin fashion, with poles. Topsoil went to the gardens to be used for compost making or to level up garden surfaces.

From the outset this dam had a plan, and a purpose. Each of the 16,000 wheelbarrow loads taken out of the pond during the years was aimed in a certain generally recognized direction: a shallow pond with a spillway and an emergency overflow, a body of water that could be siphoned into the garden and that reduces fire hazard in the dry season and provides excellent skating in winter.

At odd times on this dam-building project as many as a dozen people were working at the same time. They had never all been together before and probably never would be again. They were of different ages, sexes, races, political and religious beliefs. They had all come because they wanted to and stayed for the same reason. With rare exceptions, they were not being paid for their work. If they stayed until noon they would share in the same simple, abundant vegetarian lunch.

Relations with the pond were not always successful. One negative item was leaks. At various times serious openings appeared under the 40-foot-long concrete core we built in the 20-foot-wide earth dam, and around the 8 x 10-foot concrete block that provides our main spillway and through which runs the bottom-level tile which drains the pond.

Why should such leaks occur after we had taken the greatest possible care to make it all water-tight? Possible explanations are legion: a mouse run, a muskrat burrow, a frost crack in the concrete, the various rates of expansion and contraction of the concrete and the earth surrounding it. Perhaps even so small a break as an earthworm run might provide the means for the first seepage. With that tiny start a body of water can begin to undercut, bypass and wave a gurgling goodby to the most imposing dam.

Experienced engineers console us with the assurance that there is no such thing as a leakless dam. We are inclined to agree. Scott began damming up a small brook in Morris Run, Pennsylvania, when he was about five or six years old. He has been building dams at one place or another ever since. We have studied beaver dams and visited such notable works as the Hoover Dam in the western United States and the Aswan High Dam in Egypt. Everywhere the story is the same. No dam ever reaches the level of perfection that is mapped out by its planners and builders. If you fence in water and wait long enough, the confined water will find a way over, under, through, or around, and go rushing, bubbling, leaping from high to lower levels.

From its beginnings as an unkempt swamp, the pond area had provided a home for bullfrogs and peepers who began, while ice was still melting in the spring, to enliven the neighborhood with their peepings, croakings and serenades. They still sound out every spring. Backwater is a logical place for frogs' eggs and for the generations of tadpoles that come with each spring. Frogs like shallow water and mud. Much of our pond is less than two feet deep—a real frog paradise. They move away temporarily when we drain the pond once a year, and cut and pile up the sods that have accumulated in the bottom. When the sods have dried a bit, we wheel them to the sod-pile section of our topsoil reserve and use the resulting rotted sod for gardening. Each freshet deposits its quota of sand and silt in the pond. Each midsummer finds us stripping a quota of pond bottom and piling up topsoil for compost making and other purposes.

The Chinese drain their ponds and ditches, making special provision for the survival of their fish. They clear ditches and ponds of all accumulated refuse. When the ponds are emptied of silt, the gates are put back in the dams and the ponds are refilled. The accumulated silt and usable trash from the bottom are spread on the land or on compost piles. The product, as with us, will be a pile of first-class rotted sod which can be used in greenhouse, in mulching fruit bushes and trees, in compost making or transplanting.

What we are doing on a few square yards of a North American farm, the Chinese are doing on a nationwide scale. They are planning their agriculture, dovetailing it with the changing seasons and the weather and building their farming base.

What the Chinese are doing on a national scale, the Soviet Union is attempting on a continent-wide scale. Eurasian rivers, among the largest on the planet, which have flowed north for millennia are being turned around, made to run south into the Central Asian deserts. Twenty years ago this was an engineers' dream; today millions of desert acres are being irrigated and cultivated. Another twenty years and the desert wastes of barren

Central Asia may be feeding and clothing a great section of the human race with its harvests of cereal grains and cotton.

Our tiny postage-stamp pond is a miniature reclamation project that offers us exercise in its construction, irrigation, sods, topsoil, ice to skate on in winter and a major capital asset in case of fire. We began our work on the pond in 1953. Twenty-five years later we are still excavating, deepening, enlarging.

"There are some People that care for none of these Things, that will enter into no new Scheme, nor take up any other Business than what they have been enured to, unless you can promise Mountains of Gold."

Jared Eliot, Essays upon Field-Husbandry
in New-England, 1760

"To have a great capital is not so necessary as to know how to manage a small one, and never to be without a little. It is not large funds that are wanted, but a constant supply, like a small stream that never dies."

William Cooper, A Guide in the Wilderness, 1810

"Gardening is not only an innocent and healthy, but a profitable occupation. It is not alone by the money which is made, but also by the money which is saved, that the profits of a pursuit should be estimated."

Thomas G. Fessenden, The New American Gardener, 1828

"A certain amount of money, varying with the number and empire of our desires, is a true necessary to each one of us in the present order of society; but beyond that amount, money is a commodity to be bought or not to be bought, a luxury in which we may either indulge or stint ourselves, like any other. And there are many luxuries that we may legitimately prefer to it, such as a grateful conscience, a country life, or the woman of our inclination."

Robert Louis Stevenson, Men and Books, 1888

"Do not give up in despair because you have a small income and resign yourself to living meanly, in a hand to mouth fashion. Self denial and saving and resolute abstention from luxuries will solve the problem."

Mary Hinman Abel, Practical Sanitary & Economic Cooking Adapted to
Persons of Moderate & Small Means, 1890

"Live within your income and make it cover the truest kind of living.... The moral of it all is to live just a little below the probable limit, whatever that may be, rather than to assume a greater income than is quite certain."

Ellen H. Richards, The Cost of Shelter, 1905

"Whereas it matters little on Medlock Farm whether the cost of living goes up or down—it is not so much the market price of a dozen ears of corn that concerns us as that we have our own corn on the cob. No matter how low it goes it will still be cheaper to grow it than to buy it."

Henry Tetlow, We Farm for a Hobby and Make It Pay, 1938

CHAPTER 8

OUR CASH CROP: BLUEBERRIES

HOMESTEADERS in the United States, as elsewhere, need a cash crop. Scrimp and manage as they will, they cannot live in the midst of a money economy without using some cash money, if only for the purchase of postage stamps.

We produce 85 per cent of our food and all of our fuel, except gasoline for the car. We must pay cash for spare parts, replacements, hardware. We pay our rent when we pay our local taxes. Some of our clothes we make, some we buy in thrift shops and at rummage sales; a few clothes we buy new. We use and buy no habit-forming drugs, including alcohol, tobacco and caffeine. Our supply of printed matter, postage and stationery comes to us via our Social Science Institute, to which organization we hand over all royalties and lecture fees. Our travel expenses are paid by those who ask us to talk.

Surrounded as we are by a cash-credit economy, we need a certain amount of cash income each year. If the amount of needed cash can be figured out in advance, we can stick to our rule of no credit purchasing and no interest slavery.

We went to Vermont expecting that our cash income would come from our woodlot: saw logs, firewood, poles and posts, greens for decoration, pulp wood. Our first year in Vermont convinced us that the easiest way to provide cash was to make maple syrup and convert a good part of our syrup crop into maple sugar. This we did for years.

Our Maine farm does not have a dozen mature sugar maples on its entire acreage. After several years' experience with selling lettuce, spinach, asparagus, peas and other vegetables, we decided in favor of berries as our cash crop.

Like Maine, our area of Vermont had been largely occupied by wild blueberries and huckleberries. We frequently discussed the possibilities of blueberry culture with our Vermont neighbors. Our experimenting began in a small way with less than a hundred two-year-old hybrid blueberry plants, carefully selected for their frost hardiness. Only in the third or fourth year does a plantation of hybrid blueberries begin to pay its own way. When we left Vermont in 1952 this experimental blueberry plantation had begun to bear substantial crops. Our Vermont experience showed us that the hardier hybrid blueberry plants would survive and produce satisfactory crops even with winter temperatures of 45 degrees below zero.

Hancock County, Maine, where we had settled, was one of Maine's "blueberry counties." Many Hancock farms included extensive tracts of wild blueberries which were burned over every second year, and in the alternate year yielded good crops of wild berries, which were an important local cash crop. The local county agricultural agent each year sent out a series of letters to growers of wild blueberries giving advice, particularly about spraying and dusting.

One of our first moves in Maine was to visit the local county agent and consult with him about the advisability of hybrid blueberries as a cash crop in Maine. His advice was brief and decisive: "Don't waste money or time planting them; they won't survive our cold winters." As we had grown them in the much colder Vermont climate, we thought they would survive in Maine, so we started with a few plants in our garden and then chose a quarter-acre plot of sandy loam, sloping to the south and west, lying to the east of our chosen pond site. The area had not been plowed or cultivated in recent years. Some of the white birch and spruce trees on the plot were a foot in diameter.

We cleared about a hundred feet square of this vigorous young forest. We cut all trees and brush as close as possible to the ground. We carted the brush away and piled it in a hollow along a small adjoining stream. The trees we cut up for firewood. In the autumn we mulched the entire patch with a layer of spruce sawdust and piled on as much spoiled hay as we could gather together. We did not plow, harrow or otherwise turn over the land. We dug no stumps. We merely planted around them. (In the early years the blueberry land was full of tree roots. As time passed and we continued mulching and weeding, the roots rotted out, enriching the land. After a dozen years the patch was virtually free of stumps and roots.)

In the spring we set stakes 6 x 6 feet each way, dug good-size holes, and set in 228 two-year blueberry plants, filling in the topsoil around each plant and tramping it hard. We used no fertilizer.

There are fifty or more named varieties of hybrid blueberries, ranging from early to late, from small to large, from hardy to delicate. We set out twelve varieties, with some from each group. By so doing, we extended our picking season from late July to the freezing point in late September or early October.

How many hybrid blueberries do we pick each year? In 1957 we picked 5½ quarts; in 1958, 60 quarts; in 1960, 120 quarts. In a word, it was seven years before we had blueberries for sale. Thereafter the pick rose steadily to 655 quarts in 1965; 1034 quarts in 1970; and 1296 in 1971, which was our banner year. Since then we pick around 800 quarts.

Our blueberry bushes are petted and pampered. The bushes are well pruned and well fed. At the moment, our earlier planted bushes are 6 x 6 feet apart; the later planted bushes, when we found out how large they grew, are 7 x 7. We would recommend 8 x 8 feet apart, as our larger bushes are already crowded and must be heavily pruned to fit into 6-foot rows.

Like most fruit bushes or trees, hybrid blueberries once set are there for at least twenty to twenty-five years. After the second year they cannot be moved to advantage. They may be dug out and replaced. But if new two-year plants are set in their places, it will be at least four or five years before a crop of any size can be harvested.

We hold the height of the bushes to seven feet, which is the height of the cedar posts which support wires and the secondhand nylon fishnet that excludes birds during the picking season.

Ideally we allow each bush to consist of six to seven major trunks, on the side branches of which the fruit buds and berries grow. Of these six to seven laterals, some should be new wood from the previous year and three or four can be older stems. This method allows for a complete replacement of the canes every third year. Since the best crops of the best berries are likely to be borne on second-year wood, this method of continuous bushtop renewal gives us an advantage parallel to that of the grower of wild berries who burns off his tops every second year.

While we are on the subject of pruning, we might mention that the hybrid plants in our area are often the victims of a parasite called witches'-broom, which grows in alternate years on fir trees and blueberry plants. Witches'-broom grows sometimes from the root; at other times it gets a start on a branch high on the bush. Wherever it appears, we cut out the soft brown twigs.

Early in our experience with blueberries we fertilized at pruning time in the spring and again at the end of the crop season. But new growth, stimulated by this procedure at the end of the growing season, is likely to be frozen out during our severe winters. Latterly we have fertilized only in the spring. Our pruning is done during the good days in late winter or in the spring before the buds have begun to swell. We prune and fertilize heavily in order to increase the size of the berries and the volume of the crop. Under these conditions we get a reasonably abundant crop each year.

Spring feeding follows spring pruning. It consists of about one pound per bush of a meal composed of soybean meal if we can get it. When soy meal is scarce or excessive in price, we use cottonseed meal, linseed meal and as a last resort cornmeal. With the soy we mix equal parts of ground phosphate rock and granite dust. Over the meal we spread compost, eight to fifteen pounds per bush, depending on size and appearance. We top off with sawdust (about a peck for a good-size bush) and then spread hay or straw in the spaces between the bushes. As the hay is tramped down by weeding or picking we replace it.

Blueberry bushes prefer a sandy loam or gravel soil somewhat acid in character. We use no lime and no wood ashes on our blueberry plants and aim to keep the soil on the acid side. Each feeding includes a generous ration of peat moss per bush. In Michigan, where peat bogs abound, we have seen an entire blueberry plantation in a peat moss bog. The plants were about ten years old and seemed to be doing well.

Who picks our berries? Generally we pick them ourselves, as we know which are riper; if the berries are picked too early, they are sour. Sometimes the berries are picked on shares, one quart out of four for the picker. Pickers who are newcomers generally go for the biggest berries and leave the smaller-fruited bushes. They also eat a lot of berries. One woman who came to buy berries asked, "If I pick them myself, can't I have them for less?" "No," said Helen. "The price should be higher because you'll eat so many."

Picking is easy and pleasant. With the birds singing and the frogs croaking and the wind blowing and the sun shining, it is nice work. With good picking conditions (berries ripe and abundant and not too much conversation), one can get ten or twelve quarts in an hour, but not everyone can move that fast.

Blueberries make us a moderate cash crop. They ripen on the bushes and (unlike raspberries, which must be picked as soon as they are ripe) they stay there until they are picked. Taken into our cold cellar, they remain in good condition for days or even a week if necessary, without apparent disadvantage or loss of firmness or flavor, which cannot be said of strawberries or raspberries.

Everybody likes ripe blueberries, even our native neighbor friends who first scorned them as "not up to the wild ones; tasteless." After a few presentation quarts they now come and buy them. Animals like blueberries too, especially deer and raccoons and a great variety of birds, including the seagull—a big bird with a huge appetite.

Since our blueberry plants began bearing, we have never had a crop failure. The pick has been greater in some years and smaller in other, depending largely on the weather. But each year there is a sizable and marketable cash crop.

"I am the warmth of the hearth on cold winter nights. I am the shade screening you from the summer sun. My fruits and restoring drinks quench your thirst as you journey onward. I am the beam that holds your house; the door of your homestead; the bed on which you lie, and the timber that builds your boat. I am the handle of your hoe, the wood of your cradle, and the shell of your coffin."

Sign on a tree in a public park in Madrid, Spain

"A tree: the grandest and most beautiful of all the productions of the earth."

William Gilpin, Remarks on Forest Scenery, 1791

"The duty of a forester consists in preserving order and beauty, furnishing timber or copse, and providing a succession of young trees for falls of timber, additional plantations, other uses, or decay or accident in any part under his charge."

John Loudon, A Treatise on Forming, Improving & Managing Country Residences, 1806

"There are few farms in the United States where it is not convenient and profitable to have one or more wood lots attached. They supply the owner with his fuel, which he can prepare at his leisure; they furnish him with timber for buildings, rails, posts and for his occasional demands for implements. . . . In most woodlands nature is left to assert her own unaided preferences, growing what and how she pleases, and it must be confessed she is seldom at variance with the owner's interest."

R. L. Allen, The American Farm Book, 1849

"According to the common estimate of farmers, the woodlot yields its gentle rent of six percent, without any care or thought, when the owner sleeps or travels, and it is subject to no enemy but fire."

Ralph Waldo Emerson, Country Life, *in* Natural History of Intellect (vol. XV), 1904

"So far we have concentrated most of our bucolic attention on food: That is as it should be because it is the most important thing the land produces. But it also yields a number of non-edible things: the woodlot, for example. Year for year, the experts say, trees pay out better than grain crops."

Henry Tetlow, We Farm for a Hobby and Make It Pay, 1938

CHAPTER 9

TREE CROPS IN MAINE

TREE CROPS have played a significant role in the life of human beings for a great part of written history. Evidently, trees will continue to be one of the basic resources available to mankind.

Before men learned to domesticate animals or to cultivate the earth, they secured an important part of their food supply directly from trees. They used tree leaves, tree roots, tree sap, tree bark, tree shoots, tree flowers and tree fruits for food. As the use of fire became widespread, wood, which is derived from the bodies of trees, was used for warmth and for food conditioning. Until recently, tree bodies in the form of lumber were the chief structural material. Even today, in an era dominated by minerals and metals, wood has a great variety of uses.

Every climatic belt inside the polar extreme has tree crops for which it is peculiarly suited. Maine is no exception. Apple trees grow wild all over Maine. Originally they were crab apples, with a minimum element of usefulness. Johnny Appleseed and his contemporaries introduced into New England fruit trees and berry bushes developed in Europe, elaborated in North America and presently providing the varieties that dot the Maine countryside. In the hedges and thickets, along the highways, in former pasture lands presently growing up to brush, there are endless volunteer apple trees.

Our farm in Maine is well situated for growing hardy fruit. A century ago a large part of the farm was occupied by a prosperous apple orchard. When we bought the place in 1951 a few of the original trees from this old orchard were still bearing. They were splendid specimens of orchard antiques—some of them must have been at least a hundred years old.

Where we have cleared on our Maine farm we have found scrub apple trees among the brush, holding their own in the growing forest on our woodlot. Several of the volunteer apple trees stand out each spring crowned with masses of apple blossoms.

When we do our annual clearing in the woodlot, if we find promising apple trees we clear an open space around them, prune the trees as we would any promising young fruit tree, thin out most of the fruit buds and check on the remaining buds to see if they will fill out. We have observed that when apple trees grow from whips into promising young trees, they behave like any forest tree. They grow up with the neighboring shrubs and trees, competing for a place in the sun.

One apple tree near our blueberry patch was of this forest type, with blossoms and fruit at the top, forty feet above the earth's surface. The tree at stump level was about eight inches in diameter. The tree looked like a vigorous grower, so we cleared around it and left it standing by itself when we put in our blueberry plantation in 1953-54. The tree bore a Greening-type apple, of moderate size. The crop was borne on the top of the tree. Almost every apple was marred by destructive apple scab.

Could we convert this wild thing reared in a young forest into a disciplined and productive bearer of the kind of fruit that appeals to human beings? We decided to experiment.

We climbed to a point on the apple tree about fifteen feet from the ground where there was a whorl of side branches and sawed off the top of the tree at a point where it was about five inches in diameter. In a word, we cut the tree in half and took off the entire top, which had been bearing most of the blossoms and fruit. We pruned the lower half of the tree into some semblance of an orchard tree. For three or four years the tree bore few blossoms and little fruit. Today the Greening tree looks like an orchard native and is bearing a good crop of good apples.

We found a pair of what we consider volunteer apple trees standing rather close together when we took over the Maine farm. The trees were near our garden site and close to our compost-making area. Both trees were so close to a ditch that their roots were being undercut by spring runoff. One of them was leaning at an angle of 20 degrees. Both trees were volunteers. Both bore Cortland-type fruit, but so far as we know they had not been grafted. The leaning tree was the more vigorous grower and was bearing larger crops. Apples from both trees make good juice and applesauce.

We began with these trees by moving the stream well away from their roots. We fertilized and mulched them generously. Size and quality of the fruit increased. Apple scab, which had been bad in both trees, diminished notably, although we did not dust or spray. We thinned the fruit rigorously, picking off scabby and wormy apples. In good apple years, they produced large crops. In the 1975 season, a rather good apple year for us, we picked twenty-five bushels of apples from the two trees. Size of apples was good, and the quality was excellent. They kept in the root cellar until early spring.

Thus far we have been writing as though the chief product of forestry were the fruit yielded by trees, when as a matter of history and experience the chief crop yielded by forests is wood: wood for fuel, wood for building, wood for furniture, wood for paper, wood for a thousand and one objects.

There was a time not many years ago when important parts

of the Americas, Asia, and Africa were still occupied by virgin forests grown through centuries. Today all of the remaining forested areas are under heavy pressure to turn standing timber into a cash crop. As the world's population increases, the need for wood increases.

Large areas of the earth's land surface are better adapted to producing tree crops than any other product. Steep hills, narrow valleys, thin soil, rough climatic conditions make farming and gardening difficult. For such areas tree crops are natural. Much of New England falls into this category. For ages it has produced high-quality forest products. If the human beings moved out of New England for a century or two, we have every reason to assume that similar forests would again establish themselves.

The Chinese and the Albanians in their overall thinking about land use have developed this formula: on mountains and steep slopes up to the treeline, forests; on more gradual slopes, orchards and vineyards; on land that is flat or nearly flat, open cultivation. Following such a formula, much of Maine would be forested; its more gradual slopes would bear orchards and vineyards. Only relatively level land would be subjected to open cultivation, without the consequent threat of erosion.

Homesteaders who settle in New England and who take for granted the need for tree crops will see to it that the weeding and thinning of the woodlot occupies a high place on the list of priorities.

In trimming out our woodlot we follow a simple formula. We decide what trees will do best in a given area—swampy, rocky, hilly. How close together should trees stand in a young, growing forest? The answer depends on the age of the forest and the type of tree. Balsam for the Christmas-tree trade can be planted or thinned to 6 x 6-foot distances. When of marketable size, every second tree can be taken out. Trees should not crowd each other, but the sun can be almost excluded from the forest floor. In the garden we refer to "thinning" and "weeding." In the woodlot the same principles and the same terms may be used.

In a moderate-size Maine woodlot, our chief objective is to provide logs for milling, fuel for heating and cooking. Wood for heating should if possible consist of hardwood. In our region near the coast, hardwood is scarce. We have no oak or beech— two of the trees that provide wood with a maximum of heat units. Black cherry and white ash come next. Then come spruce, hemlock and balsam fir.

Felling trees is a simple matter if axes and saws are in good order. Small trees, up to eight or ten inches in diameter, present no problem. Larger trees, particularly if there is a thick stand in the woodlot, may be troublesome and, in the case of very large trees, dangerous. A competent woods worker can usually determine almost exactly where a given tree will fall when it is properly notched and sawed.

Once the trees are marked and down on the ground, all branches are chopped or sawed off. The trimmed tree trunks are sawed into lengths. If the project is a commercial one where high wages are paid, tree trunks are cut into logs and pulp wood. In our small-scale woodlot operation, economy is the determining principle. We cut some logs and pulpwood, but mostly firewood for heating and cooking. So we save branches that a commercial lumberman would scorn, and cut them into stovewood lengths. For us, good limb wood, well dried, is as good firewood as you will get anywhere. It cuts up easily and burns magnificently. For hot fires we know nothing better than well-dried limbs.

About four-fifths of our Maine farm constitutes a woodlot that matures year by year. About one-fifth is cleared land that we mow or scythe each year to keep back the encroaching woods and maintain the grasslands in hay for mulching and compost making.

We do not own a mowing machine (which we would use perhaps six or eight hours in the year), so we try to hire a neighbor to come in with his machine for an hour or two. As there are few functioning mowers in the neighborhood, we have equipped ourselves with scythes which we use in the most necessary places. Early every morning for about two months Scott is out swinging the scythe for his pre-breakfast exercise. One notable summer day last year, eight or ten neighbors contributed their time and energy and skill to hand-scythe from dawn to dusk and cleared a whole meadow for us. It was a Breughel-like scene with figures of men, women and children moving over the field.

In cutting trees or keeping back encroachments on meadows, we have enlarged the cleared area of our farm somewhat during the past quarter-century. We regret each acre that we pilfer from the reforesting process. Nature, here in Maine, moves from the bare earth to splendid tall timber. We regret any steps that we take in opposition to that process.

Almost everyone who settles in New England is tempted to clear some land. Trees, big and small, perennials and annuals, are cut off, their roots are destroyed and the earth is left bare and open to elements which immediately set in motion the forces of erosion. Wind blows; water runs; sun burns; fire destroys. Under such conditions one would think that in the course of time the soil would disappear and only the rocky skeleton of the countryside would survive. Land clearing, plus brush and trash burning, should have brought rocks to the surface years ago. But that just does not happen even on waterless land. On the contrary, the hills and valleys of New England have attracted and sheltered a multitude of plant life and wild animals for ages.

Instead of erosion seizing the initiative and disposing of every thing movable or burnable, natural forces make soil, enrich it and utilize it as a base for: the first year, annuals; the second year, shrubs; in a decade, young saplings on the way to becoming stately trees.

Anyone who is rash enough to try to keep New England free of trees and foliage has taken on a Herculean task. You may interfere with the process, but you cannot stop it. You might as well try to cure water of the urge to run downhill. Under existing conditions you cannot keep an acre of Maine land free of vegetation without cutting, clearing and mowing. If you let a back pasture lot go unmowed and untended for a time, it passes through a regular sequence from grass through brambles to brush composed of alder, birch and minor softwood, to semi-hardwoods like ash and soft maple and then, if the soil is ready, to yellow birch, and hard maple and ultimately to spruce, pine, hemlock and other softwoods.

The forces which made the greening-up process unavoidable, operating through centuries before Europeans came to North America, had covered the state of Maine with a blanket of green that extended from ground cover to magnificent tall timber. There was a time, not too long ago, when some of the finest ship-building timber on the planet was growing in Maine. At that time, Bangor, Maine, dubbed itself lumber capital of the world, basing its claim on the boast that it handled more lumber than any other city in the world. Maine's virgin forests have been devoured by the increasing demand for wood and still more wood. Today, in Maine, mature trees are a rarity. The murmuring pines and the hemlocks which once covered the bulk of the state exist only in song and story. The sequences of forest reproduction are interrupted as soon as young trees have reached a size that will make pulp wood. They are rushed to the pulp mills and converted into newsprint that announces price-cuts on supermarket bargains. For first-class lumber Maine now imports from the southeast, the northwest, Norway, Sweden and the Soviet Union.

If human beings would keep their hands, axes and saws to themselves for a very few generations, the Maine climate and soil, left to the normal processes of forest reproduction, would once again reestablish a magnificent growth of superb timber.

"The greatest value is received before the wood is teamed home.... It warms us twice, and the first warmth is the most wholesome and memorable, compared with which the other is mere coke.... Consider how the broker collects his winter's wood.... Postponing instant life, he makes haste to Boston in the cars, and there deals in stocks, not quite relishing his employment,—and so earns the money with which he buys his fuel. And when by chance I meet him about this indirect and complicated business, I am not struck with the beauty of his employment. It does not harmonize with the sunset.... If I buy one necessary of life, I cheat myself to some extent, I deprive myself of the pleasure, the inexpressible joy, which is the unfailing reward of satisfying any want of our nature simply and truly."

Henry David Thoreau, Journal, October 22, 1853

"I found chopping, in the summer months, very laborious. I should have underbrushed my fallow in the fall, before the leaves fell, and chopped the large timber during the winter months, when I should have had the warm weather for logging and burning, which should be completed by the first day of September. So, for want of experience, it was all up-hill work with me."

Samuel Strickland, Twenty-seven Years in Canada West, 1853

"How much more interesting an event is that man's supper who has just been forth in the snow to hunt, nay, you might say steal the fuel and cook it with! His bread and meat are sweet. My employment out of doors now was to collect the dead wood in the forest, bringing it in my hands or on my shoulders, or sometimes trailing a dead pine-tree under each arm to my shed. An old forest fence which had seen its best days was a great haul for me."

Henry David Thoreau, Walden, 1854

"In families where a strict and searching parsimony is necessary in every department of expense, if a generous spirit can be indulged anywhere, let it be in making the fireside a place of brightness and cheer, where, of a winter's night, the oak back-log hisses, and the hickory fore-stick glows till an infectious warmth pervades the family circle, and January seems no less joyful than June."

Joseph and Laura Lyman, How to Live, 1882

"There is a good deal of difference between a timber forest and an ideal farm woodlot. The latter must serve a variety of needs. The more different kinds of wood it contains, the better; and there should be trees of all sizes and ages, so that the production of available material for various uses will be steady. Our biggest single need is for firewood. Although we use four fireplaces pretty steadily from early fall into later spring we have seldom had to cut up a whole mature tree for fuel alone: weed trees, fallen trees, and the topwood of trees cut for posts or other purposes supply ninety percent of it."

Henry Tetlow, We Farm for a Hobby and Make It Pay, 1938

Chapter 10

WOOD FOR FUEL

WOODING-IT (in the vernacular) has been a basic source of income, a pleasant leisure occupation and a health-preserving avocation ever since human beings learned to make and use fire for their purposes. The practice is still popular, even in centers dedicated to technology, mechanism and automation. Wooding-it heats homes and helps in food preparation every day in millions of homes and homesteads all over the planet.

Wooding-it can be practiced by any homesteader or householder. It requires only a few simple hand tools which anyone can learn to use effectively. It occupies spare time that might otherwise be spent in front of the TV and keeps even decrepit oldsters out in the open while they make a real and substantial contribution to family income and to family comfort around the crackling open fire.

On a recent visit to England we dropped in to see a friend, Gordon Latto, who has a home in the country within commuting distance of London. No sooner had we finished our exchange of greetings than, at Scott's request, Gordon took him to a corner of his side yard and introduced his woodpile. A neighbor had been making some housing alterations that necessitated the cutting of several trees. Instead of letting the trunk and large branches of these trees go to the dump, Gordon had the good sense to have the drayman bring them to his backyard. There they lay, ready to be sawed to fireplace length. When cut, piled and dried out, the wood could be wheeled to a woodshed which opened directly on to the living room with its open fireplace.

Scott rolled up his sleeves, thanked his host for putting two newly filed saws and a sharp axe at his disposal and spent the rest of the morning happily fitting the wood to the fireplace. After days spent in airplanes, and nights in hotel rooms, the relief to him of sawing wood for hours was truly wonderful.

Horace Greeley, onetime editor of the *New York Tribune,* loved wooding-it as much as Scott. In 1868, he wrote in his *Recollections of a Busy Life:* "The woods are my special department. Whenever I can save a Saturday for the farm, I try to give a good part of it to my patch of forest. The axe is the healthiest implement that man ever handled, and is especially so for habitual writers and other sedentary workers, whose shoulders it throws back, expanding their chests, and opening their lungs. If every youth and man, from fifteen to fifty years old, could wield an axe two hours per day, dyspepsia would vanish from the earth, and rheumatism become decidedly scarce. I am a poor chopper, yet the axe is my doctor and delight. Its use gives the mind just enough occupation to prevent its falling into revery or absorbing trains of thought, while every muscle in the body receives sufficient, yet not exhausting, exercise. I wish all our boys would learn to love the axe."

Wooding-it has another advantage of overriding significance. From the decision to cut or not to cut a certain tree, through all the processes of felling and fitting, wooding presents a series of choices, decisions, tests and experiments that often preoccupy or perplex the woodworker. With experience, shrewd judgment, quickness of eye and nimbleness of foot, the successful woodsman, in half an hour or half a day, can point to a heap or pile of fitted wood as a concrete testimonial to his competence and persistence. Any tree correctly felled, any log properly split and stacked, gives a chance to evaluate, test out and get results time after time, hour after hour. Each tree, log or stick is a problem in its own right with its possible outcome of usefulness. In the north temperate zone, wooding-it will continue to be an important source of livelihood for a long time.

We cook and heat with wood. Since we have a woodlot, the outside energy needed to keep us fed and warmed in cold weather comes from a source under our own control. Wood and stoves make us independent of imported fuel.

Where we live in Maine we estimate our woodlot needs thus: a family-size cookstove will consume about four cords of moderately good dry wood in the course of a year; a chunk stove able to heat a couple of rooms in a house will require an equal amount of moderately good wood in a year.

Well managed, a growing woodlot of ten acres properly thinned and weeded should furnish an adequate supply of wood if the fuel is stored and well dried. We have two chief sources of wood. The first is our woodlot of about fifteen acres of young and old growth. The second is the driftwood that each tide and especially each storm brings into our cove. Occasionally, whole trees drift in.

Last year one of the logs that ended up in our woodshed was fifty-one feet long and two feet in diameter at the large end. It was water-soaked and consequently very heavy. We guessed that it was hemlock because of the large number of enormous knots. We sawed it into twelve pieces on the beach, loaded them with difficulty into our pickup truck and hauled them to our wood yard, where they stood around like huge Stonehenge blocks for a season while they dried out. They were then split and stored away under cover.

Usually tidewater wood comes in the form of logs or four-foot billets cut for firewood or for the paper mills. Many used timbers from demolished wharves and jetties and the construction industry end up on our beach. About half of the wood we burn is driftwood. Even when dried it is not good wood for stoves or fireplaces, since it produces creosote which clogs the chimney. But we enjoy using up an otherwise waste product. It also cleans up the beach.

Products of the woodlot and of tidewater are cut to three lengths: logs, which are either 8 or 12 feet long, billets, which are either 38 or 48 inches long; and miscellaneous wood, which is cut into stove lengths.

Our wood needs are governed by the size of the fireboxes in our heating and cooking stoves. Our heaters can handle wood up to 28 inches in length and our kitchen stove firebox will take nothing longer than 16 inches. To economize time and facilitate handling our wood supply, we cut all of our wood to a uniform length—16 inches for kitchen wood and 19 inches for chunk burners. The 16 inches is determined by the firebox. The 19 inches is the result of a decision to let wood go to the woodshed in only two lengths—kitchen and chunk burner. If all wood comes in these dimensions, piling is relatively easy. If wood comes in random lengths, piling is more laborious and unsatisfactory.

Conditions for drying wood are not too favorable in coastal New England, with its fogs, mists, high overcasts, fierce winds and nagging precipitation. For a brief period after wood is cut, it may be left in the open to season, harden and, if there is any sunshine, dry off superficially. For best results, both cooking wood and wood for heating should be kept under cover.

In the drying-off stage, we cut tree trunks and branches 5 inches or more in diameter into 8-foot lengths and pile these on skidways. A skidway consists of two poles or small logs laid 4 feet apart and blocked up sufficiently to keep the bottom logs from being rotted by contact with the earth. If there are many logs, it pays to divide them with stickers, poles or odd bits of lumber so that there is air space between the lower and upper layers of logs.

As a result of our experience in the mountains of Austria, instead of laying limb wood and poles on the ground where they attract moisture, we stand them on their butt ends in teepeelike formation. Logs and billets we cut to size. Everything else, long or short, goes into a teepee if it is 4 inches or less in diameter at the butt end.

Teepee construction is simple. We drive an 8- or 10-foot stake into the ground. Against this stake we lean poles and limbs, butt down, in concentric circles. Larger teepees are 8 or 10 feet in diameter at ground level. Some teepee poles are 18 or 20 feet long. Teepee wood, instead of lying on or near damp ground, stands up in sunshine and fresh air. Rain and moisture run off it and it dries out quickly.

Since we live in New England weather conditions, which make dry wood almost a must, in setting up a homestead we therefore set aside part of a building or a separate building for wood.

The woodshed itself is of the simplest construction, open on four sides to let in a maximum of fresh air and sunshine. Our main woodshed is built on a rock outcrop. We picked four outcropping rocks, cleared them carefully and built on each of the rocks a wooden form. The four rocks and their piers made a rectangle 12 x 14 feet. The four forms were built on the uneven rock outcrops so that the tops were at the same level (10 to 18 inches from the ground). Into these forms we poured concrete made of six parts gravel, three parts sand and one part cement, well mixed into a sticky mass.

At the center of each of the four piers we set a piece of iron one inch in diameter and about two feet long—half in the form, the other half standing vertically in the air—at each of the four corners of the prospective woodshed.

We planned to have the woodshed about 7 feet above the

ground at the plates. So we cut four cedar logs 7 feet 6 inches in length, bored a hole 12 inches deep in the top end of each log and, as soon as the concrete piers had hardened, set the four logs, butt end up, on the inch bolts embedded in the concrete.

We braced the four corner posts into position. We divided the top of each post into four segments and cut away the three outside segments, leaving the inside quarter of the post with a 6-inch projection and two shoulders to carry the 6 x 6-inch spruce plates. These plates had been hand-hewed at the ends, ready to make the halved corner joint at each of the four corners.

One-inch dowel pins were driven vertically into the corner posts and horizontally into the projecting inside quadrant of each corner post. Each corner post was braced into position by two 6 x 6 hand-hewed spruce timbers, their ends cut at 45 degrees, and pinned into position by one-inch dowel pins.

The ridgepole was a spruce hand-hewed timber set on the plate at each end and held up in position by a 6 x 6-inch hand-hewed post.

The next operation was to drive a ring of twenty-penny nails halfway into each corner post, lift the corner forms four inches and pour a stiff gravel-sand-cement concrete into the elevated forms, tying the four piers, the four posts and the four plates firmly to the rock outcrops on which the new structure was to rest.

As good luck would have it, a building contractor was tearing down an old and very well built house in Harborside. Into one pile he had heaped the 2 x 6 x 12-and 2 x 6 x 14-foot roof rafters, which bristled with fragments of broken wood and projecting rusty nails. It was as unsightly a mess as one could imagine.

We stopped by to have a word with the contractor and noticed the heap of old rafters. Said the contractor: "Anyone with a twenty-dollar bill can have that heap of trash." We produced a twenty-dollar bill, loaded the nail-studded rafters into our truck, drove home with our treasure trove, pulled out a thousand and one nails and had enough sound 2 x 6 timbers to provide rafters for the new woodshed.

The building was to have a roof of 28-inch by 12-foot aluminum sheets. The load of 2 x 6 scrap rafters from Harborside not only gave us rafters for the new building but gave us enough sound lumber to provide 2 x 6 nailing strips to carry the aluminum roof. By using the 12-foot rafters we were able to provide an overhang of almost 4 feet on the two drip sides of the woodshed roof.

We therefore had a woodspace of 12 x 14 feet, plus a comfortable, relatively dry space under the overhanging eaves on both drip sides. In this dry space we could lay out wood and work it up on rainy days, or stack wood temporarily while it was awaiting piling space.

The four sides of this woodshed were four piles of two-foot wood, laid ends to the weather. Inside this covered, woodpiled shelter, through which the wind whistled but into which only the finest snow could be driven by a high wind, we had a workplace for rainy days that was gradually filled by piled wood as we accumulated our supply for the succeeding winter.

In the woodshed, in addition to an old axe and a pulp hook, we keep a set of measure sticks about the size of ordinary wooden rulers. Each is plainly marked with a crayon—16 inches for the kitchen firebox, 19 inches for the chunk burners, 24 inches for the schoolhouse stove. The measures have holes bored through them and hang together on a nail driven into one of the corner posts.

With a measure stick in the left hand and a 30-inch bow saw in the right hand, we are prepared for anything up to a log or billet about 8 or 9 inches in diameter.

If a half hour comes along on a rainy day with nothing else to do, we can spend time in the woodshed under cover and with something practical and productive to show for each saw stroke. In addition to three 30-inch Swedish pulp saws, we have a 36-inch and a 42-inch Swedish bow saw which we use for logs more than 8 inches in diameter.

One of the most difficult jobs associated with self-sufficiency on the land is keeping the place and the tools neat and tidy and in place. On a general farm, even a small one, this is a constant problem. Each season has its particular needs, and each job has its appropriate tools. Sometimes, even from day to day and hour to hour different implements are needed and should be in place.

In the woodshed, in addition to axes and pulp hooks, we keep saws, shovels, forks. We keep our saws sharp and have a place to hang each saw when it is not being used. If tools are always cleaned after use and put into place, they are likely to be found when needed. Kept sharp and in good order, these tools can last a lifetime. In our woodshed we still have a double-bitted axe with a 30-inch hickory handle that Scott used as a young man around 1900. To be sure, the axe is worn down, stumpy and now used chiefly for grubbing, but the handle is still in one piece and it's a handy tool to have around the place.

After every morning or afternoon of work we gather up the tools we have been using, clean them with strips of burlap cut for the purpose and put them into their allotted place in the woodshed. A big machine like a cement mixer needs washing and scraping after every large or small job if it is to be kept in condition. We had one that turned by hand and mixed concrete faster than we can mix with a shovel in a wheelbarrow, but it was too much trouble to keep clean and to house. When we found it standing idle after some years, taking up room in the shed, we gave it away.

Wheelbarrows are among our favorite tools. We maintain a battery of four metal contractors' barrows with head-on dumpers attached. We use them generally for moving bulky or heavy materials. For all our concrete work in Maine we used wheelbarrows. Only during the last few years did we discover a new plywood barrow made in Vermont. It has two wheels and therefore takes a wider runway than a single-wheel wheelbarrow and carries more of a load. For light, bulky material like hay it is vastly superior to a wheelbarrow, although it takes up more space when stored.

If you occupy a cabin on a ship, or the equivalent in space, you have small choice but to keep things tidy. Space is limited and superfluous objects simply cannot be tolerated. But if you live on one or more acres, there are immeasurable possibilities for litter and clutter. With a front yard, a back pasture and a woodlot to fill up, stray pieces of wood lumber, tin cans for the dump, an odd bit of worn-out machinery, a car minus some tires, a broken cultivator or hay rake appear here and there until the whole place takes on the appearance of an unorganized junkyard. A modern homestead fills up with superfluity and waste that soon lead to disarray and chaos. Order in the woodlot, the woodshed, toolshed, yard and home are essential in the practice of the good life.

Unless wood is very expertly piled, it is likely to settle one way or another and, sooner or later, tip over. A pile of standard cord wood, 4 feet long, will generally stand up if it is less than 6 feet high. Shorter lengths always present problems. All wood in our woodshed is less than 48 inches in length. Our 16-inch wood is always a problem in any pile over 3 or 4 feet high. With a tight roof over our heads and some form of protecting siding, it is always possible to toss 16-inch wood at random into a stack. At the end of three or four months of such stacking, almost any wood will be dry enough to burn. In the woodsheds of both of Scott's grandfathers, this was their custom. They had the unused space—more than they needed—so they just sawed, split and tossed the firewood into stacks that reached the woodshed ceiling.

We enjoy both sawing and splitting and we are especially

happy with neat, even, erect, self-respecting woodpiles. With 4-foot wood this is no problem. With 16-inch wood it is a problem that must be faced with piles of more than 4 feet in height.

As we saw our limb wood and pole wood, we pick out some straight pieces an inch in diameter, cut them to 32 inches and have a small pile of these pieces handy as we pile. Instead of piling one pile at a time, we pile two, side by side. As the piles go up side by side, for each 12 inches of height we lay a 32-inch binder across both piles, and a binder every 3 or 4 feet sideways, and go right ahead piling over the binders. This gives us in effect a 32-inch-wide pile self-tied together as it goes up. The chances are that two such piles will stand up until needed for the stove.

When the pile of 16-inch wood has reached the required height, if it has been skillfully made it will be a work of art. If the piler wishes to take one more step in refining his artistry, he can use a piece of 6-inch board 3 or 4 feet long, stand it vertically or lay it horizontally along the completed pile and tap it with a light axe, bringing all of the ends to a line as even as any wall.

We go over all brush carefully and trim branches down to a diameter of one inch. And the branches of less than an inch in diameter? If we lived in Western or Central Europe we would treat this brush with respect. Here in New England most people leave it where it falls unless, like us, they take seriously (1) the problem of forest fires and (2) the conservation of our diminishing forest wood supply.

We are developing a technique of faggot making that follows the European tradition. Most West Europeans are hard put to get any burnable material—be it fossil fuel or wood currently produced. Consequently, like people in all parts of the world where wood is scarce, they pick up every available fragment of burnable material, including brush, and use it for cooking or heating. This has resulted in the European faggot: a bundle of twigs or branches, cut to size and bound together by twisted grasses, twigs or other likely material including waste string.

Our faggots are of two kinds: those of kindling size, used to start fires; and faggots made up of pieces of brush wood and limb wood from an inch to an inch and a half in diameter. This material when gathered should be at least partially dry; it should then be broken or cut to firebox length and bundled in units that can be added to a small amount of paper and ignited. If well made and dry, the faggots burn as readily as paper and are almost surefire with the first match.

We have built convenient troughs made of a base piece and two side pieces in which to assemble faggots. The base piece is at least 8 inches wide. Nailed to the edges are two 4-inch strips. Notches are made at convenient intervals so that each faggot is bound together by two strands of binding material. Binders are slipped into the notches; the trough is filled with cut-to-length or broken pieces and the binders fastened with easy-to-untie knots of scrap string or rope. If the string is good for two or more uses, so much the better. These bundles may contain anything up to a dozen or more pieces of brush or wood.

We know no other American homesteader who goes to the trouble of making up these faggots. We have found them invaluable in using up small pieces of wood otherwise difficult to pile and therefore tossed away or left neglected.

So much for wooding practices. Like any other activity, wooding can be just a chore and a bore, or it can give the wood handler a chance to put artistry into the trade. There are several ways to perform almost any act—an efficient, workable, artistic way and a careless, indifferent, sloppy way. Care and artistry are worth the trouble. They can be a satisfaction to the practitioner and a joy to all beholders. For us, efficiency and artistry always pay off because of the satisfaction of doing a job well.

We live in an age of quick and easy heat and power supplied by kerosene, gasoline, natural gas, fuel oil, electricity. The supply of these fossil fuels is sharply limited, less and less adequate to meet the increasing demand. All are produced and sold to consumers at high prices, which will increase as the years pass. The energy squeeze in 1973-75 created a big demand for wood and was a foretaste of what must happen as the supply of fossil fuels diminishes with population growth.

The purchase and sale of these sources of energy trespass on one of our basic formulations for the good life: "serve yourself." Those who can meet the demand for wood from their own woodlots will have an invaluable source of economic stability and security.

photo: Richard Garrett

"When thou hast chosen a convenient and fit plot of ground to digge a garden in, then must thou in handsome manner castying the utter compasse of it (as eyther four square, or round or otherwyse) enclose the same round about, and besett it and fence it throughout before you go about to dresse up or sowe any thyng within the same. For Gardens must be well fenced and closed about, before there be any thynge sowen in them."

Thomas Hyll, First Garden Book, *1563*

"All your labor past and to come about an Orchard is lost, unless you fence well. For you can possess no goods that have so many enemies as an Orchard. Fence well therefore, let your plot be wholly in your own power."

William Lawsen, A New Orchard and Garden, *1676*

"I am amused to see from my window here how busily man has divided and staked off his domain. God must smile at his puny fences running hither and thither everywhere over the land."

Henry David Thoreau, Journal, *February 20, 1842*

"When we have stones to contend with, we raise them above the surface by the help of levers. By these means, stones of half a ton weight can be more easily lifted from their beds. The larger ones are generally drawn off the fields to make the foundations of fences, and those of a smaller size are used in the contruction of drains."

Samuel Strickland, Twenty-seven Years in Canada West, *1853*

"More sensible is a rod of stone wall that bounds an honest man's field than a hundred-gated Thebes that has wandered farther from the true end of life."

Henry David Thoreau, Walden, *1854*

CHAPTER 11

STONE WALLS VERSUS WIRE FENCES

WE HAD lived in Vermont for almost twenty years, where we had fairly friendly relations with our neighbors and a consequent de-emphasis on fences or fencing. We dislike fences on principle because they shut people and creatures out. We like wild animals. One of our first experiences in Maine was watching two does and their fawns playing on our meadow. The little deer were like overgrown puppies, chasing each other back and forth over the greensward. While the young deer raced and circled, tumbled and butted each other, the mother deer browsed and watched. It was a happy family scene.

We were delighted with the fairly regular sightings, all to be seen through our house windows. There had been many deer in Vermont but they never came near the house, which was close to the road and had no extensive meadows about it. Here was a dividend on which we had not counted.

There were wild creatures aplenty around our isolated house. Except for short summers, the house we bought had been unoccupied for a few years and the wild animals had come to accept the place as deserted. By and large they were unafraid. One raccoon came to our back door and we lured it into the kitchen with a piece of bread. It prowled about the room and had to be got out with another piece of bread.

We later found varied reasons to keep the wild things out in the woods where they belonged. In Vermont we had tried without success to grow grapes. The vines survived the hard winters but the summers were too short for the grapes to ripen. We thought we would try them out in Maine. A hundred feet north of our house there was a rock outcrop that faced directly south. This outcrop seemed to offer us just the opportunity we wanted. A well-fertilized bed along the rocky edge could be enriched. A trellis could be built over the rock, across which the grapevines could trail and where they would be protected against the north winds and have the advantage of sunlight. The rock would absorb heat during the day and radiate it at night.

Accordingly, we made a grape bed at the base of the rock ledge, bought some carefully selected grapevines and looked forward to a crop of delicious grapes by the third year. The grapevines did their part. They took root and grew sturdily. By the end of the second year our cherished vines were thriving against the rock outcrop. One more year and we could anticipate a crop of grapes.

Came the third season. The grapes had lived through two winters. They budded out properly and the young leaves began to appear. Early one bright morning we chanced to look up toward out prospective vineyard. Dawn light showed us two half-grown deer standing in front of our grape trellis nibbling the vines. We got field glasses for a better look. With dismay we watched while the deer ripped off each partly grown grape leaf. Leaf by leaf, they were being daintily plucked from the young vines. When the deer had finished their morning snack there was not a green leaf or a bud remaining on the grape arbor. That was the end of our grape venture unless we were prepared to fence in the outcrop.

Between this rock outcrop and the house we planted a dozen Rugosa roses, which we found in a nearby cove growing just above high-tide mark. Rugosa rosebushes grow, at best, to a height of five to seven feet. Once established (as they were along the coast), they thicken to an all but impassable bramble patch and therefore make an excellent hedge. They are showy green in spring, rosepink or white when in flower. By mid-August the petals are replaced by a reddish yellowish rose apple or rose haw that can be as much as two inches in diameter. When mature, these rose apples contain much more vitamin C than the best citrus. To make Rugosa still more attractive, they are a decorative shrub, beginning to flower in early summer and continuing to flower and fruit until frost cuts them off in the autumn. We are loyal friends and admirers of Rugosa's foliage, flowers and fruit.

From the dozen plants we now have thirty-five hills in our planting. Each year they are heavily pruned and thinned and fertilized generously with rotted sod dressing and a home-mixed protein meal and mulched with seaweed fresh from the shore. We prune and treat the Rugosas about like raspberries. The hills are four to five feet apart in each direction. Additional young plants, of which there are many, are dug out. Each year a third of the old plants are cut away. In their places, two or three young plants are allowed to replace those that are being removed so that each hill retains from four to seven plants.

One year at thinning time in early summer, Eliot Coleman, a near neighbor, took forty of our young plants to establish a plantation of his own. Of the lot he lost only one; thirty-nine lived and provided him with the basis for his present extended planting of Rugosas, from which he in turn gives away numerous plants.

When we began our Rugosa patch, we did not fence it. By the third year the deer had discovered it. That year they sampled the rose apples. The next year they began on the tender leaves early in the spring. By the following year they were eating the leaf and flower buds from the roses. That year we did not get a single rose hip from our plantation. That same year we put up a wire fence.

One more item in this list of reasons that led us to fence our vegetables and fruit: Traditionally we plant sweet corn—usually from eighty to a hundred hills. For a number of years our corn was molested only occasionally. Finally this molestation became serious. One year, from a hundred corn hills we got not one single ear of mature corn. All were destroyed by raccoons before they ripened.

Rabbits, woodchucks, squirrels, porcupines all caused damage so serious that we had to adopt countermeasures or do without, as in the case of grapes and the sweet corn. After much discussion and heart-searching, we decided to keep the animals out of our garden if we could. This has meant a six-foot woven wire stock fence for the garden and the Rugosa rose patch and a wire and net cover over the blueberry quarter-acre in which we raise our cash crop.

Woven wire fences are good for only a few years—a dozen at best. After that they begin to wear or rust out. When our fence began to go to pieces, we were forced to replace it with new wire or find a substitute. Finally in Maine we went beyond wire protection and built 420 feet of stone wall around our entire garden area.

Certainly a wire fence is the cheapest form of protection against garden predators, but it does not give total protection. Beside our garden and west of the house, there is a small patch of lawn. Early on summer mornings, with the dew heavy on the lawn grass, a small army of slugs and snails would cross the lawn while the grass was wet, go through the fence into the vegetable garden, have their early morning snack and get back across the lawn to their regular quarters before we had finished our human breakfast and readied ourselves for the day's work.

At the worst of this invasion period we would take a container into the garden shortly after daylight, pick up to 500 slugs by count and dispose of them before coming in to breakfast. For a time this was a regular morning practice. As we replaced the wire fence by a five-foot stone wall we eliminated this threat to our supply of fresh green food almost 100 percent. The commuting slugs could not or did not climb over the wall.

Other items in the same category are perennial weeds—such as milkweed, thistles and witchgrass—which pass undeterred under or through a fence into a garden. A stone wall stops this invasion.

There are other arguments in favor of a stone wall. It is better looking. It is homemade. It lasts longer. On the other side of the argument, the stone wall takes much more time to put up and, if it is done at hourly wages, costs so very much more that the average gardener cannot afford it.

We have one strong argument in favor of our building stone walls: we enjoy working with rocks. In Vermont, stone was plentiful and well shaped for building. We found the same ample supply in Maine. A heap of fieldstone almost anywhere in New England will yield a surprisingly large number of what we call "builders."

In Maine as in Vermont we had a place off the mowing on the edge of the woods where stones were sorted and stored. Wherever we went we picked up "good" stones and carried them home, especially if they had one or more good "faces" or smooth sides. Lacking this virtue, they were classed as "uglies" and put in a pile for fill in foundations or roads. We seldom broke or cut stone, but picked from the stone pile the one that seemed most likely to fill the next place in the wall. As these stone piles grew, it became more and more evident that the time was coming when they simply had to be used.

During our first dozen years in Maine, nothing much was done with the accumulated stones. The piles grew in bulk and also in number. Finally, early in the 1960's we decided that the solution for the worn-out and rusting garden wire fence was a stone wall around the garden. We agreed that the project should be a part-time job. It could be our tennis and/or golf. Both of us preferred building with stone to playing tennis, golf or any other game. It was relaxing, in the open air, usually in sunshine. It was constructive and lasting. It was not the subject of an urgency or deadline. It would be our pleasant avocation.

The garden wall project had a unique advantage: it could be carried on for an hour or two, dropped for a day or two—or a week or a month—and then picked up again at our next opportunity.

The 420 feet of garden wall required as many feet of foundation trench. As the texture of the ground varied from one point to the next, this trench was dug to a depth that varied from 30 to 48 inches. With hardpan or rock ledge below, 30 inches was enough. With softer earth, 4 feet put us below the frost line.

The foundation trench was dug with mattock, pick, bar and shovel. The digging was done carefully so that we could use the sides of the trench to act as forms to contain the concrete and rocks while setting. On top of the foundation we put forms which would contain our stone wall. All of our forms were 18 inches wide and of various lengths. The forms were leveled and plumbed and braced strongly enough to hold the rocks and concrete.

Into these forms we put a bedding of concrete, then added the stones with their flat sides to the forms. Behind them we tamped the sticky concrete until it occupied every niche and cranny between the stones. Stone upon stone went into the wall, with at least an inch of concrete in between. When the concrete set, the form could be removed, or another form could be placed on top of the first one and leveled, plumbed and filled in its turn.

Building such walls depends largely on the available stone. Each of our walls begins as a pile of fieldstone, small and large, thin and thick. We set aside stones with 90-degree angles as corner stones, flat even stones as floor stones, stones with one flat face as wall stones, stones with no good faces as fillers or uglies.

During fourteen seasons of never-ending, varied, enjoyable open activity, the garden wall building went on. At times two or three people composed the work crew. At other times the number of participants was much larger. Most of the time we worked at it alone. The job was finished in the autumn of 1971, when Helen was 67 and Scott was 87. We give our ages to show that almost anybody at almost any age is capable of building a wall such as ours.

The total cash outlay for the garden wall was about $450, largely for the cement. If we had paid professional masons to do the job of building us such a stone wall, stone-faced on both sides and three to four feet underground, the cost would have been in the thousands of dollars. And we would not have had the pleasure and experience of doing it ourselves.

There were no fixed rules for the guidance of this fourteen-year volunteer enterprise. We just played it by ear, when and as we liked. Its duration outlasted any other activity of this kind in which we have ever participated. It was a collective enterprise too, in so far as many people who took part in the wall building learned some of the necessary techniques. Undoubtedly, however, the real value of the experience lay in three directions: first, its long-continuing occasional nature; second, the small numbers engaged on the job and the absence of any compulsion; and third, throughout the fourteen years on the job, although there was much discussion and exchange of opinion, there was little or no argument or bickering and, so far as we can remember, no quarrels. What an interesting and positive example of successful and constructive mutual aid!

We regret the need for fences, walls and other obstructions to free movement. If they must be built, we would hope that as many of them as possible could be solid, beautiful and provided, like this quarter-acre garden, with at least three gates, closed only when necessary, and available to anyone who has the wit to turn a wooden button.

"For the building of houses, townes, and fortresses, where shall a man finde the most conveniency, as stones of most sorts."

Captaine John Smith, Advertisements for the unexperienced Planters of New England or anywhere, *1631*

"The advantages of stone buildings are their great durability; their seldom wanting repairs; their greater security against fire; and their offering to the owners places of abode of greater comfort, both in cold and hot weather....It may be thought by many that to erect such an one would be a great undertaking, yet it may be done without either great expense nor much difficulty. Hammered or chisseled stone is adapted to public buildings, or the houses of the wealthy, and is expensive; but comfortable, decent houses may be built with common stone, such as we would use for good field walls....Their happy owners may live freed of that continual intercourse with the paint pot, the lumber yard, and the .cut nails of all sizes and dimensions. A stone house substantially put up, will last three hundred years, and will require little or no repairs for the first fifty years."

J. M. Gourgas, in The New England Farmer, *January 1828*

"If I were commencing life again in the woods, I would not build anything of logs except a shanty or a pig-sty; for experience has plainly told me that log buildings are the dirtiest, most inconvenient, and the dearest, when everything is taken into consideration. As soon as the settler is ready to build, let him put up a good frame, roughcast, or stone house, if he can possibly raise the means, as stone, timber and lime cost nothing but the labour of collecting and carrying the materials. When I say that they 'cost nothing,' I mean that no cash is required for these articles, as they can be prepared by the exertion of the family."

Samuel Strickland, Twenty-seven Years in Canada West, *1853*

"These stone dwellings last forever, and need few or no repairs, so that money is well invested in them. Their quality does not deteriorate with time, like that of brick or wooden buildings."

Harriet Martineau, Our Farm of Two Acres, *1865*

Chapter 12

BUILDING STONE STRUCTURES

In Vermont, rock was everywhere, especially granite, excellent for building. We have found that Maine stones are as plentiful (though not as large and rarely granite) where we now live and are on the whole more colorful. Both Vermont life and Maine life were dominated for us by building with stone. Any day outside the deep-freeze season, after we had a look at the weather and consulted our date book, we would try to fit in some stonework, which we always found interesting, productive, creative and collective.

In Vermont we put up about a dozen stone buildings: a three-room cabin we built down the road off our land, to gain experience before we tackled our own home; a main house with connecting woodshed and sugar-packing room; a guest house and a workshop; a woodshed; a lumber shed; a garage; a greenhouse; a study for Scott on top of a huge boulder in the woods; and two guest cabins in the sugar bush—one occupied for years by Richard Gregg. With the log cabin we built to experiment on and to sell, we left quite a community of buildings when we moved to Maine after nineteen years in Vermont.

In Maine, from 1952 to date we have put up nine stone and concrete constructions. One of the first jobs was the spillway and concrete core for the earth dam that gave us our acre-and-a-half pond. Other undertakings early in our stay were several water tanks for garden and blueberry plantation, and a new tank for our bubbling spring. Another project was the 420-foot stone wall which encircled our quarter-acre vegetable garden. In the northwest corner of this garden wall we built a greenhouse, with the stone wall as a backdrop and sun reflector. To the west of the greenhouse, also along the garden wall, we built a stone garage.

Finally, we have been building three stone buildings on a small tract overlooking Penobscot Bay as a future homestead for ourselves. This big project was begun in 1972 by clearing the forest which had been in possession of the area long before Columbus discovered America. These acres had not been cultivated or built upon because they included a piece of low land lying between two stone outcrops which ran from the neighboring hills to the narrow, sandy strip of beach bordering the bay.

After much discussion, and some sounding and testing, nearly everyone decided the spot was too wet and swampy—not an auspicious building site, although having a superb view over the bay. An alternative site, which Scott favored, was to perch the projected stone buildings on a high section of ground also overlooking the bay. A building on this site would face north and could have no cellar unless one were blasted out of the rocky outcrops. It would also be difficult to get spring or well water up to the house. Helen favored the low area on account of the sunset view. She got her way.

The first finished project on the new place was a stone and concrete outhouse, completed in 1973. City-bred people may think it strange to launch a building plan by first constructing an outhouse. However, on any extended building undertaking far removed from ordinary utilities, putting up an outhouse the first thing is a matter of course.

It was built on a side hill with good drainage. The foundation was attached to a fairly smooth ledge with a pitch of 12 or 15 degrees. At the bottom of this pitch there is a wooden shutter hinged at the top and large enough to make the task of emptying the outhouse simple. The wastes slide down this incline and are easily shoveled out. If a generous amount of sawdust and soil is sprinkled by each user, the result will be a mature, odorless compost. The important thing is to provide enough earth and other absorbent material to handle the volume of waste deposited. We have found sawdust and wood dirt more effective than ashes.

The first time we emptied this particular outhouse (we had the same kind in Vermont), we were planting tulip and daffodil bulbs around the new house site. We placed the bulbs in depressions in the ground where we wanted a bed, and covered them lightly with compost. Then we went to the outhouse with shovel and wheelbarrow. We took out the material left from a summer's use (two wheelbarrow loads) and covered the bulbs with it. Then we put on more compost and topsoil. The bulbs benefited from the natural fertilizer, and the stuff was dry enough to leave the wheelbarrow and shovel clean at the end of the job.

Our outhouse was designed and built with hand-hewn timbers, a metal roof and a heavy Dutch door. Keith Heavrin, our near neighbor, and Scott did the foundation; Helen did all the stonework; Keith hewed the timbers and did the other necessary woodwork. It turned out to be a beautiful edifice and has been called "the prettiest outhouse in five counties."

We also have a composting toilet, or earth closet, in the main house—a Swedish Clivus Multrum. Outhouse and inhouse are useful in that they both return composted material to the land. The night soil will be used mainly under apple trees, as mulch, to stimulate their growth. As knowledge and practice of ecology grows, and water becomes a scarcer commodity, earth closets may take precedence of wasteful water closets.

Before we tackled our second stone building project on the new site, we had to put in roads. Ordinarily, that would involve buying many truckloads of expensive town gravel. We decided to look around for some on our own place.

The hill to the south of our new site rose high above the level on which we planned to do our building. It was a steep, ledgy outcrop, its rocky shoulders showing at various points among the young trees which covered the area with typical Maine coast vegetation, from the mosses and teaberry plants through alder and pineberry, white birch and soft maple, ash and black cherry to a few stately cedars and spruces.

Test digging on this rocky outcrop showed up a base of soft brown sandstone made up of small rock fragments the size of a hand to big rock masses. The rocky crag also had a covering of loam or forest soil so much sought after by gardeners for choice plants. Here was a fabulous treasure to be had for the taking: rich earthen pockets; rocks for the building; and stone chips just the right size for road foundation—millions of them.

Our roads were generally 10 to 12 feet wide. We established their levels, made provision for drainage and then laid down a solid bed of stones and chips from 8 to 15 inches deep. In wet places we began with large stones. On top of these stones we placed a layer of stones about the size of coconuts. On top of them went a layer of stone chips, finished off with a top-dressing of tidewater gravel.

This pattern of road construction is borrowed from the thousands of miles of hard roads that Roman engineers built in Europe, North Africa and the Near East about two thousand years ago. Some of the Roman-built roads and bridges are still in use. As with the Romans, no backhoes, tractors or heavy machinery were used in building our roads.

Results of this landscaping have yielded building rocks by the thousands, tons of coarse material for road building and topsoil for gardening. Best of all, the digging has uncovered a sheer rock precipice consisting of tier above tier of jutting rock ledges, set on the hill at various angles and providing a rugged backdrop for the stone buildings we have erected during the past three years.

The second unit of our stone and concrete building project was a garage-workshop-storeroom 25 feet wide and 50 feet long, with a metal roof painted brown to blend into the landscape. Why start with a garage and workshop? Why not do what is usual: get to the house first and let the lesser buildings trail along in due course?

In 1971 and 1972 there was little seasoned lumber to be had in the state of Maine. Trees stood in the woods on Monday; by Friday they had been cut and hauled to the sawmill. Within the following week they were being shipped out to construction jobs. We aimed to put our lumber in the open shed and leave it there to dry while we were building the house.

The garage-workshop involved digging 144 feet of foundation trench. The trench was 16 inches wide and at least 30 inches deep unless we hit bedrock, when we stopped digging. Most of the trenches were 30 to 40 inches deep.

When we reached a level at or below the frost line, we scattered 4 or 5 inches of fist-size rocks over the bottom of the trench and poured in a sloppy concrete mixture—one that would run into every nook and cranny. At the next stage we put in, on top of the small stones floating in concrete, a line of boulders as large as available and of a size possible to handle. Maximum width of the boulders was 12 inches, always aiming to leave a minimum of 2 inches between the side of the boulder and the wall of the trench, and with a minimum of 2 inches between boulders.

We continue this procedure until the trench is full, tamping and adding stones so long as they are covered by at least an inch of concrete. We aim to dig and fill 15 to 20 feet of trench at one time, then continue with another installment, until the foundation is completed up to ground level.

The foundation is left rough on top so that the wall of rock and concrete will have something to grip. Then comes the time to set the wall forms level and plumb and build the wall, which will be 12 inches thick. Our forms are 18 inches wide with a 2 x 3 spruce stud every 24 inches. They are held apart by 12-inch spacers and held together by a strand of telephone wire at the top and bottom of the form. The wire runs around the 2 x 3 studs if possible.

In building jobs as big as this, we like to begin with one corner, fill the form, then build a second corner. We then set forms and fill in the space between the corners, measuring carefully and frequently to keep the wall straight. We lay in metal reinforcing—especially at the corners. Thereafter there will be horizontal reinforcing each 9 inches as the wall rises— two lines of reinforcement to each 18-inch form.

At doorsill level, preparations are made to set in door frames, which along with the window frames can be set in either flush with the outside wall, flush with the inside, or midway. All three methods were experimented with on this building. Forms are shifted as we work up the wall until we reach plate level.

Keith Heavrin did the hand hewing of the timbers, the form work and general carpentry on this building. He stayed with us up to plate level. Then we had to put on the roof. Fred Dyer and his team did the job.

As the forms were removed from the walls, Helen did all of the pointing (which is filling in between the various rocks with a rich mixture of concrete). This is a one-man (or, in this case, a one-woman) job, as everyone handles the pointing mixture and trowel differently and the finished impression should be uniform in appearance. In all our various buildings and walls in

Vermont and Maine, this was Helen's special prerogative. She rarely let anyone (Scott included) handle the pointing trowel.

Who did the rest of the stonework? Just the two of you? No. Our work team consisted of the two of us if no one else was around; many particularly enjoyable days we quietly worked away together, with no outside help. But we get endless visitors and they usually want to help with whatever we are doing. The majority of them, boys and girls, men and women, have had little or no experience with such work, but they learn the ropes fairly quickly and many times become useful members of a smoothly functioning team. Or else they remember some errand they had to do in town and leave suddenly.

When we found how many workers were available on any set day, we paired them off. A couple of people made the mixes in the wheelbarrows and wheeled them to the job. One or two people were needed to keep the master mason (Helen) supplied with stone, which she insisted on handling herself.

With the roof on and the doors and windows in place in the new utility building, we had a tight, dry structure to store our piled lumber, our cement and our tools. On many jobs lumber is dumped and scattered about outside on the assumption that it will be soon used and that in the meantime no harm will be done if it is wet now and again. We proceed on an opposite assumption. On any construction job, we try to order our heavy supplies such as lumber and cement ahead. We like to keep them under cover and in order, stacked properly. Of course we take care of our tools, keeping them clean, oiled and out of the weather under some roof.

With the garage and workshop roofed in and a properly covered supply depot established, we were prepared in the spring of 1974 to make the preparations for building the house proper. It was to be two-storied, stone to the plates, with two bedrooms upstairs, each having a balcony. Helen designed the house to fit into the landscape. She wanted an alpine-type building with a broad sloping roof, creosoted heavy hand-hewn timbers, and pine paneling and bookcases in a large 20 x 30-foot living room with big windows looking over the bay. A Dutch architect friend drew up the first plans from Helen's initial drawings.

The first step was to dig a cellar under half of the projected house. Fred Dyer, a friend and local building contractor, looked the site over carefully and guessed that, although low-lying and wet, it could be used if extensive drainage were installed. With his cooperation we decided where the house cellar should be. Fred and his crew took on the job of putting in the cellar.

They excavated, drained, built the necessary forms and had transit-mix machines bring in the concrete and pour it. This was something new for us; every other cellar we had dug and built ourselves. However, this was bigger and wetter than anything we had tackled and we were glad to let Fred take charge. He let us help when it came to the actual pouring. The cellar when completed ran under the kitchen, hallway and bathroom. It is 52 feet long and 12 feet wide. We amateurs hand-dug and -filled foundation trenches for the balance of the house. We were ready to go on with the building of the house itself in the early summer of 1975.

At this point destiny moved into our building program with the appearance of a first-class cabinetmaker named Bretton Brubaker. A year earlier he had ridden a bicycle from his home in Ohio and turned up at our place, having read *Living the Good Life* and wanting to see what we were up to in Maine. He built a log cabin on a neighbor's camping lot and occupied it one winter. Then he got a job helping to refit an old schooner, the *Nathaniel Bowditch*. We visited the ship and saw some fine cabinetwork he had done. When it came to selecting a woodworker who could cooperate with us in building the new house, Brett was a logical choice, and he agreed to take on the job.

One of his first inspirations after seeing our plans for a simple, sturdy and longlasting house was a suggestion for the heavy timbers we wanted for the window and door frames. In Vermont we had plenty of big timber and had hand-hewed what we needed from our own stock. Here in Maine we had no big timber and would have to buy it.

Brett saw an ad in the local paper of a fertilizer factory being dismantled in a nearby town. The heavy mill timbers were being put up for sale. Brett went to have a look. He reported that they had many fine 6 x 12-inch oak timbers up to 24 feet long. The timbers had carried the mill roof studs and were bristling with 20- and 40-penny nails but were sound and serviceable. We bought two truckloads of the oak. Brett built an ingenious nail-puller and extracted the nails, smoothed up the timbers and used them to make all the door and window frames in the new house. With bar, winch and tackle he snugged the heavy timbers into place with little help. Like Helen, he wanted the fun of doing it all himself.

From then on, Brett was the genius of the place and did singlehandedly all the woodwork that had to be done. We and various visitors did all the stonework; Brett took care of the setting up and building of the forms. He proved an indefatigable and meticulous worker, a perfectionist of the first order. Perhaps we can best sum up his contribution by describing him as a one-man precision job, comprehensive and outstanding.

Two individualists really built the house. With Helen insisting on laying every stone, from outhouse through two large buildings to the high chimney, and with Brett tackling the careful carpentry and the cabinetwork alone, it might be termed a one-man, one-woman house.

Although others had a hand, Helen was in charge. She decided the overall plan, dimensions and layout. She designed and helped execute the inside furnishing and finishing. She handled every stone personally, choosing it, trying it out and putting it in its permanent place in the wall. Scott was allowed to mix the concrete in his favorite wheelbarrow, and dozens of unnamed helpers put in many days' work here and there on the house construction. But it really was Helen's and Brett's house.

A friend of Brett's, Forrest Tyson, was a retired electrical engineer and professor of electronics. Forrest had practiced and taught electrical engineering at the University of Hartford. He was good enough to help plan and set up the electrical installations of the new house. It was wonderful to work with friends on all these jobs.

We planned to heat this house and cook with wood. We put four flues in the massive chimney. A door on the north side on the house opened directly on the woodshed and had a storage capacity of eight cords. It was built open, with three piers, and covered by an extension of the house roof.

Earlier in this report we quoted a visitor as asking what we did for fun and enjoyment. There are many things we enjoy doing about the place: Helen prefers one and Scott another, but we both agree on one thing. Give us a good-size job of building with stone and concrete, with time and materials to do the work well. Now that the house is built, and we are living in and enjoying it, we look around us at piles of rocks still unused and wonder: "What next? Perhaps another garden wall? A green-house? A sauna?" Time will tell.

"*The private buildings [in Virginia] are very rarely constructed of stone or brick, much the greatest portion being of scantling and boards, plastered with lime. It is impossible to devise things more ugly, uncomfortable, and happily more perishable....The inhabitants of Europe, who dwell in houses of stone or brick, are surely as healthy as those of Virginia. These houses have the advantage, too, of being warmer in winter and cooler in summer than those of wood; of being cheaper in their first-construction, where lime, and stone, is convenient, and infinitely more durable.*"

Thomas Jefferson, Notes on Virginia, 1784

"*The evil in our architecture lies principally in this—that we build of wood. From this custom much immediate as well as remote inconvenience is to be expected. The comfort arising from celerity and dispatch does not make up for the numerous considerations of perishableness, want of safety, and call for repairs....Bachelors only ought to build of wood—men who have but a life estate in this world, and who care little for those who come after them.*"

Anonymous, in The American Museum, *October 1790*

"*I may remark here, in way of warning to those who undertake the renovation of slatternly country places with exuberant spirits, that it is a task which often seems easier than it proves.*"

D. G. Mitchell, My Farm of Edgewood, 1863

"*Many a farm of ample acreage is left to the rheumatic labor of advancing decrepitude....There is no strength for repairs, no ambition for improvement, and no expectation of more than a bare subsistence.*"

Commissioner of Agriculture, Farming in New England, 1871

CHAPTER 13

REMODELING OLD WOODEN BUILDINGS: DON'T!

DETAILS about the state of decay and dilapidation of farm buildings in the New England countryside are neither entertaining, constructive nor edifying. We write about them here because we want readers to realize what they have ahead of them if they tinker with old buildings. We lived in such houses for years, put up with their inconveniences and inadequacies, repaired, patched, reroofed, retimbered and otherwise spent valuable time and money on the projects.

We are aware that old buildings have an appeal for people fed up by the slapdash tawdriness and lack of grace and beauty which are so often met with in the "developments" that are going up all over the country. We agree in rejecting such graceless structures. But that is no reason for accepting and refurbishing old buildings that, no matter how patched, repaired and rebuilt, are still old buildings, even if the shingles and the paint are new.

We began homesteading in Vermont in two clusters of badly built wooden buildings, which were made of hit-or-miss materials and styled as the fancy of the moment or urgency or preoccupation had dictated. In a word, they had been thrown together. In each case there was a house built on a hole in the ground apologetically called a cellar. Each house was surrounded by a ramshackle woodshed, an outhouse, a chicken coop, a bathhouse.

When there had been a breakdown that needed repair, or signs of decay, the spots were plastered over or nailed or wired, patched or fastened back together with bits of lumber, rope, binder twine, chicken-coop netting or any other material that offered itself. Repairs had been haphazard, with no pretense at workmanship.

Of course there were exceptions, pleasant old houses, particularly in neighboring villages or towns, but we did not choose to settle in such. They were beyond our financial means at the time and outside the range of our interests. We wanted to live on a farm, on some isolated back road.

In Vermont, the Ellonen house where we started homesteading in 1932 was up the Pikes Falls road 7 miles from Jamaica, a village with a post office, country store, a bank and a church, and 3 miles from Bondville, which was little more than a country crossroads. In Maine, our Forest Farm is a little more than 2 miles from the post office and 6 miles from the nearest village (South Brooksville), 22 miles from the nearest town (Blue Hill) and 50 miles from the nearest city and airport (Bangor). On both of our homesteads in both states we started out with poor old second- or third-hand buildings of wood. In both places we tinkered with the decrepit places and finally built houses of stone for ourselves.

The Vermont house and barn needed roofing when we bought it. The house was ancient, with a poor excuse for a cellar, an outside toilet, and water from a pump in the kitchen. Our earliest building job in Vermont was to build a stone-walled, pine-paneled living room with a stone fireplace on the ground floor.

Some years later we acquired the place next door. It had a better cellar that included a spring of good water, but the house was in even worse repair than our original farm house. For the next two years we used the old house as a toolshed, carpentry shop, and shed for freshly sawed lumber direct from the mill. When we no longer needed it as a storage place, we tore it down and built a stone guesthouse and workshop on the site.

With the dried lumber and with rocks we had been gathering for years we built a new stone house against a split boulder on the edge of the woods about a hundred feet above the original wooden house. The split glacial boulder was 26 feet long and partly buried in the earth, from which it rose 9 feet above the surrounding terrain. We came across the boulder while cross-country skiing in the woods. The boulder was overhung with limbs from surrounding trees and smothered in brush and brambles. We paused in our skiing to examine the boulder more carefully, We decided that it was perfectly plumb and looked like the wall of a house. To that rock we attached the living room of our first stone Forest Farm.

The house near Harborside, which we bought from Mary Stackhouse in the fall of 1951, was reported to be about a hundred years old. It certainly looked it and more. In its later years it had been used by woodsmen and hunters to house tools and supplies, and as a place to eat noon meals and occasionally stay overnight. When Mary bought the building it was in a bad state of repair. Tradition says that when she took it over, the back door was hanging by one hinge.

Mary was an artist of sorts with a modest amount of money to spend. Elwyn Dyer, who worked on the place as a carpenter, estimated that she had a thousand dollars to spend and house plans that called for ten times that amount. She had the work crew tear down most of the existing buildings, and pick out the best of the timbers, floorboards and siding from the wreckage. From this material and additional stuff they put up a five-room dwelling and a small barn-garage which used to be a boathouse. When Mary ran out of money she still had a spot for a fireplace that she planned but never built, a place for a woodshed that was never constructed and the beginnings of a garden that was never organized.

When we took over the place in 1951-52, the roofs of both house and barn were in poor shape; the floors downstairs were sagging; north winds blew right through the house, which was not insulated. For the next twenty years we spent time, energy and money repairing and remodeling the old wooden buildings. We did most of the work ourselves, so the money outlay was not large, but year in and year out we had to tinker, repair, replace.

We reroofed the house and garage, replacing wooden shingles with asphalt ones, and replaced some roof boards in the process. We replaced the wooden boardwalk porch back of the house with a stone and concrete terrace that connected house to barn. The barn-garage had been set on wooden corner posts dug into the ground. In the course of years these posts, in contact with the earth, rotted out. We jacked up the buildings unit by unit and replaced the wooden posts by stone and concrete piers with foundations below the frost line. The living-room floor was laid on 2 x 6 spruce joists rather too close to the ground. As a result the joists rotted and the floor settled. Elwyn tore up a large part of the living-room floor, replaced the joists and relaid the floor.

We tore a hole through the living-room south wall and built a stone fireplace. On the north and east sides of the house, at the second-story level, we put up a balcony for yodeling and to sleep on in good weather. After a dozen years this balcony became unsafe. It came down and we used the best of the rotted wood in the fireplace. At the end of all our work we had an old house.

Most home makers attempt to save money by making at least temporary use of an established building instead of devoting materials, time and money to the construction of a new one. It seems to us now that time, money, materials and effort can be used to better purpose elsewhere.

We have argued over the matter at length in our own family.

We have gone over the issues with friends and neighbors. Like so many problems, it can be discussed endlessly. Everyone has opinions and experiences. Not only have we gone over the pros and cons of old buildings versus new construction, but we have tried out one aspect of the problem after another for forty years.

Our conclusion is emphatic. Do not spend time and materials in reconditioning old structures. Nine times out of ten it is better, cheaper and in the long run more satisfactory to build new and with the best materials available.

Building a shelter for self and family is not a fly-by-night affair. You will probably live many years in the new quarters. See to it that the design, the materials and the workmanship are the best obtainable. Economy, standards of workmanship, aesthetics and historical experience all press for excellence.

Our advice on the remodeling of wooden buildings would be something like this:

1. The cost of repairing and remodeling old buildings is about the same as the cost of new buildings. Probably in the end the cost will be a bit more. Certainly in our experience it will not be less.

2. In remodeling, if some materials are reused in the new structure, particularly if they are of wood, they will rot out much sooner than new ones.

3. Unless the overall pattern of the old building was letter-perfect and repeated letter-perfect in the new one, the result will be a clash of styles. The structure will lack uniformity and integrity—will be neither old nor new.

4. Anyone who builds has ideas and concepts which are part of the personality and should not be lightly cast aside. Unless the remodeler and rebuilder is an antiquarian, doting on the old, believing in the old and following it slavishly, we would recommend: Build according to your own personality; do not adapt to someone else's life style and tastes.

If you are not tied to the past, if you are mechanically inclined and creative, build new every chance you get, with the best materials that come to your hands, and do it yourself. Work out and develop your own designs. As you proceed and are painstaking, each new venture will be a chance to express your own ideas and to improve your skill as you strive to work out the very best product of which you are capable. Following such practices you will create and learn—learning and creating at the same time.

photo: *Richard Garrett*

"He is wyse, in my conceyte, that wyll have, or he do sette up his howseholde, two or thre yeares rent in his cofer."

Andrew Boorde, A Dyetary of Helth, 1542

"Every work for the next day is to be arranged, whether for fine or rainy weather, and the farm-books to be made up for the transactions of the past day. Besides these, he should have another book, for miscellaneous observations, queries, speculations, and calculations, for turning and comparing different ways of effecting the same object....Loose pieces of paper are generally lost after a time, so that when a man wants to turn to them to examine a subject formerly estimated or discussed, he loses more time in searching for a memorandum, than would be sufficient for making half a dozen new ones; but if such matters are entered in a book, he easily finds what he wants, and his knowledge will be in a much clearer progression, by recurring to former ideas and experience."

Arthur Young, The Farmer's Calendar, 1805

"I would encourage every family to live within their means. If there be a way— and such a way there certainly is—of living as comfortably and happily, on very small means, as we now do on much larger ones, it is certainly desirable to know it, especially in times like the present. 'But suppose the means are very small, what then?' Why, then, live within very small means."

William A. Alcott, Ways of Living on Small Means, 1837

"No one will deny the importance of urging rich and poor alike, in the present state of things to try and economise the fuel and food which they may have at their disposal. The sooner we make up our minds that what we regretfully speak of as the 'good old times' with their good old prices will never come again, the sooner we shall cease to look fondly back on a cheaper past, and brace ourselves helpfully and bravely to face the increased cost of the necessaries of life."

Lady Barker, First Lessons in the Principles of Cooking, 1886

"Everything depends both on what has been and what is to be. Which suggests the need for a good system of records....It is not the fellow weeding the onions in July who is getting the most out of his farm; it is the man who, in January, is planning what kinds and quantities of onions to plant next Spring....It may be possible to run a farm well without the help of a carefully worked out plan, but if it is I have never seen it done."

Henry Tetlow, We Farm for a Hobby and Make It Pay, 1938

CHAPTER 14

PLANS, RECORDS, AND BUDGETING

HUMAN beings are persistent planners and record keepers. Stone Age men chiseled their records on massive boulders. Those who came later used horn, wood, baked clay, animal skins and vegetable fibers. Whatever the medium on which men have listed their prospects, outlined their purposes or detailed their plans, humans have recorded the past, surveyed the present and made their proposals for the future as a matter of record.

Written records have a multitude of uses. They are as important to the gardener and the garden as they are in most other fields of human interest and endeavor.

Successful gardening begins with a survey of the proposed garden spot—an evaluation of its possibilities and limitations. It continues with a freehand outline of the project. Soon after it is put on paper, the freehand sketch is finalized by putting into your garden book a working drawing, still in free hand, but outlining the general garden project.

If possible, the garden should slope gently toward the south. Certainly it will aim at maximum exposure to the sun, and a minimum of shadow from trees or buildings or even from taller garden crops. If tall corn or pole beans or other crops are contemplated, they should be arranged in a manner that will throw the least possible amount of the garden area into shade.

A second important consideration is crop rotation. With rare exceptions the same garden crop should occupy its place in the garden for only one season. In the second and third seasons, different crops should occupy that space.

Irish potatoes do better if planted on a fresh green sod each year. We arrange this by having four plots side by side, each plot 15 x 30 feet. We begin the rotation by planting potatoes in plot 1 which, ideally, was occupied by a green sod the previous year. Meanwhile plots 2, 3, and 4 are planted to other crops.

The second year, potatoes go into plot 2. Plot 1 meanwhile is planted to squash. The third year, potatoes go into plot 3 and squash into plot 2; plot 1 is planted to grass and clover. The fourth year, potatoes are in plot 4. Squash goes into plot 3. Plot 2 is bearing a ragged green sod and plot 1 has a rich green sod. The fifth year, potatoes take over the green sod of plot 1. Squash occupies plot 4. Grass seed is planted on plot 3, and plot 2 is allowed to develop a green sod of its own.

Here is a minor crop-rotation sequence. Each fifth year the same crop returns to its 15 x 30-foot land strip. Between any two returns there are three years devoted to particular crops: one to squash, and two to green sod.

In our garden, as presently laid out, there are two paths which divide the garden roughly into four segments. Each year one of the four segments produces tall peas, a second produces pole beans, a third produces cucumbers, melons and tomatoes, and a fourth, small truck. Each year these four crops move on to a new garden location, rotating the crops into a new position.

Gardens have a fifth segment—semi-permanent crops, such as asparagus, artichokes, rhubarb, strawberries, which continue without any annual rotation for a number of years. Strawberries stay in one place for two or three years. Rhubarb and asparagus beds, once established, last a decade or more. Semi-permanent crops should be grouped together and so located that they interfere as little as possible with garden routine.

Biodynamic gardeners advocate bed culture instead of row culture. Most organic gardeners in the United States lay out their gardens in sections and plant almost everything in rows. Exceptions are made in the case of pole beans, corn, cucumbers, potatoes and squashes, which are planted in hills. Using hand- or power-driven machines, gardeners are able to go over their rows in short order. Weeds are eliminated and gardening correspondingly simplified.

Bed gardening is quite different. Beds are raised several inches above the surrounding garden area. Sometimes the beds are boarded or planked along the sides. Generally they are made by heaping up the soil to form the bed, making the bed itself so narrow that it can be worked from paths on both sides without treading down the soil of the bed.

This is not a modern invention. Chinese and French advocates of intensive gardening have planted in beds for centuries. The French method is usually quite small in scale; the Chinese often extend their beds for hundreds of feet across relatively level land.

Generally they are about a yard wide, skipping a space to provide a walkway between, then heaping up a second raised bed parallel to the first. The garden thus becomes a series of raised beds, uniform in width, with narrow walkways between them, producing drainage ditches for wet land and irrigation ditches for dry land.

The raised beds are planted and serviced by pairs of workers, one working along the ditch on one side of the raised bed, the other working the opposite side. By bending and reaching, two workers cover the entire bed, keeping their feet in the path, without stepping on the bed. Any soil, but especially a clay or gumbo soil, thus treated, remains light and flaky, making the pulling of weeds easy and allowing the plant roots to penetrate the soil.

The benefits are obvious. In our previous row-culture gardens we have packed down the loose soil by rolling it, beating it down with a spade or even walking on the seed row after it was planted. With bed culture the gardener keeps his feet in the walkways and does not pack down the seed rows at all, but makes every effort to keep the soil open to sun and air and capable of absorbing a maximum of moisture.

If the beds have been properly prepared and the soil is flaky and friable, sunlight and air penetrate the soil freely, water is absorbed into the soil as it falls with a minimum of evaporation or runoff and thinning and weeding are greatly facilitated.

Beds may be planted crossways in short rows, or longways in long rows, or the seed may be broadcast, raked or rolled in, and give the workers a chance to thin the plants to proper distances and at the same time to pick out the weeds. The most impressive result of bed gardening is the relatively high yield per square yard of garden due to the greater density of plants.

In bed gardening, as in row gardening, it is essential to know what has been planted and at what date. We meet this need by having a number of plant markers—wood, plastic or heavy waterproof paper on which we note with a ballpoint pen the date, variety and any other necessary information.

The same information, noted down in a garden book, provides the gardener with a record so that a glance at the book will tell the story of that particular bed, row or hill.

Like any other complex and confusing situation, a garden book (or a box of index cards kept up to date), enables the gardener to proceed from day to day and season to season with enough information to know what is happening in various parts of the garden and for like periods in various gardening seasons.

One can go further, making a detailed garden plan in advance and checking off the various items as the plan is carried out.

This brings us to an item of the greatest concern to home-steaders and any other experimenters—the role of bookkeeping (a) in making plans, (b) in carrying the plans into execution, (c) to establish the limits within which plan and fulfillment must operate and (d) to balance accounts at the end of the operation, to show at a glance whether the operation has involved a profit, suffered a loss or broken even.

Behind every successful enterprise there is not only a plan but also a series of preparations that will make the success of the project more likely. A decision to set up a homestead is not a casual affair but should be the outcome of careful thinking, a series of firm decisions and the determination to see the project through to a satisfactory conclusion. The first three years are the most difficult and critical. It takes at least that length of time to try out and check on the requirements and the possibilities.

Anyone who attempts to abandon a market economy and move into a use economy faces a period of transition that will certainly eat up months or perhaps years, during which the security of the old economy is absent and the hopes and promises of the new economy have not yet materialized. This gap must be filled by an amount of working capital sufficient to provide goods and services during the transition interval. Anyone planning to make such a shift must be prepared to provide the necessary goods and services for existence during the interval.

Most of our friends and acquaintances who have shifted from a market economy toward or into a use economy had laid aside enough to provide food, clothing and shelter for at least one transition year. Some prepared for two years or even three.

Others have arranged to keep working part-time for months or years of the transition. In the case of groups larger than family size, some of the members have continued for years on regular jobs in the market economy, contributing the surplus of their earnings to the group treasury.

The first requirement is fellow workers. Only an exceptional individual—a confirmed hermit—can set up a successful homestead alone. A would-be homesteader should have a tried and experienced partner or partners. Perhaps we should say, the more cooperators the better, but at least one who will stick to the project and see it through.

A homestead, to be successful, must operate day and night for 365 days in the year and for several years before it is "out of the woods." It is a big assignment for any individual to be continuously on duty and responsible week after week, year after year. Both the responsibility and the necessary labor should be shared. Only the "right people" will succeed in homesteading.

Experience is a good teacher. If one or more of the prospective homesteaders are tried and true, so much the better because they will have learned some of the skills that are necessary for such a project.

A homestead presupposes a piece of land as the base for operations, enough land to make success likely or even possible. The land should be suited to the needs of the proposed homestead. If possible it should be owned and unencumbered by mortgages or other obligations.

The homestead will require working capital—that is, a supply of cash or at least credit sufficient to carry the enterprise for at least two, and better still three, years without any net income from the project itself. Of course there will be some income which can be added to the working capital, but that is uncertain and not to be counted on. The initial working capital should be sufficient to carry the project through an extended trial period.

During that trial period the project should acquire the needed tools and equipment, paid for out of the initial working capital.

Skillful bookkeeping is another requirement. Someone on the project must be responsible for all of the necessary paperwork, including the maintainance of a cash balance sufficient to cover all necessary and likely expenses.

If two or more people are engaged in the experiment, they should be seriously and honestly determined to make the experiment succeed, to think through each day, week, month and year. In a word, each step should be anticipated, put on paper, discussed, modified if necessary, agreed to and then carried out.

Each day, week and month should have a working program, put down on paper, and referred to constantly as a guide and determining factor. The whole project might be referred to as a "three-year plan."

Most homesteaders have sharply limited resources. In that case, if they hope to succeed in their homesteading adventure they would be wise to follow the old adage: "Pay as you go." If the homesteader is wise, he will do his utmost to keep his spending inside his income and to avoid borrowing and interest slavery as he would any other evil.

The homesteader should distinguish between current expense and capital outlay. The budget for each year should contain a balance sheet, with current receipts on one side and current expenses on the other. Every effort should be made to end each year with a surplus or profit rather than a loss or deficit.

The budget surplus, like any other profit, can be consumed for personal needs and wants, or it may be put back into the business by buying new tools or other equipment or by laying in stacks of raw materials.

Sugaring in Vermont yielded a surplus or profit each year, but it required capital spending to replace worn-out equipment. Each year sap buckets were damaged, piping was replaced and new tools were purchased. Each year we set aside a part of our sugar-business surplus to cover such depreciation.

We also decided to insure the sugarhouse and its contents. Sugarhouses were littered places, fires in the evaporator were hot and many syrup and sugar makers suffered serious fire losses. We went to an insurance agent. Oh yes, he would insure our sugarhouse and contents for $500, but the risk was great and the premium was high. The policy would cost us annually 25 percent, or $125.

We thanked the insurers and went our way. Each year we took $125 from the sugar-business surplus and put it aside. At the end of four years we had $500. With this money we built a second sugarhouse, installed a duplicate set of sugar tools and equipment so that in case the first sugarhouse burned during the sap season we could finish out the season in the second sugarhouse. Incidentally, if we had a big run of sap we operated both sugarhouses at the same time and were able to double our output in a single good sap day.

United States big business has installed methods of book-keeping—cost accounting, depreciation, special funds and installations—that gobble up surpluses and avoid tax collectors. One thing we small fry can learn from big business is to keep careful records, anticipate the future and avoid trouble in one of its many forms.

Plans and records can be as important to little business as they are to big business. Well-kept records tell the story of any enterprise and in the long run become the basis from which the history of the enterprise can be written.

photo: Richard Garrett

"Sit down and feed, and welcome to our table."

William Shakespeare, As You Like It, *1599*

"Every man shall eat in safety, under his own vine, what he plants; and sing the merry songs of peace to all his neighbours."

William Shakespeare, Henry VIII, *1612*

"See that your victuals are prepared in good order and on time so that when the brethren return from their labors in the fields, that they can bless you and eat their food with thankfulness, without murmuring."

Mother Ann Lee (Shaker Founder), *1780*

"Thrice happy days! In rural business passed.
Blest winter nights! when, as the genial fire cheers the wide hall,
His cordial family with soft domestic arts and hours beguile....
Sometimes, at eve, his neighbors lift the latch,
And bless unbid his festal roof; while, o'er the light repast and sprightly cups,
They mix in social joy; and, through the maze of conversation,
Trace whate'er amuses or improves the mind."

John Armstrong, The Art of Preserving Health, *1838*

"I had more visitors while I lived in the woods than at any other period of my life. I have had twenty-five or thirty souls, with their bodies, at once under my roof....But fewer came to see me on trivial business. In this respect, my company was winnowed by my mere distance from town."

Henry David Thoreau, Walden, *1854*

"Over the river and through the woods to grandfather's house we'll go."

Lydia M. Child, Thanksgiving Day, *1870*

"Digging was not what any hand yearned for. Some are born to dig; others have digging thrust upon them."

E. F. Green, A Few Acres and a Cottage, *1911*

"Doorbells are like a magic game, or the grab-bag at a Fair—You never know when you hear one ring who may be waiting there."

Rachel Lyman Field, in Taxis and Toadstools, *1926*

"She left no little things behind, excepting loving thoughts and kind."

Rose Henniker Heaton, The Perfect Guest, *1930*

CHAPTER 15

VISITORS AND HELPERS

HUNDREDS of people came to see us and our farm in Vermont. The thousands of young people who now come to our farm in Maine are the same type of seekers. They have heard or read about our Forest Farm and are curious to learn what it has to show or teach. They are ready for anything that makes an idealistic appeal and that is fairly far from standard community practice. They are unattached except in the very limited sense of selective mating. They are apolitical, impatient of restraints—especially when governmentally imposed.

Increasingly they are turning their backs on a world community that has tolerated war and is preparing for the contingency of one in the future. They are ardently in favor of peace in a broad sense, but are not ready to accept a commitment to any organization that works collectively for the cause. Almost universally they favor "freedom": that is, the pursuit of their personal goals and fancies. They are not joiners and generally not members of any group more specific than is implied by the adoption of a specific diet or the practice of some yoga exercises.

They are wanderers and seekers, feeling their way toward an escape from orthodoxy and superficiality, with the nervous dissatisfaction that characterizes people who do not have a home base in any real sense. Perhaps they can best be described as unsettled. Never before in our lives have we met so many unattached, uncommitted, insecure, uncertain human beings.

There are, of course, those serious few who are consciously and conscientiously working toward an ideal in which they believe and to which they attach themselves. They are definitely looking for a niche in which they might play a more effective part in helping to develop a new and better life style.

Many young couples, singles and groups came to us wanting land. They had limited means. Most of them had traveled from coast to coast looking for a place that they could afford and that would offer possibilities for a satisfying alternative way of living. They were homeless between two worlds.

We had a hundred acres or more (our deed read 140 acres, but it turned out to be a good deal less, and at the moment we have only 26 acres left). We decided to share what we had with the right young people. We sold a large slice of land to Susan and Eliot Coleman, a promising young couple, for what they could afford to pay; another slice to Jean and Keith Heavrin; and later, the tip-end away from the water to Greg Summers. All were prepared to homestead. All cleared their land and put up the necessary buildings.

The Colemans went in for raising vegetables and fruit as a cash crop and made a great success in market gardening. The Heavrins built a fine house and deep cellar, added a large pond, went in for animal husbandry and did construction work as a source of cash income. Greg Summers, who had an art background in Wisconsin, raised a good garden in the woods and took printshop jobs to bring in the necessary cash.

A real problem was the large numbers of singles and couples who wanted to spend a few days, a week or a summer working with us, learning and practicing gardening and building. We received hundreds of letters from them asking if they could come and work and camp. Where could they stay? On part of the Colemans' cleared land we put some cabins and heating and cooking arrangements and provided the bare necessities for backpackers and helpers. Each open season the campground was utilized.

The young people who gathered there were strangers to each other but readily found things in common. The shifting population worked wherever and whenever they felt disposed. Meals and garden produce were provided where they worked. They had musicals around the campfire. They attended our Monday night meetings where everything from compost to communism was discussed weekly. They went to square dances in the neighborhood. On the whole, it seemed as though they had worthwhile and happy times. It was a free and easy, loosely knit community formed of people who came and went. Some of the campers and workers became our very good friends, corresponding and coming back at every opportunity.

Parallel activities are going on in various parts of Maine and elsewhere in New England and the United States, where by various means land is being secured and homesteads, collectives and communes are being established.

We do not remember having one black youngster come, or one daughter or son of a coal miner, nor do we recall young people whose parents worked in textile factories or steel mills. We had daughters and sons galore of merchants, of doctors, teachers, lawyers, bankers and public officials—people who had been born into affluence of a sort, raised in comfort if not pampered in luxury. They had had little or no real work experience. They might have washed dishes, run errands, sold merchandise or taught school for short times, but they had stuck at nothing for long. Occasionally we had a visitor who had worked on a farm and knew his or her way around. Some few had real skills. They were among the exceptions.

We realize that the few thousands of young people who come

our way are not necessarily representative of American youth in the decades following war's end in 1945. It is quite possible that the young people who stop by at Forest Farm are leftovers who do not fit into the current picture and are deliberately seeking another life style. They are part of the process of self-selection during which those inclined or ready to line up with the Establishment have made their choices and are securely part of the typical American scene. In one sense our visitors are a motley crew. Through trial and error the sheep are being separated from the goats—or, the goats from the sheep.

Before we moved from Vermont to Maine, the trickle of visitors had become a stream. During the next years in Maine it became a flood. By the 1970's the number of visitors by head count has ranged between 2000 and 2500 in the course of a year. It often reached dozens in a day.

How do we cope with this visitation? By a single and generally followed rule. When visitors come unannounced we continue doing what we had planned to do for that day and that time of day. If we are writing, we go on writing. If we are working, we go on working. This is not to the liking of those who want to sit around and talk about this or that. However, we have to keep on our jobs in order to get anything done.

Many visitors are willing, eager and enthusiastic. Some few prove to be experienced people who know how to handle tools and what to do with them. Some make real contributions to the projects on which we are engaged.

We had a few glacial boulders that had found their resting place on our land. The largest of these boulders must have weighed between a quarter and half a ton. It was in our way and we decided to move it about thirty feet. One of us alone could not budge it, even with a crowbar. Five of us could handle it only if we worked as a team, following the directions of a temporary leader or foreman. With an explosive or a series of drilled holes and wooden lugs, we might have broken the rock, but only by spending a long time on the job. In any case, we wanted it in another place. Finally, with bars and chains and the help of a four-wheel truck, we shifted it to its new dwelling place. Teamwork had paid off.

Necessarily, with the numbers of visitors ranging from one or two to a dozen or a score in a single day, our helpers had to be grouped together in one or more work teams. Of course, there were always drop-ins and dropouts. But if we had reason to believe that two, three or four experienced and reliable people were to be on hand, we organized as many crews as we could handle effectively on that day. We divided up workers according to inclination and experience. Most crews consisted of three to five people under the direction of one or two experienced workers. With these crews we could dig foundation trenches, pour concrete, cut brush and above all build roads. People who had skills exercised them. Others of less experience learned.

If the two of us were alone, there was no problem. We could work in the house, in the woods, in the garden, or at building. If there were more people we tried to adapt to their number. Building was not their forte; masonry we did not dare let them handle. On gardening we could usually use only a few experienced people. Work in the woods with sharp tools was dangerous if not handled by knowledgeable folk. So we usually came down to clearing land or building roads when there was a crowd. They did not always like this; they would rather sit and talk, but we went at the job anyway, with those who were willing.

Perhaps the hardest work they did was on the craggy rock pile. They called themselves "the chain gang" but they sang and worked with a will, with occasional rests and lapses. Some tenderfoot visitors, facing a rocky hillside cleanup job for the first time in their lives, were put off by the roughness of the work. Some were unprepared to get their hands into common dirt, while others were attracted by the archaeological excitement of uncovering down to bare rock. To some it was tedious, to others exciting and fascinating.

We laid out a road network and proceeded to build the roads: with large stone, with small stone and gravel on top. Where did we get this material? From the beach on our cove and from the rocky outcrop beside our house site. We attacked the cliff with axes, picks, bars, mattocks, forks, shovels. We cut off trees, shrubs, brush. We dug out roots. We scraped the woody surface with trowels, carefully collecting, from the pockets of forest, soil which we saved for landscaping or garden. The feminine members of the group usually picked this easier sitting-down job, although there were sturdy girls who preferred to work fiercely with mattock or axe, or wheel the heavy loads of rock or miscellaneous refuse away from the working face of the cliff to the roadways being built.

Large rocks went to their allotted piles to use for terraces if they had good faces, to be used in foundations if they were uglies. Medium stones were carefully sorted into builders, corner stones and uglies. The rough balance was shoveled into the wheelbarrows and wheeled to the road we were constructing around the buildings.

We are writing about our visitors during the period of construction work on the new house and grounds. During the last five years we have worked off and on at this time-consuming project, fascinating in its way, and we are still at it. It has involved the participation of neighbors, friends and chance itinerant help, some of which has become semi-permanent and paid. We and they, we hope, have enjoyed our contacts together. There has been an apprentice-learning side to our endeavors, a sociological-communal side, a constructive side and an entertainment side. The results generally were educational, healthy, beautiful and useful.

We have not yet mentioned the culinary side of our day's work, which was Helen's domestic contribution. After a morning's work in woods and garden or at road or building work, we were called at noon. We gathered our tools, cleaned them and put them in place. Then we trooped in to lunch. Weather permitting, we ate outside on the stone patio that adjoins the kitchen. Chance visitors who were on hand at noon were also invited. Each luncheon guest received a wooden bowl and wooden spoon. Soup was dipped out, with always seconds or even thirds available in the tureen. Season permitting, green leafy vegetables were on the table, and sprouted grains. Bowls of uncooked rolled oats, oil and raisins ("horse chow"), boiled wheat, millet or buckwheat were served. These cereals were eaten with an amalgam of peanut butter and honey called "Scott's emulsion." "Carrot croakers" were popular journey cakes with a grated carrot base. Apples usually topped off the plentiful though simple meal.

The number of hungry mouths at these lunches ranged from half a dozen to over twenty on some days. We tried to serve an abundance of simple, fresh, nourishing vegetarian food: food that was ethically and dietetically sound and sufficiently filling to satisfy people, mostly young, who had spent four hours in hard physical work. With ravenous appetites, the spread usually disappeared in short order. Officially the meal lasted for an hour. If there was interesting talk and no other pressing work, people stayed on longer.

This brief review of our experience with two generations of helpers and associates during the last few years hardly does justice to what is really a period of transition and transformation. Changes are taking place, deeply affecting the young, and we—with our lives almost over—observe them with mixed feelings. We believe the groundbreaking work we have done with our own homesteading and the missionary end of it in letting people come and observe has been worth while through the years. We would like to continue to have interested visitors drop by. We are glad to have willing helpers when they want to assist in any of our projects. But by 1976 the handling of hundreds of visitors had become so serious a problem that we put up a sign at the entrance of Forest Farm stating that our mornings were our own and that we could accept visitors from 3 to 5 in the afternoon only. In 1978 we declared a sabbatical (our first) in order to get to some necessary writing (this book included) and we would see visitors only with advance notice. We regretted this seemingly inhospitable step but had to take it in order to get any amount of consecutive work and writing done.

We would like to take every opportunity to help young people in their serious search for a life style that would make sense to them. All are possible recruits for a general effort now under way to stabilize and improve man's earthly living space. For a long period we have done our utmost to raise popular interest and determination to the action point. We hope to continue to do so as long as our energies last. As we near the century mark of our lives we find we must limit our contribution to part-time.

*"Now hear from me what and how great the wealth a frugal diet brings.
Well, first, good health you shall enjoy.
What ills mixed foods effect you may believe, if you but recollect
How on your stomach once sat simple fare."*

Horace, Ofellus, 30 B.C.

"House-Wives persuade themselves that the more cost they bestow, the more rich things they jumble together, the better and more nourishing their Food must be; and more nourishing indeed it is, but of Diseases, and evil Juices, whereas plain, coarse, cheap, simple Foods are much more friendly to Nature, and consequently more strengthening and restorative."

Thomas Tryon, The Good House-Wife Made a Doctor, 1692

"A very spare and simple diet has commonly been recommended as most conducive to Health."

Dr. W. Kitchiner, The Cook's Oracle, 1822

"Simplify, simplify. Instead of three meals a day, if it be necessary, eat but one; instead of a hundred dishes, five; and reduce other things in proportion."

Henry David Thoreau, Walden, 1854

"Recipes for cookery in the colonial days were for the plain fare of a plain, hardworking people, more intent on survival than elaborate service. The home-hewed wooden trenchers served as plates, one for two people, or the table board might be hollowed into bowls along the edge. The spoons were of pewter or of wood, whittled out by the men of their family in the evening hours before crackling fires."

Gertrude I. Thomas, Foods of Our Forefathers, 1941

"The palate has been confused, dulled and degraded by a hundred and fifty years of food sophistication and processing and by at least fifty years of ever-intensifying and misleading publicity for time-saving substitutes, palate-ticklers and pre-digested or factory-compounded mixtures."

Edgar J. Saxon, Sensible Food for All, 1949

"Wholesome food and drink are cheaper than doctors and hospitals."

Dr. Carl C. Wahl, Essential Health Knowledge, 1966

CHAPTER 16

WHAT WE EAT AND WHY

WHAT IS man's natural food? Surely not the mishmashes and inadequate, denatured .items displayed on the shelves of supermarkets. They are bad-natured, instead of good-natured, foods. The artificiality of their worked-over substances should be apparent to the most casual and conventional food shopper.

There is hardly anything natural in the food stores anymore. The grains are puffed, pounded and supersaturated with sugar for boxed breakfast cereal. The meats are injected with hormones, colored and full of antibiotics. The juices are filtered, flavored and carbonated. The overprocessed canned fruits are sweetened beyond measure. Sugar is also included in the packaged soups, soft drinks, salad dressings, sauces, dessert mixes, ketchup and even peanut butter. The raw vegetables in the stalls are sprayed and dusted; the raw fruits gassed and coal-tar dyed; the ice creams notorious for their heavily sweetened, artificially flavored compounds.

Restaurants and food bars where so many go for their meals offer quick-service items that may have been standing on the stoves for hours, losing vitamins, and before that sitting in warehouses and trains and closets for weeks and months. The foods that are bought and eaten in the United States are handled and handled and handled again. By the time the hungry diner is served, his dinner is doctored and tampered with and far from natural.

Where do we turn for good, healthy, nourishing, unadulterated food? To our own gardens, of course, and our own kitchens. Grow your own; cook your own—or, better still, eat your own food raw. The best and simplest food in the world is unprocessed, picked by yourself from the garden or the trees or the meadows or the woods and eaten raw before the vitality has fled. This is vital, this is nourishing, this is good-natured food.

Five minutes away from contact with the earth or mother plant is enough to start the wilting disintegration process in lettuce and other delicately leaved greens, and deterioration in the more solidly constituted vegetables and fruits.

As for food preparation, the less and the simpler the better: the better for the housewife in time spent, the better for the food itself in vitamins saved, and the better for the body in vitality added. Processed foods are those that have been cut, peeled, cooked, frozen, pickled, pasteurized, spiced, colored, smoked, flavored, chemicalized and otherwise adulterated.

We never have gone in for denatured food and have kept away from store food whenever possible. Eating out, especially in restaurants, is never a pleasure for us. One winter we were in Asia and the Near East for almost five months. During that time we never entered a restaurant to eat. We frequented the local markets, bought greens and fruits and cheeses and ate in our rooms. The food we consumed was as fresh, as simple and as unprocessed as we could find. It was far healthier and safer and cheaper than eating at restaurants.

We can be and are largely self-sufficient in food. Self-sufficient means that we can feed ourselves. During half a century of gardening there has never been a time when we have lacked a supply of organically grown produce. This food comes directly from the garden for a large part of the year. During the late fall, winter and early spring we have three additional sources of supply. (1) It may come from the sun-heated greenhouse where we grow lettuces, parsley, radishes, leeks, kale, spinach. (2) It may come from our root cellar where apples, potatoes, carrots, onions, beets, rutabagas and other root vegetables are stored in bins of autumn leaves. (3) It may come from our stock of bottled soups and juices and applesauce which we put away during periods of surplus production and use when the garden is in deep freeze.

We use several grains in our diet, which we do not grow on our farm: wheat, oats, millet, buckwheat, rice, corn, are bought from the local coop. With the exception of apples and pears, we have no local source of tree fruits. Berries grow well with us: blueberries, strawberries, raspberries. Grapes we have found need a longer season. We buy and use vegetable oils: olive, peanut, safflower. We buy citrus and bananas in a local wholesale market. With these noted exceptions, we come as near to our ideal of food self-sufficiency as seems presently practicable.

From ordinary grocery stores or supermarkets we may buy occasionally citrus, bananas, avocados, cheese, yogurt and sour cream (though we are turning to tofu and soybean milk instead of dairy products).

Bread is a time-consuming product and so easy to glut on, particularly when laden as it usually is with butter, jam, cheese and other things. Instead of spending hours making and baking breads from manipulated dough, we eat our grain unground and unkneaded. Bread is so easily swallowed unchewed; grains are grittier and require mastication, which is good for the teeth, gums and digestion. If tough and hard, like raw wheat berries, we soak a couple of handfuls overnight, and simmer on the stove for a morning. If a softer grain, like millet or buckwheat, we cook for less than half an hour. Rolled oats we eat uncooked.

Put on the table, hot or cold, these grains are eaten with a bit of oil and sea salt, or with an amalgam of honey and peanut butter, and sometimes chopped-up apples. We do not use white flour in our home and rarely any flour, grinding our own grains when we want some.

We buy in bulk through our local cooperative or health-food store and always have stocks of staples on hand, stored in barrels or tins. We could almost qualify for a health-food store with our supplies of wheat berries, rolled oats, buckwheat groats, cracked wheat, oat flakes, soybean flakes, barley, lentils, millet, rice, cornmeal, popcorn, dried beans and peas, mung beans, raisins, prunes, dates, peanuts, peanut butter, almonds, sunseeds, herbs, honey and oil.

We rarely buy canned or frozen vegetables and fruit, or snack foods, and never the cake mixes, puddings, desserts, pizzas, cookies, pastries and instant goods that crowd the shelves of food shops.

We try to avoid sugar and refined sugar products, substituting instead honey, maple syrup, molasses and sweet fruits such as dates, raisins, prunes.

Living in a climate not adapted to a year-round fruitarian or raw diet, we adapt and simplify as much as possible. The basics of our diet are simple: our own herb teas and fruit for breakfast; soup and grains for lunch; salad, one cooked vegetable and some applesauce for supper. Day in, day out, these are our meals. There may be a few additions occasionally—such as sunflower seeds or nuts to the breakfast; or tofu or cottage cheese to the supper—but these are the fundamentals.

There is an easy ritual to our mealtimes, which are eaten at 7, noon and 6 o'clock. On a bare wood table we set wooden bowls, wooden spoons and chopsticks. Soup, salad or dessert is all served in the same wooden bowl. This simplifies dishwashing. We are not quite down to Diogenes' standard of simple living:

when he saw a boy drinking out of his hands, he threw away his only utensil, a cup. Nor do we adhere to Gandhi's determined silence at meals.

Our meals are sociable times when conversation can range from garden work to world politics to latest UFO sightings. We approximate the experience of William Alcott, who wrote in 1837 of a meal he shared with friends: "With their plain dinner, and pleasant conversation, they pass half an hour or even more; sometimes sitting till 1 o'clock, especially if they have company. If the most illustrious visitors are present, they add nothing to the bread and potatoes, or whatever plain dishes they happen to have on the table, except perhaps some one kind of the best fruit of the season; and they never make any apologies" (*Ways of Living on Small Means*).

We have not yet mentioned that we do not eat meat. We regard vegetarianism as an essential part of the good life, in its ethical and humanitarian as well as health aspects. To us, leaving off flesh-eating is taken for granted. If not a requisite to living a good life, let's say it is to *us*. We cannot conceive of kindly, considerate, aware people consuming carcasses of perceptive, defenseless animals who were raised in captivity for slaughter. We think that the gross and selfish custom will be abandoned in years to come, as the eating of human flesh has been largely abandoned. If not for humanitarian or health reasons, then for economic and world-hunger reasons the vast population must eventually turn to vegetarianism. It is well known that the breeding and feeding of animals for slaughter uses more land than raising vegetable crops which can be eaten direct, without passing through animals' bodies.

For kindness, common sense, economy, simplicity, aesthetics, and health reasons, we eat nothing that walks or wiggles. This leaves a certain latitude as to eggs, milk, yogurt, cheese, honey, butter. We go very lightly on these animal products but do not eschew them altogether. We don't buy a dozen eggs a year, but eat them when served in food away from home. We haven't bought a quart of milk in years, though we get it in some foods served to us.

We eat yogurt and on festive occasions ice cream. Cheese, particularly cottage cheese, we may eat once or twice a week. We think vegetable oils better for us than butter, and they involve less exploitation of animals.

Taking honey from bees certainly exploits the bees, even if it does not starve or kill them; it robs them of the results of their intensive labor. We still eat honey but question it morally, as well as on account of its concentration of sweetness. On the whole, we go easy on sweetening, using a minimum of honey or maple syrup. We think most Americans overdo the sweet thing. They also overeat on protein and cereal starches. We live on a very low protein diet, with seeds, nuts and a few vegetables and fruits supplying what we get. Cereal starches we eat only once a day.

We prefer live foods and raw foods, eating them as fresh as possible, while they are still vibrant with life. If food is to be cooked, baking is better than boiling, and both better than frying. We try to keep the diet simple, with few mixtures, and preferably one food at a time. We have gone on mono-diets— for example, eating only apples for days on end, or subsisting on juices, or fasting on water only—for ten days at a time. We find this salutary, cleansing and restful for the body, let alone the easement for the housewife. One day a week we aim at twenty-four hours on just liquids, either juices or water. We enjoy these days of fasting and look forward to them as one of the high points of the week.

Not eating (so long as one is not starving) can be as enjoyable as eating. Just as shaving the head completely of hair can give one a godlike feeling of lack of clutter, so going without food can give one a feeling of freedom and release that is real emancipation.

Time and again we are queried on our sources of protein. Where, we ask in return, do the cows, elephants and rhinoceros —all sturdy, strong creatures—get their protein needs supplied? From grass, from foliage, from green things, is the answer. They do not eat refined, cooked, pickled, dehydrated, pasteurized, spiced, salted, canned, or otherwise conditioned materials. They are simple creatures eating nature's way. We try to be the same: simple-living people surviving on simple food, home grown, organically grown, and simply prepared. Our foods are vital, nutritional and economical. For fifty years we have thrived on such, and plan to continue so until our last days.

"There is no man nor woman the which have any respect to them selfe that can be a better Phesycion for theyr owne saveguarde than theyr owne selfe can be, to consyder what thynge the whiche doth them good, And to refrayne from such thynges that doth them hurte or harme."

Andrewe Boorde, A Dyetary of Helth, 1542

"It is undeniably one of the most important Businesses of this Life to preserve our selves in Health. But there is scarce one Man or Woman of a thousand that does in earnest consider and pursue the means of preserving their Health, but either lives at Random, or at least takes up with the pernicious Notions of Custom, Tradition and Blind Guides, whose Prescriptions of Diet are most improper and prejudicial, their Medicines Nauseates to Nature, and their Physick a close Confederate with the invading Disease."

Thomas Tryon, The Good House-wife, 1692

"It is most certain that 'tis easier to preserve Health than to recover it, and to prevent Diseases than to cure them."

Dr. George Cheyne, An Essay of Health and Long Life, 1725

"We should strengthen and beautify and industriously mould our bodies to be fit companions of the soul, assist them to grow up like trees, and be agreeable and wholesome objects in nature."

Henry David Thoreau, Journal, January 25, 1841

"I have been asked sometimes how I could perform so large an amount of work with apparently so little diminution of strength. I attribute my power of endurance to a long-formed habit of observing, every day of my life, the simple laws of health, and none more than the laws of eating. It ceases any longer to be a matter of self-denial. It is almost like an instinct. I have made eating with regularity and with a reference to what I have to do, a habit so long that it ceases any longer to be a subject of thought. It almost takes care of itself. I attribute much of my ability to endure work to good habits of eating, constant attention to the laws of sleep, physical exercise, and cheerfulness."

Solon Robinson, Facts for Farmers, 1869

"The whole of the material for growth comes from the food we eat. Wear and tear is made good from foodstuffs. There must be a fund to meet depreciation, and this depreciation is made good by food and food alone. The energy for work comes from the slow utilization and combustion of food in the cells of the body."

V. H. Mottram, Food and the Family, 1925

"We are rarely ill, and if we are, we go off somewhere and eat grass until we feel better."

Paul Gallico, The Silent Miaow, 1964

CHAPTER 17

WE PRACTICE HEALTH

WE LIVE in a society that takes sickness for granted and looks upon abounding health as lucky or exceptional. There are family doctors by the thousands all over the Western world who practice medicine by prescribing pills and drugs. Doctors (and dentists) are experts on sickness. Only a minority are practitioners of health.

Early in their history the Chinese are reported to have paid doctors their regular fees so long as people remained well. If and when a person became ill, the medical fees stopped until the patient was restored to health.

We, in the West, follow an opposite practice. We pay our doctors when we get sick and continue to pay them while we remain sick. The longer and the more serious the sickness, the longer the medical fees are paid. The lesson of such a situation is obvious to any reasoning being. If the doctor is paid when his clients are sick, the more often they are sick the more often the doctor will get a fee. Equally, the longer the sickness lasts and the more often the doctor is called in, the larger the income of the doctor.

Doctors often object to this reasoning. All the same, economic forces are potent factors in any society. Doctors, dentists and druggists and their families buy their groceries and pay their rent and taxes out of the money supplied by people who are in need of their services.

We cannot forget the story of the society lady who woke up one morning with a red blotch on her cheek. Much disturbed, she called up her family doctor and made an appointment to see him. The doctor looked carefully at the disfiguring spot and shook his head dubiously. "Is it that serious, doctor?" the lady questioned anxiously. "Rather serious, Madam," answered the doctor. "If you had waited for an hour or two before coming, the spot would have disappeared and I would have lost my fee." All doctors are not so frank.

The question "Who is your family doctor?" suggests that you expect to be sick and will therefore need help, so you keep a family doctor. The person who expects to be well does not need a doctor. He takes health for granted.

We homesteaded in Vermont for nineteen years without having a family doctor. We have homesteaded in Maine for more than twenty-five years equally free of permanent medical advice because we have been chronically well. In a word, we have practiced health by conducting ourselves in a way that keeps us well.

There is an old saying that practice makes perfect. Following this precept, those who want to be healthy must practice health. They must work at it. Like any other activity, the practice of health involves one or more choices. We choose to live quietly and simply, to exercise in the open air, to keep sensible hours and not overdo physically. We choose to exercise our bodies not in gymnasiums or on golf courses or tennis courts but doing useful outdoor physical work. We choose to live in the country rather than the city, with its polluted air, noise and stress. We prefer clean fresh air, sunshine, clear running water. We choose to cut our own fuel in our own woods rather than pay the oil barons. We design and construct our own buildings. We grow and prepare our own food, rather than shop in the super-markets.

There are endless choices we all make daily and yearly—even hourly. One of our older neighbors came back home from an operation that was necessary to remove a cancer from his lip. Our friend was an inveterate chain cigarette smoker. He and the rest of his family had no doubt that cigarette smoking had resulted in the cancer. Back from his operation and surrounded by his family and friends, he reached for a cigarette, looked at it for a long moment, took out a match, snapped it with his thumbnail as was his wont and lit his first post-operational cigarette. He had made his choice. He preferred smoking to health. All choices are not equally as simple and single-tracked.

Early in life both of us faced up to a series of choices regarding health. These choices were never cut, dried and easy. Usually the decisions, especially about food and drink, forced us to separate ourselves from the customs of family, friends and acquaintances. We faced alternatives, in attitudes to life and current practices. Generally our young friends went along with the crowd: it was so easy to say yes, thank you. It took courage, knowledge and determination to say no, thank you, especially when some tasty edible was being offered. Early in our mid-teens we were faced with the choice to go along with the crowd or to choose habits that would establish and preserve health.

When we say that we practice health, or that we are healthy, we mean that the organism is operating according to plan and purpose as judged by its function and its product.

The human organism—physical, emotional, mental, spiritual —is the sum total of a human being alive and in good working order. This human organism has been evolving toward its present form on earth for at least two million years, and possibly a great deal longer. Over these vast reaches of time and sequence the processes of biological selection have matured the human organism into a wide range of variations of the present-day human being, with the same general contour, but differing in size, shape, color.

Human organisms are alive, growing and developing in successive stages of their life process or cycle. They generate their own energy patterns, converting energy intake into the wide variety of functions possessed by a complicated apparatus like the body, emotional structure, mind and spirit of a normal human being.

Like any other natural process, human energy is expressed in an aggregate of living cells, tissues, organs and members, which make up the human body. Not only are these coordinations highly complex, coordinated, specialized fragments of a complex whole, but, so far as we are able to determine, no two of these specialized organisms are identical in form, structure or function. Each is unique, living its own individual life span under its own individual direction—similar, but never identical.

The life processes we see operating in humanity at the present moment have been repeated numberless times in the past and are being lived (repeated) in the present, similar but not uniform in manner, each integer or life unit possessing its own unique identity through the minutes, hours, days, years, centuries and millennia.

It would be a mistake to lay too much stress on the multiplicity of individual life acts, stages and processes. On the other hand, it is impossible to pass the life process by without calling attention, with great admiration, to its multiplicity and its diversity and its continuity.

We make these observations in a country that abounds in complex mechanisms, each with its own multitudes of standard replacement parts and fittings—sewing machines, generators, typewriters, planting and harvesting machines. Doubly impressive is an organism that is as complicated, that is alive and capable of reproducing itself endlessly, given the necessary energy and raw materials. The result is trebly impressive when we note that the human organism cannot only duplicate itself arithmetically, but that it can proceed analytically and critically evaluating the product during the operation.

When a mechanism can turn out a needed or wanted product, we say it is in good working order. When an organism can do this, we say it is in good health. That is, the organism is producing the results that it was developed to produce. Through direct and indirect experience we convert a more or less helpless infant at birth into a trained, skilled, experienced adult capable of performing one or more of the multitude of operations necessary to produce a work of art, a telephone system or a suspension bridge.

The important factor in the situation is that we are consciously aware of the entire process, know when and why we fail and are increasingly certain that if we follow the necessary procedures we can establish and maintain the quality and length of our lives. In other words, we can avoid sickness and ill health by adopting life styles that bypass illness and stabilize good health.

We are proclaiming human health as the condition of body, emotions, mind and spirit that all self-respecting human beings should strive to achieve. We believe that we should practice or maintain health as we practice any other human virtue. On second thought, health should probably head the list of primary objectives toward which humans should strive.

We are not professional healthists. We are mere laymen. Our claim to champion the cause of health is based on four note-worthy facts: first, both of us have been well and have practiced health since we were in our teens. Second, both of us are now healthy in old age. Third, we have and have had no family doctor. Fourth, we are active in organizations that advocate and practice health.

We round out this chapter by setting down some of the essential aspects in the practice of health.

1. Sufficient knowledge and experience are necessary to know what practice of health involves. Scott's mother was a health fan at the end of the nineteenth century, with six children to bring up. As high-school students, Scott's generation was exposed to the teachings of Bernarr MacFadden and other health enthusiasts of the period, who published literature, gave lectures and held classes and workshops in which they called into question the health pattern of the Establishment on the ground that it accepted sickness as an essential feature of human life and maintained an elaborate apparatus of institutions and trained personnel which was paid and financed for looking after sick people. Helen's parents were theosophists, involved in Eastern philosophies, were vegetarians and believed in healthful practices.

2. Instead of the negative attitude of treating sickness after the organism breaks down, the healthist proposes practices that make people well and keep them well. Such a view makes illness subnormal and to be replaced by practices that establish and maintain health as normal.

3. Health therefore should be taught and practiced consistently as an essential feature of good citizenship. This means, of course, that doctors and other health professionals should set an example to their patients by being well and staying well. Health workers should be living and shining examples of abounding health: Physician, heal thyself.

4. Since the human being is fueled or energized by taking nourishment into the alimentary canal, healthists should know what solids and liquids are necessary to maintain health and see to it that the food intake corresponds to the best that health science has attained. Food intake should be properly balanced chemically. It should be fresh, free of poisons or deleterious substances. Food should be whole and unprocessed where possible (cooking is a form of processing). Food should be supplied in proper quantity as well as be of proper quality. Since

the body is built up and its cells are replaced by the food-drink intake, the greatest care should be taken by health authorities to see that only the best of building materials are supplied to the citizenry—especially to the children of today who are the adults of tomorrow.

5. Health depends not alone upon food and drink. Sunshine, fresh air, pure water and exercise are equally important elements in health. Balanced, healthful living requires at-oneness with all aspects of nature.

6. Sufficient shelter, good housing and adequate clothing are essential to health, especially in climatic belts where bad weather is encountered.

7. Tension is to be avoided, in the interest of health. This is particularly the case in urban living under conditions of congestion, high speed, noise and other irritants which impair and undermine human well-being. Those who advocate health should live wisely and sanely, socially as well as bodily.

"O happy who thus liveth! Not caring much for gold;
With clothing which sufficeth to keep him from the cold.
Though poor and plain his diet, yet merry 'tis, and quiet."

Elizabethan Song Book, *circa 1588*

"I never had any other desire so strong, as so like to covetousness as that one,
which I have had always, that I might bee master at last, of a small House and
large Garden, with very moderate conveniences joyned to them, and there
dedicate the remainder of my life, onely to the culture of them, and study of
Nature. And there, with no design beyond my wall, whole and entire to lye, in
no unactive ease, and no unglorious poverty."

Abraham Cowley, The Garden, 1666

"It must be owned, indeed, that the Town hath its Pleasures as well as the
Countrey. But how alluring soever the Pleasures of the Town may seem to us,
whilst Health and Strength and the Gaities of Youth last, Envy, Malice and
Double-dealing do so frequent the most busy Parts of the World, which tend to
mar all those Delights. We shall be inclined to declare in Favour of the
innocent Simplicity of a Countery-life. As long as the World lasts, the
Pleasures and Entertainments which Gardening and Agriculture afford, will be
the pursuit of wise Men."

John Laurence, A New System of Agriculture, 1726

"Our life is a busy round of a great variety of occupations, all tending to health
and chearfulness. We rise every day with the sun, and in the cool of morning,
employ ourselves in business which requires some strength. The garden takes
up much of our time. In the afternoon we read and work. In the evening I take
to my tools and labour again, either hoeing, digging, chopping wood against
winter, or any work of the season that is necessary. Such generally is the round
of the day . . . . Our happy little farm yields us a constant amusement of a most
rational and agreeable kind."

Arthur Young, The Adventures of Emmera, 1767

"Countrymen in general are a very happy people; they enjoy many of the
necessities of life upon their own farms, and what they do not so gain, they
have from the sale of their surplus products; it is remarkable to see such
numbers of these men in a state of great ease and content, possessing all the
necessaries of life, but few of the luxuries of it."

Anonymous, American Husbandry, 1775

CHAPTER 18

A REWARDING WAY TO LIVE

LIKE multitudes of people all over the world, we are seeking a good life—a simple, balanced, satisfying life style. Like them, our aim is to lend a hand in shaping the planet into a homelike living place for successive generations of human beings and for the many other life forms domiciled in and on Mother Earth, her lands and waters.

Immediate needs for a good life are food and shelter, as a basis for survival. Beyond these basic necessaries are amenities like education, recreation and travel, which make life more satisfying and rewarding for individuals and small local groups such as families and other collectives.

We begin our listing of good life attributes with our four-four-four formula: four hours of bread labor; four hours of professional activity; and four hours dedicated to fulfilling our obligations and responsibilities as members of the human race and as participants in various local, regional, national and world civic activities.

Bread labor provides the basic essentials of living normal, healthful, serviceful lives. The work of the world must be done and we should all share in it. Professional activities enable us to specialize and contribute our mite to the world's sum total of skills and competencies. Association enables us to share experience and knowledge with our fellow beings.

The four-four-four formula should be specific as well as general. Everyone, rich or poor, young or old, can contribute somewhat to the world's physical work. Bread labor can and should be performed by every able-bodied human being from age 7 to 77 (though Scott at 95 is still carrying his end of the load). Bread labor should be an obligatory and honorable phase of the daily routine in which everyone can take an active part as a matter of course. This daily contribution to the work of the world will make a vigorous, self-supporting society.

The personal interests and skills of each human being will be another contribution that will produce inventions and artistic achievements from which society will also benefit.

Civic responsibilities and activities taken on by all adults will benefit the whole society and bring people together in common interests of survival and well-being.

If we would have things done, we must be prepared to do them. This principle applies to the life of the individual; it is even more urgent when issues of group concern are up for consideration. Those who would be well served serve themselves, individually and collectively.

With us Westerners in the present century this principle deserves double emphasis, because in our immediate past we have overemphasized the individual to the detriment of the group. Groups have grown larger, more numerous and more complex. Doubling populations automatically shift attention from individual to group activity. Increase in size, coupled with growing complexity and interdependence, must play down the individual and upgrade the group and group problems.

Since the Mexican Revolution of 1910, through the Russian Revolution of 1917, the East European, Asian and African revolutions that followed the wars of 1914, 1936 and 1945, and the upheaval in China that began as early as 1899, a third of mankind has launched a movement for collectivist socialist-communist action that places group welfare above individual interests. Up to this point of social evolution, life, liberty and the pursuit of happiness in terms of eighteenth-century perspective dominated the planet-wide struggle for a better life. The socialist-communist revolutions of the present century subordinate individual happiness for the bourgeoisie to well-being for the entire group. In the face of growing sociological challenges, we in the West have continued to underscore the eighteenth-century formula of freedom, independence, and self-determination.

Through the years, the authors of this book have seen steady and persistent efforts by individuals, and by social groups, to protect and conserve the natural environment. There are vast regions in the socialist countries and in Scandinavia and other parts of Europe in which conservation of nature is a first charge. This is an aspect of civic responsibility that should come to the fore more generally.

The essence of life consists in living. In the words of Robert Louis Stevenson, "To travel hopefully is better than to arrive, and the true success is to labor."

From earliest childhood to the final insecure steps of old age, those who put the most into life get the most out of life. This applies to quantity of life and quantity of output. Theory guides; practice determines. The uniting of theory with practice provides a higher degree of assurance and promotes a more rewarding body of dependable guidance for individual and group living.

Muscles grow strong and responsive with exercise. Muscles of the spectator go flabby and shrink. This rule is equally applicable to the problems of physical function and social action.

Personally, we in our entire homesteading venture have endeavored to keep our social as well as physical muscles in shape. We tried, as a couple, and insofar as we could in groups, to set up and continue a life pattern to maintain health and sanity in a period of social insecurity, conflict, disruption and disintegration.

We began experimenting with an alternative life pattern nearly half a century ago, in 1932. We were not young, but we were adventurous. Our first steps were tentative. As we proceeded, we became clearer in our thinking and surer that the course we were following was right for us.

We were trying out a life style that was not new in history, but was new in our generation. We left city living, with its civilized polish and its murky poverty, and launched out into a simpler, more self-sufficient life in the country.

Our general aim was to set up a use economy for ourselves independent of the established market economy and for the most part under our own control, thereby freeing ourselves from undue dependence on the Establishment.

We wanted to provide ourselves with the economic means that would free at least a third of our time and energy to carry on our professional work and our interest in improving the social environment.

Specifically, we have provided ourselves during more than four decades with the basic necessaries of life in exchange for a sufficient amount of planning, persistence and hard work.

We have been able to carry on our writing and research. Scott has written six books since leaving the city, only one of which saw the light of day in the commercial book market. Six additional books were written jointly with Helen. She has continued her lifelong interest in music and has added secretarial, editorial, writing and house-building skills to her accomplishments.

In our forty-odd years of homesteading we have reshaped old ideas and practices and tried out new ones. Never for a moment did we sit back and say to ourselves: This is it; we have learned all there is to know about homesteading; we have arrived.

On the contrary, the further we went with our bread labor, our professional activities and our civic work, the more we realized that we had only scratched life's surface. There is so much more to experience, to do and to learn that only many lives ahead will give us time and opportunities to fulfill all we hope to do.

We have done our best to contribute to the knowledge and possibilities of homesteading in New England for four decades.

We have been able, from our home base, to initiate a considerable number of young people into the possibilities of learning a way of self-sufficient living. We helped them to get started on a life style more satisfying than that of the average young American.

Through writings, speaking, workshops and other means of reaching the public, we have tried to show what can be accomplished by oldsters.

We have manifested that health and vigor can be maintained to a degree consistent with efforts to live simply and sanely.

We have done what we could to conserve and improve the natural environment and to make its facilities available for social advancement.

Driven by whatever urge, motivated by a wide variety of interests and convictions, all human beings, early in their lives, are possessed by the wish and the will to live a satisfying and rewarding life. Speaking for ourselves, we, at advanced ages, are still questioning, investigating, searching and aiming to build a more rewarding and more creative life. For those who are so minded and so willed, we have written this book.

If we have helped a number of people to get started on a life style more satisfying than that of the average United States citizen, they have in turn contributed measurably to the building of our own lives. They have helped us with gardening and with building. By the exchange of insights, experiences and skills, they have cooperated as fellow workers in our joint efforts. We thank them and salute them as we continue in our own varied fields of productive and creative endeavor.

EPILOGUE

"O what peace, what privacy and securitie is to be found in the country! No silken curtains, no costly arras, no gold or silver plate, no sumptuous jewels, no embroyderd garments, no coaches nor sedans, with an unprofitable and troublesome traine of attendants, are there in request. The expenses we must be at there are both frugall and necessary; there is nothing to incite us to a lavish imitation of every ridiculous prodigall, that claps his revenues upon his back, and by the way of bravery comes at last to beggary. The countryman's household-stuffe is but ordinary, his tables and chairs are of plaine timber, his beds neither carv'd nor gilded. The cups he drinks in are in the winter of wholesome earth or the seasoned oke, and in the summer of glasse. His richest habit is a plaine coate or cloke, worne first by his own sheep, afterwards shorne and spun for himself; an able horse, a man-servant and a maid are all his retinnue. And truly this plaine husband-man, both in reguard of the utensils of his house, his provision and course of life, is and ever shalbe in my opinion far more happy than either the nobleman, the courtier, or the citizen. And if we consider him for uprightnesse and purity of conscience, I believe there is no man so irrationall, but will confesse him to exceed them all."

Don Antonio de Guevara, The Praise & Happiness of the Countrie-Life, *1539*

"Truly I cannot but here take Occasion to exhort all Philosophic Gentlemen to employ a reasonable Share of their Thoughts and Experiments on the Subject of Agriculture as a more becoming Exercise and Relaxation than Hunting or Cards; and to be sure, more conducing to the Health of the Body, the Strength of the Mind, and to the Capacity of Generosity in the Fortune, than many other fashionable but criminal Excesses. For it ought to be observed that it is an Employment which will at once contract their Wants, and give a larger Ability to supply them; 'twill give greater Relish to the Enjoyments of Life, and make every Part thereof sweetly varied between Ease and delightful Labour."

John Laurence, A New System of Agriculture, *1726*

"The reader must not take it for granted that in going into the country we escaped all the annoyances of domestic life peculiar to the city, or that we fell heir to no new ones, such as we had never before experienced. He must remember that this is a world of compensations, and that nowhere will he be likely to find either an unmixed good or an unmixed bad. Such was exactly our experience. But on summing up the two, the balance was decidedly in our favor."

Anonymous, Ten Acres Enough, 1864

"This book is the fruit of years of labor in a great and good field. It certainly contains much that will be useful to all classes who till the earth or live in farmers' houses....Though not perfect, farmers (and their wives) will find this book a useful one. If not invaluable, I hope it is one that they cannot afford to do without....Usefulness instead of elegance has been aimed at....To those who know the name of the author (and the number is large) I hope this book will be a welcome bequest. I hope it will be the means through which that name may live in love and honor with your children and children's children, around many an American hearthstone."

Solon Robinson, Facts for Farmers, 1869

"If we had ample means and could choose any kind of life we wished, we would choose what we have chosen. And when I say we, I mean we. There are many differences between a man's viewpoint and a woman's, even though they may live side by side in the same house year in and year out. But there must be a profound unshaken unity underneath the difference if they are to make a success of such a life as we have lived, because the things that must be passed by are things that one or the other might consider indispensable. As for children, I cannot help but think that they gain far more than they lose, in happiness and experience. By and large, it is the best life for children. And later, they must make their own choice."

Gove Hambidge, Enchanted Acre: Adventures in Backyard Farming, *1935*

BIBLIOGRAPHY

Alcott, William A. *Ways of Living on Small Means*. Boston: Light & Stearns, 1837.
————. *The Young House-Keeper; or, Thoughts on Food and Cookery*. Boston: George W. Light, 1842.
————. *The Young Woman's Guide to Excellence*. New York: Clark, Austin & Smith, 1852.
Aldrich, Chilson D. *The Real Log Cabin*. New York: Macmillan,1928.
Anonymous. *How a Small Income May Be Made to Go Far in a Family*. London: Fry, 1745.
————. *Six Hundred Dollars a Year: A Wife's Effort at Low Living Under High Prices*. Boston: Ticknor & Fields, 1867.
————. *The Young Housewife's Book; or, How to Eke Out a Small Income and Insure Domestic Happiness and Plenty on a Limited Scale of Expenditure*. New York: Garrett, 1851.
Baker, O.E.; Borsodi, Ralph; and Wilson, M.L. *Agriculture in Modern Life*. New York: Harper, 1939.
Balfour, Eve Balfour. *The Living Soil*. London: Faber & Faber, 1949.
Barborka, Clifford J. *Treatment by Diet*. Philadelphia: Lippincott, 1936.
Barr, Stringfellow. *The Pilgrimage of Western Man*. New York: Harcourt, Brace, 1949.
Beecher, Catharine E. *A Treatise on Domestic Economy*. Boston: Marsh, Capen, 1841.
Booth, Edward Townsend. *Country Life in America*. New York: Knopf, 1947.
————. *God Made the Country*. New York: Knopf, 1946.
Borsodi, Ralph. *Flight from the City*. New York: Harper, 1933.
————. *This Ugly Civilization*. New York: Simon & Schuster, 1929.
Brimmer, F. E. *Camps, Log Cabins, Lodges, and Clubhouses*. New York: Appleton, 1925.
Bromfield, Louis. *Pleasant Valley*. New York: Harper, 1945.
Brownwell, Baker. *The Human Community*. New York: Harper, 1950.
————, and Wright, F. L. *Architecture and Modern Life*. New York: Harper, 1938.
Carque, Otto. *Natural Foods*. Los Angeles: Carque, 1926.
————. *Rational Diet*. Los Angeles: Times Mirror Press, 1926.

Cary, Harold. *Build a Home—Save a Third*. New York: Reynolds, 1924.

Colby, Evelyn, and Forrest, John G. *Ways and Means to Successful Retirement*. New York: Forbes & Sons, 1952.

Copley, Esther. *Cottage Comforts with Hints for Promoting Them, Gleaned from Experience*. London: Simpkin & Marshall, 1832.

Corey, Paul. *Build a Home*. New York: Dial, 1946.

———. *Buy an Acre*. New York: Dial, 1944.

Cruger, Mary. *How She Did It; or, Comfort on $150 a Year*. New York: Appleton, 1888.

Cruikshank, E. W. H. *Food and Nutrition*. Toronto: Macmillan, 1946.

Culverwell, Dr. Robert James. *How to Be Happy (An Admonitory Essay)*. New York: Redfield, 1850.

Davis, Adelle. *Let's Cook It Right*. New York: Harcourt, Brace, 1947.

———. *Vitality Through Planned Nutrition*. New York: Macmillan, 1949.

Demarquette, Jacques. *Le Naturisme Intégral*. Paris: Editions du Trait d'Union, 1931.

Dempsey, Paul W. *Grow Your Own Vegetables*. Boston: Houghton Mifflin, 1942.

Evelyn, John. *A Philosophic Discourse on Earth*. London: Martyn, 1676.

Faulkner, Edward H. *Plowman's Folly*. Norman: University of Oklahoma Press, 1943.

Fed, Rockwell F. *10,000 Garden Questions*. New York: Doubleday, Doran, 1944.

Flagg, Ernest. *Small Houses: Their Economic Design and Construction*. New York: Scribner, 1922.

Gannett, Lewis. *Cream Hill*. New York: Viking, 1949.

Gould, John. *The House that Jacob Built*. New York: Morrow, 1947.

Greenberg, David B., and Corbin, Charles. *So You're Going to Buy a Farm*. New York: Greenberg, 1944.

Gregg, Richard. *Voluntary Simplicity*. Wallingford, Pa.: Pendle Hill, 1930.

Greiner, T. *How to Make the Garden Pay*. Philadelphia: Maule, 1890.

Gustafson, Hardenburg. *Land for the Family: A Guide to Country Living*. Ithaca, New York: Comstock, 1947.

Hambidge, Gove. *Enchanted Acre*. New York: McGraw-Hill, 1925.

———. *Time to Live*. New York: McGraw-Hill, 1933.

Hay, William Howard. *Health via Food*. New York: Sun-Diet Press, 1930

———. *Some Human Ailments*. Mt. Pocono, Pa.: Pocono Haven, 1937.

———. *Superior Health Through Nutrition*. New York: Hay, 1944.

Highstone, H. A. *Practical Farming for Beginners*. New York: Harper, 1940.

Hodgins, Eric. *Mr. Blandings Builds His Dream House.* New York: Simon & Schuster, 1946.

Hopkins, Donald P. *Chemicals, Humus, and the Soil.* New York: Chemical Pub. Co., 1948.

Howard, Albert. *An Agricultural Testament.* London: Oxford, 1940.

———. *The Soil and Health.* New York: Devin-Adair, 1952.

Hyams, Edward. *Soil and Civilization.* London: Thames & Hudson, 1952.

James, George Wharton. *The Indians' Secrets of Health.* Pasadena, Calif.: Radiant Life, 1917.

Jensen, Anton H. *How to Eat Safely in a Poisoned World.* Lincoln, Neb.: Jensen, 1949.

Jones, H. A., and Emsweller, S. L. *The Vegetable Industry.* New York: McGraw-Hill, 1931.

Kaighn, Raymond P. *How to Retire and Like It.* New York: Association Press, 1951.

Kains, Maurice Grenville. *Five Acres and Independence.* New York: Greenberg, 1935.

Kallet, Arthur, and Schlink, F. J. *100,000,000 Guinea Pigs.* New York: Vanguard, 1933.

Kellogg, Charles E. *The Soils That Support Us.* New York: Macmillan, 1941.

Kemp, Oliver. *Wilderness Homes.* New York: Outing Pub. Co., 1908.

King, F. H. *Farmers of Forty Centuries.* New York: Harcourt, Brace, 1927.

Kingsford, Anna. *The Perfect Way in Diet.* London: Kegan Paul, 1904.

Lindlahr, Henry. *The Practice of Nature Cure.* New York: Nature Cure Library, 1931.

Lindlahr, Victor H. *The Natural Way to Health.* New York: Natural Nutrition Society, 1939.

———. *You Are What You Eat.* New York: Natural Nutrition Society, 1942.

Lovell, Philip M. *Diet for Health by Natural Methods.* Los Angeles: Times Mirror, 1931.

———. *The Health of the Child by Natural Methods.* Los Angeles: Times Mirror, 1927.

Lyman, Laura and Joseph. *How to Live: The Philosophy of Housekeeping.* Philadelphia: Thompson, 1882.

McCann, Alfred W. *This Famishing World.* New York: Doubleday, Doran, 1918.

———. *The Science of Eating.* New York: Doubleday, Doran, 1931.

McCarrison, R. *Nutrition and National Health.* London: Faber & Faber, 1944.

————. *Studies in Deficiency Diseases.* Milwaukee, Wis.: Lee Foundation for Nutritional Research, 1945.

Monier-Williams, George. *Trace Elements in Food.* New York: Wiley, 1949.

Morgan, Arthur E. *A Business of My Own.* Yellow Springs, Ohio: Community Service, 1946.

Mumford, Lewis. *The Condition of Man.* New York: Harcourt, Brace, 1944.

Nearing, Scott. *Economics for the Power Age.* New York: John Day, 1952.

————. *Where Is Civilization Going?* New York: Vanguard, 1926.

————, and Nearing, Helen. *The Maple Sugar Book.* New York: John Day, 1950.

Norman N. Philip. *Constructive Meal Planning.* Passaic, N.J.: Phototone Press, 1946.

Ogden, Samuel R. *How to Grow Food for Your Family.* New York: Barnes, 1943.

————. *This Country Life.* New York: Barnes, 1946.

Osborn, Fairfield. *Our Plundered Planet.* Boston: Little, Brown, 1948.

Owen, Catherine. *Ten Dollars Enough (Keeping House Well on Ten Dollars a Week; How It Has Been Done; How It May Be Done Again).* Boston: Houghton Mifflin, 1887.

Paine, Lansing M., and Webster, Polly. *Start Your Own Business on Less than $1000.* New York: McGraw-Hill, 1950.

Payne, Roger. *Why Work?* Boston: Meador, 1939.

Peters, Frazier Norman. *Pour Yourself a House.* New York: McGraw-Hill, 1949.

————. *Without Benefit of Architect.* New York: Putnam, 1937.

Peterson, Elmer T. *Cities Are Abnormal.* Norman: University of Oklahoma Press, 1946.

————. *Forward to the Land.* Norman: University of Oklahoma Press, 1942.

Pfeiffer, Ehrenfried. *Bio-Dynamic Farming and Gardening.* New York: Anthroposophic Press, 1938.

————. *Soil Fertility.* London: Faber & Faber, 1949.

————. *The Earth's Face and Human Destiny.* Emmaus, Pa.: Rodale, 1947.

Picton, Lionel James. *Nutrition and the Soil.* New York: Devin Adair, 1949.

Preston, John Frederick. *Developing Farm Woodlands.* New York: McGraw-Hill, 1954.

Price, W.A. *Nutrition and Physical Degeneration.* New York: Hoeber, 1939.

Quigley, D. T. *The National Malnutrition.* Milwaukee, Wis.: Lee Foundation for Nutritional Research, 1948.

Richter, John T. *Nature—the Healer.* West Haven, Conn.: Nature's Products, 1949.

Roberts, Isaac Phillips. *Ten Acres Enough.* New York: Miller, 1864.

Robinson, Solon. *How to Live; or, Domestic Economy Illustrated.* New York: Fowler & Wells, 1860.

Rochester, Anna. *Why Farmers Are Poor.* New York: International, 1940.

Rodale, J. I. *The Organic Front.* Emmaus, Pa.: Rodale, 1949.

————. *Pay Dirt.* New York: Devin Adair, 1945.

Rorty, James, and Norman, N. P. *Tomorrow's Food.* New York: Prentice-Hall, 1947.

Sanderson, L. D. *Rural Community.* New York: Ginn, 1932.

Scott, Cyril. *Health, Diet and Commonsense.* London: Homeopathic Pub. Co., 1950

Shelton, Herbert M. *The Hygienic System.* San Antonio, Texas: Shelton, 1947.

Shepard, Ward. *Food or Famine.* New York: Macmillan, 1945.

Sigerist, Henry E. *Civilization and Disease.* Ithaca, N.Y.: Cornell University Press, 1945.

Skinner, B. F. *Walden Two.* New York: Macmillan, 1948.

Sorokin, Pitirim A. *The Crisis of Our Age.* New York: Dutton, 1949.

————. *Man and Society in Calamity.* New York: Dutton, 1942.

Stannard, Stella. *Whole Grain Cookery.* New York: John Day, 1951.

Sternberg, Fritz. *The Coming Crisis.* New York: John Day, 1947.

Stevens, Henry Bailey. *The Recovery of Culture.* New York: Harper, 1949.

Stowell, Robert F. *Toward Simple Living.* Hartland, Vt.: Solitarian Press, 1953.

Sutherland, G.A. *A System of Diet and Dietetics.* New York: Physicians & Surgeons Book Co., 1925.

Sykes, Friend. *Food, Farming, and the Future.* Emmaus, Pa.: Rodale, 1951.

————. *Humus and the Farmer.* London: Faber & Faber, 1946.

Szekely, Edmond B. *Cosmotherapy, the Medicine of the Future.* Los Angeles: International Cosmotherapeutic Expedition, 1938.

Thompson, Homer C. *Vegetable Crops.* New York: McGraw-Hill, 1939.

Tilden, J. H. *Food.* Denver, Colo.: Tilden, 1914.

Toynbee, Arnold. *Civilization on Trial.* New York: Oxford, 1948.

Tyler, Fred. *Plan for Independence.* New York: Harian, 1951.

Van de Water, F. F. *A Home in the Country.* New York: Reynal, 1937.

———. *We're Still in the Country.* New York: John Day, 1938.

Vogt, William. *Road to Survival.* New York: Sloane, 1948.

Wagner, Charles. *The Simple Life.* New York: McClure, Phillips, 1904.

Waksman, Selman H. *Soil Microbiology.* New York: Wiley, 1952.

Walker, Roy. *The Golden Feast.* New York: Macmillan, 1952.

Warren, Eliza. *Comfort for Small Incomes.* Boston: Loring, 1866.

Wend, Milton. *How to Live in the Country Without Farming.* New York: Doubleday, Doran, 1944.

Wrench, G. T. *The Wheel of Health.* New York: Schocken Books, 1972.

Wicks, William S. *Log Cabins.* New York: Forest & Stream Pub., Co., 1889.

Williams, Howard. *The Ethics of Diet.* London: James, 1907.

Wilson, Charles Morrow. *Country Living.* Brattleboro, Vt.: Stephen Daye, 1938.

Wright, Frank Lloyd. *On Architecture.* New York: Duell, Sloane & Pearce, 1941.

———, and Brownell, Baker. *Architecture and Modern Life.* Harper, 1938.

Young, Arthur. *Rural Economy.* Burlington, Vt.: Neale, 1792.

Young, Mildred Binns. *Functional Poverty.* Wallingford, Pa.: Pendle Hill, 1935.

———. *Participation in Rural Life.* Wallingford, Pa.: Pendle Hill, 1940.

INDEX